FROM HERE TO THE NATIONS

When God came in all his glory to a small church in Toronto in 1994 and the fruits of that initial outpouring spilled over into an Anglican Church in London England, I was not only sceptical but somewhat hostile. Prompted and cajoled by my wife Lois I paid a visit to this British Church where parishioners were falling off their chairs supposedly overcome by the power of the Holy Spirit. Despite my Pentecostal pride in what I believed to be understanding of the Holy Spirit and his ways and genuine offence at some of the things I witnessed that day, the Lord captivated my heart in a very unexpected but profound way.

As a direct result of the impact of this visit my church took up an offering to send my wife, myself and one of our leaders to the Church in Toronto where God was continuing to pour out on vessels descending from all corners of the world. The week that my wife and I spent receiving from the father can never be fully described by mere words. We fell in love with Jesus all over again he took his place at the centre of our lives, and subsequently our church family. He became our first love. He healed our hearts and we found we had come home.

Upon our return God in his Grace poured out on our little Church in Sunderland and there began 4 years of nightly meetings, untold miracles and visitors pouring to visit us from all over the world. That season became known as "the Sunderland Refreshing" and was the beginning of what can only be described as the best of the rest of our lives. Twenty years later and the father is still pouring out and producing wonderful fruit, it is truly amazing.

Finally how we love our family in Toronto and especially our dearest friends John and Carol Arnott, two of the most precious sincere and faithful loving people you would ever care to meet.

How can we ever truly thank God enough for what happened in January 1994 and continues to this day.

—Ken Gott
SENIOR LEADER OF BETHSHAN APOSTOLIC COMMUNITY
FOUNDER OF HOUSE OF PRAYER EUROPE

D1555145

When I first heard about the movement of the Holy Spirit at Holy Trinity Brompton in London I honestly believed this was not the Holy Spirit. I find falling and laughing offensive! What is more, if it really was from God it would have come to Westminster Chapel first! I was both prejudiced and envious as we at Westminster Chapel had fasted and prayed, taken to the streets trying to reach the lost and putting my whole future and career on the line. We thought we deserved God's favour if anyone did! I was quite wrong to think this of course, but I could not bring myself to believe a true work of God came to an apostate Church of England, especially one filled with posh Etonian accents!

But I was wrong. It took HTB's churchwarden Ken Costa to make me see what was actually happening. I began to tremble – that I might not only have been wrong but in the tradition of those Evangelicals who in the past hundreds of years opposed the genuine work of the Spirit – from the days of Jonathan Edwards to the Welsh Revival. Having previously warned my members at Westminster Chapel that what was happening in certain places was not from God I later climbed down publicly. Some of our deacons joined me at HTB and got prayed for. We then invited the vicar Sandy Millar to come to the Chapel and pray for us. The result was that HTB and Westminster Chapel developed a lovely relationship.

When you read this book with an open mind you will see why I climbed down and subsequently embraced this offensive work of the Holy Spirit. I thank God all the time that He was patient with me and that I had the privilege to repent of my attitude and became a part of what God was doing. I pray He will lead every reader as He did me. To those who are already in this mould, you will love this book. Others will find this book troubling – as I did when I first heard of this. My prayer is that you will follow me in 'climbing down' and becoming a part of a work of God that has not ended.

I will add one more thing. Not only have I never been sorry I took the decision I did; subsequent occasions during which I got to know John and Carol Arnott have convinced me that we are dealing with people of wonderful and rare integrity. To me this means everything. They are pure gold.

I commend this book to every Christian and pray your life will be changed as a result.

—R T Kendall

MINISTER OF WESTMINSTER CHAPEL (1977–2002)

The Toronto Outpouring completely changed my life! Prior to the Revival, I was a broken, discouraged local Pastor questioning my next steps here in Pasadena. Without knowing it, I was battling forgiveness with my father, my wife, and myself. When I first went to Toronto to the first Catch the Fire conference in October 1994, I had a radical encounter with God! There was deep healing in my heart which later led to reconciliation with my wife and my father.

When I came back from Toronto I thought I was born again, again! Not only had God healed my intimate relationships with family, but The Holy Spirit led us to start our own nightly meetings at Mott Auditorium which lasted for over three years. It was through these nightly protracted revival services that our apostolic network, Harvest International Ministry (HIM) was birthed.

HIM is now in over 60 nations with thousands of churches and ministries that are aligned with this new network. Glory to God! I can't thank God enough for what came from the Toronto Outpouring and John and Carol's friendship. I know countless lives have been born again. Many believers have been revived and changed through their obedience to the Holy Spirit. Hearts have been healed, bodies set free from sickness, and destinies fulfilled. I know we would not be the church movement we are today without the rich history and friendship of John and Carol, and the Toronto Outpouring. I pray that this book will be used as a catalyst to impart revival to the heart of the reader and to take the church to another level of glory that will usher in the greatest harvest in the history of mankind!

—Dr. Ché Ahn

SENIOR PASTOR, HROCK CHURCH, PASADENA, CA
PRESIDENT, HARVEST INTERNATIONAL MINISTRY
INTERNATIONAL CHANCELLOR, WAGNER LEADERSHIP INSTITUTE

We were permanently impacted by the Toronto Blessing in 1994. While Winnie and I had had a supernatural conversion and baptism of fire back in the 70s, it took this fresh fire to burn away the religious starch that had accumulated over the years and restore us back to our "First Love."

The Lord had opened our eyes to see the Word of God and everyone, including ourselves, in a whole new way. We began to immerse ourselves in the depths of the Father's love and the costly price that was paid to make us His sons and daughters. The joy of Jesus, the joy unspeakable and full of glory we've read about in the Bible, became our daily portion and altered the way we used to preach and lead praise and worship. We became more radical and free as the glory of God intensified, and we've been able to remain in that wonderful 'first love' intimacy with our Lord ever since.

—Georgian Banov, DD honoris causa

PRESIDENT AND CO-FOUNDER OF GLOBAL CELEBRATION
GENERAL DIRECTOR OF THE BULGARIAN BIBLE PROJECT
CHAIRMAN OF THE BULGARIAN SPRING OF LIFE FOUNDATION

Some events serve as defining points in life: the day I was married, the birth of my children, those domestic dates serve to help me fit in other events as, pre-children and post-children, etc. Toronto is another of those events. History is already beginning to tell us how far-reaching and transforming the impact of the Visitation in Toronto has been.

This book is a wonderful combination of faithful factual reporting of events leading up to and since The Outpouring but also seeks to share the heartbeat of the revival and those at its head. Even its critics are kindly quoted and referred to. This is no purple patch myopic, rather an insight into how faithfulness is a key to ongoing revival.

As a third generation Pentecostal I was attracted by the reports of God moving in Toronto and went along in early 1994. I was not so much blown away as carried along in a river of intimacy of the Father's Blessing that fed my heart for revival and keeps me seeking His Face with an ever increasing zeal ever since. John and Carol Arnott are two of the most down to earth folks I know who have worked really hard to keep the revival rooted in reality by modelling it, and my prayer is that the River continues to overflow and that He continues to gives us enough to give away.

—David Campbell

REGIONAL LEADER, METROPOLITAN REGIONS, ELIM PENTECOSTAL CHURCH, UK

The outpouring at Catch The Fire Toronto changed my life. It became the platform from which I was launched into the nations for equipping the saints and an evangelistic harvest. Twenty years and forty-five nations later there have been 3,000,000 people saved through three persons' ministries who were powerfully touched by the Toronto

Blessing - the Father's Blessing. Over 25,000 churches were started in only a few people's ministries. I am sure there are millions more who have been saved and thousands more churches planted. This well documented story of how it all began is needed for the testimony of Jesus to be clearly proclaimed. May God be glorified when the fruit of His work is made known.

—Dr. Randy Clark
FOUNDER AND PRESIDENT OF GLOBAL AWAKENING AND
THE APOSTOLIC NETWORK OF GLOBAL AWAKENING

We first came in the summer of 2000. Wow! Our lives have never been the same since. We purchased the first version of the soaking kit and this led us to a journey of deep transformation through intimacy with the Lover of our soul. This book does not only recount with exactitude the events that make the outpouring of the Holy Spirit in Toronto an extremely significant historical event but it also stirs up the hope for what is yet to come.

—Pierre and Anne-Marie Goulart
CANADA

The presence of God in the Toronto revival continues to be an oasis of life drawing millions from all over the world. Cathy and I and our family have been some of those who have been privileged to live in the middle of this revival for 13 years. Our lives have been irreversibly changed not only by what god has done in us but by seeing the miraculous transformation in others over and over again. The story of this revival needs to be told. Twenty years on, read the story, *From Here To The Nations*.

—Gordon Harris
DIRECTOR OF CATCH THE FIRE COLLEGE

Our lives have been completely transformed and revolutionized by the power and love of the Father that we experienced in Toronto. Nothing compares to discovering him as a loving Father and standing in his intoxicating presence. This book captures the facts, and beyond that it captures the very heart of what God did in Toronto in 1994 and is continuing to do around the world.

—Benjamin & Sarah Jackson
CATCH THE FIRE

Heather and I have had the incredible honour and privilege of being a part of this revival from the beginning. We were ruined for the ordinary by encountering the glory of the Lord again and again. We are so grateful to John and Carol Arnott for their faithful stewardship of this move of God and always pressing on for more! This is a very important and timely book that will help anyone hungering and thirsting for God's presence, process the mysterious ways in which He moves.

—Peter & Heather Jackson
ITINERANT MINISTERS, WWW.PETERJACKSON.ORG

The outpouring of the Holy Spirit in Toronto has forever marked my life. I will never be the same. I am so glad that this amazing story of God's great grace is now in print. May this ongoing move of God spread even further throughout the nations of the world, all to bring God glory.

—Bill Johnson
BETHEL CHURCH, CALIFORNIA

My parents moved our family to Toronto in 1999, following the call of God. We were all changed, and more than anything, given tools for healing ourselves and the nations. My mother joined the staff, and after high school I joined the staff also. Now 10 years on, I have had the privilege of serving under incredible men and women of God, and watching countless lives be changed by the love of the Father.

—Jonathan Puddle
NEW ZEALAND

There is no doubt in our minds that what took place through the revival that started in 1994 has utterly changed our lives. AJ's life was characterized by abuse, eating disorders and suicide attempts. Alyn's experience of God was thoroughly intellectual and marked by doubt. What we found through the Toronto Blessing was supernatural life that transformed every aspect of our lives.

This book carefully chronicles the "inside story" of a revival by the people involved in it. You will be filled with faith and challenged in your expectations of what God can do.

—Alyn & AJ Jones
GRACE CENTER, FRANKLIN, TN

When ordinary disciples seem to have had too much new wine, someone needs to stand up and say, "This is that spoken by the prophet." (Acts 2:16) Jerry Steingard has done just that with a masterful eyewitness account of the Toronto Outpouring. Highly readable and well-documented, *From Here To The Nations* delivers an insider's view of the remarkable events that began in 1994 and have since inspired churches and believers around the world.

—Gordon Robertson

THE CHRISTIAN BROADCASTING NETWORK

I came with my wife Sandra to a Monday night meeting at Toronto Airport Vineyard Christian Fellowship. It was January 25th, 1994. I came as a tired, frustrated, dry, hurting pastor. I left transformed! In one night, God changed my destiny, I felt alive, hopeful, refreshed, reinvigorated!

I pulled out my Bible and read the book of Acts. I kept thinking that I had a different translation as there were stories and words here that I didn't recall reading before. The book now made total sense to me. The passages of people being filled, laughing and falling down all seemed normal - I knew what Luke was talking about.

Monday morning on February 1st, 1994 I began to work with John and Carol Arnott and their team. As it turns out, we are still working for John and Carol 20 years later. We've never looked back.

Not only has my job changed dramatically, but Sandra and I are now massively different than we were then. I had deep anger issues and a very critical spirit. Sandra was insecure and fearful. We were distant from the love of the Father and the fellowship of the Holy Spirit. We didn't know the grace of the Lord. Now we have all three!

The "Toronto Blessing" as the British media called it, has transformed our lives. There is simply no time to review the entirety of what God has done through of this outpouring. This book is just a taste and no doubt you can add your own story to the backdrop of revival that Jerry Steingard has so wonderfully painted.

—Steve and Sandra Long

VICE PRESIDENTS CATCH THE FIRE
SENIOR LEADERS CATCH THE FIRE TORONTO

I am ever in awe of the mysterious work of God which so obviously rests solely in His sovereign hand of grace, and yet seems in some incredible way to require our willingness to say "yes." This tremendous display of kingdom tension is so obvious in the birthing of what has come to be known as the "Toronto Blessing". I am so grateful to God for stepping into that season of history and releasing such blessing, and forever thankful to the Arnott's and others like them for stepping forward and saying "yes" to the Spirit's initiation. Blown away to have had some small part in it all, and stoked to see where it all goes from here!

—David Ruis

MEMBER OF VINEYARD CANADA NATIONAL TEAM
BOARD MEMBER - SAVING INNOCENCE

In 1994, as reports of the Toronto blessing began to spread, opinions covered a wide spectrum from, "This is the greatest move of God in our time," to "Stay away—it's the devil!" Curious, I decided to see for myself. My first visit convinced me that God was up to something big, and after returning often I saw good fruit in the lives of others as well as my own.

Since 1972, I have been a Pentecostal healing evangelist, so I was surprised when John Arnott invited me to minister at the nightly renewal meetings. The culture was very different than what I was accustomed to, yet it became abundantly clear that the passion and hunger of people who were coming from all over the world far outweighed any cultural differences.

It was an absolute joy and privilege to become a regular speaker over the ensuing years as the Toronto Blessing continued; in fact, I was told that I spoke there more times than any other guest minister. During that time hundreds of miraculous healings took place, and many more gave their lives to Christ as they experienced the Father's love. While the leaders tell me I helped them move more fully into healing and evangelism, they opened a whole new world of authentic, intimate worship to me, and showed me how to minister in way that is naturally supernatural.

Thank you, John and Carol Arnott, for modeling the Father's heart and for sharing with us what you received. The impact of the Toronto blessing continues to be felt in hungry hearts all over the world.

—Bill Prankard

CANADIAN EVANGELIST, PRESIDENT OF BILL PRANKARD EVANGELISTIC ASSOCIATION

It has been quite a ride over these past years as God has graced us with the honour of hosting His Presence! We have had the privilege of being on the pastoral team from the beginning days of this church and being eyewitnesses to the glorious manifest presence of God which poured out on January 20th, 1994 and remains with us today. We are so aware that it wasn't anything any of us have done to deserve this honour, but earnestly desire that His presence will remain and increase upon all of us yet.

So we can testify to the fact that Jerry Steingard has done a fabulous job of researching and documenting the many facets of this move of God in this book. The accounts are very accurate and thorough. There are also numerous testimonies recorded of people who have been impacted, which reveals the wonderful fruit it has produced in people's lives. Those who read it will be astounded by the reports that show the far-reaching effects that this outpouring has had throughout the world. It gives us great anticipation for more yet to come!

—Connie & Jeremy Sinnott
CATCH THE FIRE

We owe our lives, our hearts and our marriage to the Holy Spirit who we have so encountered in this glorious revival. We arrived in Toronto in August 2000 as two broken individuals and found love, significance and a spiritual home in the Father's great heart of love. We had experienced the effects of the "Toronto Blessing" in the UK and had seen many manifestations that confounded our natural minds, but when we joined the team we found out it was really about Jesus bringing us into the Father's blessing and discovering our identity as a son and daughter!

John and Carol Arnott have laid down their lives for us and loved us to life. We owe them both a debt of love. We consider it the greatest privilege of our lives to be on their team and to be sent out carrying this revival fire all over the nations of the world.

We are constantly amazed that even among the most unreached tribes in the world we see people responding to the love, presence and power of the Holy Spirit with exactly the same manifestations and extraordinary miracles as we see in Toronto or any of our Catch The Fire churches around the world. This revival is utterly transferrable and completely unstoppable and will never end until Jesus returns for His glorious Bride.

—Duncan & Kate Smith
VICE PRESIDENTS CATCH THE FIRE,
SENIOR LEADERS CATCH THE FIRE RALEIGH

It might seem almost unbelievable that the revival that broke out here in 1994 impacted my youth ministry 9315 miles away in Singapore. I remember weeping, laughing and rolling on the floor under the power of the Spirit during those years. All we knew was it was called the "Toronto Blessing" and that God was incredibly happy and was sharing His joy with us. It revived in the youth in our ministry an intense hunger and thirst for more of His Spirit.

—Kenny Rason Tan

SINGAPORE

I knew John and Carol before the Toronto outpouring began. I respected them highly and was glad to embrace the wild manifestations that came with this laughing revival. Why not laugh? A merry heart does good like medicine, and we all sure could use some medicine to heal up our souls! And the Father's love: who could argue that? Not me. I had journaled for years, and already found out that God loved me unconditionally. So there was nothing here but raw God. This is the revival the Church needed, and much of the Church still needs it.

As the Church receives the touch of this renewal, it becomes healthier and more appealing to a world that looks on and wonders, "Is there true reality and a true encounter with a living God in Christianity?" The answer is YES!

The Toronto revival is a source of living water to a dry and thirsty Church, and I for one am glad to be a part of it and to embrace it. Having been to the Toronto church 50 times in the last 12 years, it feels like my second home. I pray this revival touches your life also.

—Dr. Mark Virkler

PRESIDENT, CHRISTIAN LEADERSHIP UNIVERSITY
AUTHOR, *4 Keys to Hearing God's Voice*

My wife and I started attending TACF in 1995 on my last military posting in Toronto. We were caught up in the revival and the wonderful spiritual presence that permeated the atmosphere of the meetings. The book has allowed us to relive our transformation journey that brought us closer to God and gave us many close friends and opportunities to minister to others.

—Bryan Stephenson

MAJOR GENERAL (RETIRED), CANADIAN ARMED FORCES

From Here to the Nations

The Story of the Toronto Blessing

From Here to the Nations
Published by Catch The Fire Books
272 Attwell Drive, Toronto ON M9W 6M3
Canada

Distributed worldwide by Catch The Fire Distribution. Titles may be purchased in bulk; for information, please contact distribution@catchthefire.com.

Catch The Fire® is a registered trademark of Catch The Fire World.

ISBN 978-1-894310-42-0

The Team: Emily Wright, Rachel McDonagh, Marcott Bernarde, Benjamin Jackson, Jon Long, Jonathan Puddle, Steve Long.
Cover design: Marcott Bernarde (Catch The Fire)
Interior layout: Belinda Love Lee (belindalovelee.com)

Printed in Canada
First Edition 2014

FROM HERE
TO THE NATIONS

THE STORY OF THE TORONTO BLESSING

JERRY STEINGARD WITH JOHN ARNOTT

We dedicate this book to the unsung heroes of this outpouring of God's Spirit in Toronto; to the hundreds of people who have been on the prayer ministry teams. Night after night, the women and men wearing the ministry team badges have faithfully prayed for those who have come for a fresh touch and encounter with their Lord. They have given of themselves to minister the love of God to hundreds of thousands of hungry and desperate people, for over two decades.

We have heard that what most impressed many leaders about their experience in Toronto was not the speakers, but the love, gentleness, godliness and anointing on this little army of average-looking people who faithfully prayed for them. This book is for you.

Contents

Preface

I have long desired to publish a book telling the story of the Toronto Blessing from our side and perspective. No one was as surprised as we were at what has taken place, and Carol and I still have moments when we look at one another as if to ask "Is God really doing this, with us?" We are eternally grateful to Randy Clark and his team for coming to Toronto in January of 1994 and releasing the fiery, loving Presence of the Holy Spirit among us.

And thankfully it not just with us alone, as this move that we have shared in has gone around the world. The testimonies speak for themselves. The changed lives are abundant. The fruit is exceedingly good, as you will see.

Late in 2012, I approached Jerry Steingard to write out an honest and accurate account of what led up to this historic event; what it was like in the early days of the revival, where we all are today, and where we believe it is all going. While many books have been written that touch on the Toronto Blessing, none have yet emerged as a definitive work. Jerry is the perfect guy to write such a story.

Jerry and I have known each other for about 25 years. He became my Assistant Pastor in our Stratford church, and took over there when Carol and I finally moved to Toronto in 1992. Jerry was with us in Argentina in November of 1993 when we received prayer and impartation from Claudio Friedzon, and were never to be the same again. He was in the early Toronto meetings right from the beginning. Most importantly, he is also a bit of a historian, saving and collecting all of the various and sundry articles and newspaper reports that addressed what was happening at the Toronto meetings. He is also an excellent writer in his own right, and has endeavored to record these events as did St. Luke in presenting his Gospel account; Luke 1:3 *"Therefore since I myself have carefully investigated everything from the beginning, it seemed good also to me to write an orderly account for you...."* While Jerry is not directly involved in Catch The Fire today, he remains in close relationship with many of us and is a regular visitor. He is as much a child of this move of God as anyone.

Thank you Jerry, for partnering with me to write such an excellent volume. It is a very fitting tribute to all that the Holy Spirit has done in and through us all over the last twenty plus years.

We do still stand amazed. We are all deeply humbled at the hundreds of thousands of transformed lives. Perhaps your life is one of them. The Holy Spirit has taken us all higher and deeper at the same time. He has done "Exceedingly abundantly above all we could ask or think" (Ephesians 3:20). I hope you enjoy the read, and I hope the stories and testimonies remind you of how awesome and personal God our Father is. We know that as glorious as all of this was and is, the best is still before us!

Truly, *"in His Presence is fullness of joy, and at His right hand there are pleasures forevermore."* (Psalm 16:11)

—John Arnott

Acknowlegments

To my dear wife of thirty-five years, Pamela Joy, and our grown up children, Jonathan, Michael and Joanna; thank you for your amazing support, patience and encouragement through yet another writing project.

To my son, Michael, thank you for your professional photographic work in taking recent photos of the outside of Catch The Fire, Toronto, and for taking my photo.

To my son-in-law, Collin Gibson, thank you again for your practical assistance and support in matters related to the computer world. You've covered my back once again.

Thank you too to my mentors and spiritual father and mother, John and Carol Arnott, for more than two decades of showing us the way in terms of continually seeking after, valuing and stewarding the manifest presence of God. What a ride this has been and continues to be. Thank you for staying so playful, child-like and captivated by the beauty of Jesus and so immersed in the lavish love of the Father, through all the ebbs and flows of life.

Thank you to Dr. R. T. Kendall for reading the early manuscript and providing such encouragement to me.

Thank you to my sister, Connie, and her husband, Jeremy Sinnott, for your support over the years as well as in this research and writing project. Connie, while busy travelling and ministering, you made time to read the manuscript and provide me with vital information and perspective as well as help keep things accurate. Thank you sis. I owe you.

Thank you too to my friend, Al MacDonald who took the time to proofread the manuscript and to my dear friend and editor, Doris Schuster, of Christian Editing Services, for your sharp eye in catching my many mistakes and flaws and cleaning things up for me.

Thank you to all the incredible men and women who came through at the 11th hour to endorse this book, and moreso, to endorse this move of God. Your names have been recorded.

Finally, thank you to Jonathan Puddle and the team at Catch The Fire Books in Toronto for all that you have done to polish up and publish this material. I know it was quite the rush at the end! I appreciate your input and encouragement as well, Jonathan, after reading the first draft.

May this book bring honour to our Father in heaven as well as be a testimony of His willingness and even eagerness to unleash heaven on earth as we demonstrate a desperation and hunger for only Him.

Introduction

The outpouring of the Holy Spirit in Toronto began on January 20, 1994 and over the last two decades has circled the globe. Before our eyes, God has shown up in dramatic fashion. He has been performing an extraordinary work of grace of such a magnitude that we long for no one to miss out.

Why write this book?

This book is our attempt to track what God has done through the outpouring and how He has gone about it. We've recorded here, to the best of our ability, the gracious orchestrations of our passionate God who partners with His people in order to advance His kingly rule on the earth. In these pages, we seek to connect the dots; to follow the stories of the people and events God has used to create an ever-widening rippling effect of His Father's Blessing around the globe.

In the Scriptures, we see the Lord frequently instructing His people to record and to recall the stories of His faithful deeds for generations to come. Our faith is fortified by reading the record of what God has done in waves of renewal and revival throughout church history. That's why I believe it's very important to chronicle what God has done in an extraordinary season of divine visitation.

In some ways, it's still too early to see the full picture; the full impact and fruit of what God has done through this move of His Spirit. Yet, if we wait too long, we risk losing some of the details and accuracy of the events, testimonies and stories. In seeking to document this visitation, we are humbly aware it's impossible to track it all. What is covered here is merely the tip of the iceberg. Beneath it lies an ocean of stories, of people who have been powerfully touched and mightily used by the Lord to spread the flames of revival.

We pray that this attempt to accurately document the extraordinary things Father has performed in and through the lives of ordinary people during this season of heavenly visitation, will bring him honour. We pray too that it will inform your mind, stir your heart, and intensify your hunger as you believe and contend for further waves of His glory. May the cry of all our hearts continue to reach the throne room with the prayer, "More Lord."

Renewal, revival or awakening?

Many Christians use the terms renewal, revival and awakening interchangeably and we believe that's valid. They are referring to a season of visitation in which God comes down and manifests His presence in a very powerful and tangible way, leaving multitudes renewed, revived and awakened.

However, there is a legitimate place to seek to be precise in the meaning of words employed in order to minimize confusion and to sharpen understanding and expectations. Many evangelical leaders have concluded that:

A renewal is when God comes down and touches, refreshes and reinvigorates believers.

A revival is when God does the above plus we see prodigals and sinners come to repentance and faith in Christ in extraordinary numbers, resulting in noticeable numerical growth in churches.

An awakening is when God does the above plus we see Kingdom transformation and reformation within the fabric of societies and cultures.

In the early days of the Toronto outpouring, John Wimber encouraged us in the Vineyard not to call it "a revival" but rather "a renewal." He knew that in the early stages of an outpouring, the Holy Spirit tends to work primarily with God's people; awakening and renewing them in their relationship with God and each other. This should then lead to the next stage, historic revival, where we see many prodigals and sinners coming to Christ both in church meetings and in the marketplace. John Wimber felt that prematurely using the word "revival" might cause some to believe 'this is as good as it gets'. He didn't want us to be content with only seeing believers refreshed, but to believe and contend for so much more.

The Arnotts and their leadership team sought to respect John Wimber's request that this move of God be called a renewal. After two years, when the Toronto church was no longer in the Vineyard, they felt the freedom to use the term 'revival' to describe what they believed God was doing. Within the first year of this visitation, the church historian, Richard Riss, of New Jersey, claimed that this indeed had virtually all the characteristics or landmarks of a genuine revival. He felt that by calling it only a "renewal", we were devaluing what God was doing.[1]

In the Spread the Fire magazine in 2001, John Arnott wrote:

"Some have commented 'I don't want renewal, I want revival!' What they don't realize is that they are saying that they don't want the intimate, refreshing times of soaking in the Holy Spirit's renewing presence. They want to get involved with evangelism and the harvesting of souls. It sounds so noble, but what they are actually saying is, 'No thanks, God. I don't personally need any more of your love. I'm eager to work for You, but I really don't want to be with You.' It is as though taking time to be a son rather than just a servant is some kind of unhealthy form of self-indulgence.

However, the deep work that the Holy Spirit does in the heart causes a paradigm shift in our motivation. The person who is truly in love will far outperform the worker. Why? Because love is a stronger motivation than duty...

So the revival continues in the midst of theologians arguing over what is and what isn't God. Hundreds now are being saved, healed and brought into God's intimate love by the Holy Spirit. He is the precious key to revival, the One who causes revivals to look different depending on what He wants to do. This one is about experiencing the Father's gracious love and restoring our heartfelt passion for Jesus.

---

1   Richard Riss, Spread the Fire magazine, August 1996, p. 19; January 1998, pp. 6-7.

The promise is to the thirsty, (John 7:37) not to those thirsty for head knowledge only but for those who are thirsty to experience Him.

And it's not over; it has only begun. Regardless of what you call this outpouring of the Spirit, the real issue is that we not be content to be students of revival only but become whole-hearted participators, ones who experience revival. Revival is not just a phenomenon to be theologically dissected. Too often we analyze revivals of the past in the hope of isolating and identifying their principles so we can reproduce them elsewhere through our own efforts. What we really need to do is welcome a visitation of the Holy Spirit by catching its fire ourselves. Why not just take the Holy Spirit the way He comes, with His agenda instead of ours? I think we can really trust Him, don't you?... What a treasure His presence really is. He's the only treasure worth keeping, and He's here among us now. I want to welcome Him, value Him and keep Him at all costs and never ever grieve Him away. After all, He is revival."[2]

Even if we insist on the more narrowly defined use of the word "revival", in terms of God's manifest presence coming, resulting in mass conversions to Christ, then, after twenty years, a case could very well be made that this outpouring has begun to meet that definition. The nightly renewal meetings continued six nights a week for twelve years and they saw over ten thousand conversions and re-dedications to Christ. The Toronto Outpouring, over the years, has actually resulted in conversion fruit of millions throughout the world. Though the vast majority of conversions have not come from the Toronto meetings directly, better yet, they have come through those who have been freshly touched by the Father's powerful love and grace and have gone out into the highways and byways "gossiping the gospel". And with an army of saints freshly loved, restored and empowered going to tens of thousands of churches and into the public marketplaces of the world, who knows what that might look like in the years to come, in terms of a greater harvest of souls for the Kingdom and even reformation of

---

2   John Arnott, Living in Revival, Spread the Fire magazine, Issue 5, 2001, pp. 8-9.

cultures and nations?

The story is not finished yet, especially if we believe for another wave to ride in on top of this one. What if this outpouring is the preparation for (or the first part of) an awakening? If God's Holy Spirit, who comes with a wave of revival power and grace, is met and deeply grieved by human fear, pride, competition, control, criticism and unbelief, that season of visitation will tend to be restricted and short-lived. However, if a move of God is widely embraced and cherished, continues to grow and gain momentum in an atmosphere of humility, hunger, unity, and depth and breadth of mature leadership, it could be sustained and ultimately lead to an awakening that impacts and transforms whole communities and cultures for decades to come.

A few notes on the writing of this book

I am very thankful to John for granting me the privilege of taking on this research project, which has entailed long hours of meticulous sifting through books, magazines, newspaper clippings, old VHS tapes, websites, my personal journals, emails, and telephone correspondence, as well as personal interviews (My family couldn't understand why, through all our moves, I kept all those boxes full of videos, books, magazines, and newspaper clippings of Toronto).

It has been quite an experience going down memory lane and recalling so many of the astounding things God has done in these two decades. I have laughed. I have cried. I have been awestruck at how kind, affectionate and delightfully joyful our heavenly Father really is. I'm also freshly awakened to the fact that our sovereign God is full of surprises and that He loves us way too much to let us settle for mediocrity and defend the status quo.

In chronicling this move of God, I've been inspired by the writings of the Christian journalist, Frank Bartleman, who recorded what the Lord had done during the Azusa Street revival at the beginning of the 20th century, even though he was a fully active participant in that outpouring. John and I recognize that we are not outsiders to this move of God but rather joyful and active participants. This gives us the advantage of being first-hand witnesses to many of the events described. We also have the disadvantage of not being totally objective and unbiased, though I have done my best to present matters for all readers to make your own decisions.

What we've left out

As the page count got longer and longer, we realised we would need to focus on certain things and leave others out. I truly understand what John meant when he wrote in chapter 21 verse 5 of his gospel, "Jesus did many other things as well. If every one of them were written down, I suppose that even the whole world would not have room for the books that would be written." We have had to leave out the biographies of the many spiritual sons and daughters that John and Carol have raise up during this time. Some of their names do grace these pages, but they have not been given the attention they deserve. Also left on the cutting room floor was a large section regarding the attention the world's media has paid to this Outpouring.

John and I acknowledge that God has done much to extend His Kingdom over these last twenty years that has had nothing to do with the outpouring in Toronto. By His Spirit, He is always working and moving in and through His Church and in the lives and affairs of man around the world. We are a part of a much larger whole, and we celebrate everything He does!

PART 1 – A HISTORY OF THE TORONTO OUTPOURING

CHAPTER 1

Prophecies About the Coming Outpouring

"Surely the Sovereign LORD does nothing without revealing his plan to his servants the prophets." Amos 3:7

The Lord often prepares His people for a new season of divine visitation by speaking through the prophets. Prophetic revelation creates greater hunger, faith and expectation. It motivates the saints to intensify their prayers that He would come.

When prophetic words about a move of God are fulfilled, they reassure God's people that this is Him at work. They help us to embrace what God is doing in that hour rather than oppose and miss out.

Before we look at many of the prophetic words given prior to 1994, let's look back at a couple of examples in church history when God prophetically tipped off His people prior to a revival.

Prophecies given prior to Hernnhut and the Welsh Revival (1904)

John Hus, a forerunner of the Reformation, worked among the people of Moravia. He was burned at the stake in 1415 for teaching the Bible. Before he died, he claimed that his teaching, prayers and the persecuted Moravians were a "hidden seed" that would one day spring up into revival. Two hundred years later, John Amos Comenius, the father of modern education, prophesied that the "hidden seed" that John Hus had prophesied about would sprout into revival in one hundred years.

Count Nikolaus Ludwig von Zinzendorf was born in 1700. In 1722, he began taking in Moravian refugees onto his land. Soon he had three hundred people living in a community called Hernnhut. By 1727 there was much division among them. One day Zinzendorf came across Comenius' writings regarding community life as well as his prophecy. He looked at the date and realized it was given exactly one hundred years earlier. This stirred the faith of Zinzendorf and the refugees that the Lord was about to do something extraordinary. On August 13, 1727, as these refugees reconciled their differences and had communion together, the Holy Spirit fell in revival power.[1]

For several months in 1904, Evan Roberts was awakened by the Lord in the middle of the night and had powerful times of communion with God. During this time, Evan received a prophetic vision that catapulted his faith forward for revival. In the vision he saw the number "100,000". From then on, he was confident that revival was imminent and he was praying and believing for one hundred thousand salvations. He began to share with others at school about his vision of one hundred thousand people coming to faith in Christ."[2]

He even wrote to the editor of the newspaper and explained, "We are on the eve of a great and grand revival, the greatest the world has ever seen. Do not think that the writer is a madman."[3] Revival began in Wales the first week of November 1904 and in less than a year, over one hundred thousand souls came to Christ.

Prophecies prior to the outpouring in 1994

Dave Obbard, 1954
A prophetic vision received by a Kent-based Baptist pastor, David Obbard, suggested that revival may start in 1994. In the year 1954, Obbard was studying Ezekiel 37. In his autobiography *Ploughboy to Pastor*, he wrote:

---

1   http://wordsfromsimon.wordpress.com/2013/06/16/prayer-01-god-wants-your-prayer/, http://ruminatewithrick.blogspot.ca/2013/08/vol-74-moravian-pentecost.html; also Rick Joyner, Morningstar Journal, Vol. 5, No. 1, 1995, pp. 64-65.
2   Richard Riss, A Survey of 20th Century Revival Movements, Hendrickson Pub., 1988, p. 33; citing Eifion Evans, The Welsh Revival of 1904 (Port Talbot, Glamorgan, Wales: The Evangelical Movement of Wales, 1969), p. 64.
3   Wesley Campbell, Welcoming a Visitation of the Holy Spirit, Creation House, 1996, p. 37, citing J. Edwin Orr, The Flaming Tongue, Moody Press, Chicago, 1973, p. 8.

It came to me in this way; that as bone came to bone, so there would be a revival of interest in the doctrines of grace, which are surely the framework of the true church, but this would not bring revival itself. Also, as the sinews and flesh came upon them, so there would follow a revival of true biblical order and experiential spiritual life, but neither would these things bring revival. Following this there would be a mighty movement of the Holy Spirit, the breath of God, and the church would be raised from its lifeless state to that of an exceeding great army.

When this persuasion came to me there was presented to my mind the figure of twenty-year periods: twenty years for the bones to come together, twenty years during which Bible-based churches of born-again believers would be established on a worldwide scale; and some time during the next twenty years (i.e. from 1994 onwards) a mighty outpouring of the Holy Spirit. I can give no reason for these twenty-year periods other than to repeat that they were presented to my mind at that time.

Dave Roberts, in his book *The Toronto Blessing*, provides us with this prophecy and he goes on to comment that Obbard, during the early 1990s, viewed the ministry of Martyn Lloyd-Jones as evidence of the promotion of doctrines of grace and the growth of the charismatic movement as a contributing factor in "a return to the New Testament pattern of church life." Obbard also indicated that he had hope for the period from 1994 to 2015.[4]

Mike Bickle, 1982
In September 1982, while in his hotel room in Cairo, Egypt, Mike Bickle heard the Lord speak powerfully within his spirit, causing the fear of the Lord to come upon him. God said to him, "I am going to change the understanding and expression of Christianity in the whole earth

---

4   Dave Roberts, The Toronto Blessing, Kingsway, 1994, pp. 27-28, citing Ploughboy to Pastor, David Obbard, published privately.

in one generation."[5]

Though not specifically referring to the Toronto 1994 visitation, this word gives further context to what God is seeking to do in our day.

Bob Jones, 1984

On a Saturday morning, in April 1984, Mike Bickle was lying wide awake on his bed, about to get up, when all of a sudden he heard the thunderous audible voice of God say: "I have a revelation for you. Call Bob Jones." This shook Mike to the core. He talked with Bob Jones on the telephone a couple of hours later. Bob said, "Mike, I had an absolutely astounding experience this morning. The Lord wants me to tell it to you." God certainly had Mike's attention. He realized that the Lord had prepared him to hear revelation that must be taken very seriously.

Bob Jones went into an open vision of Joseph's dungeon (Genesis 40:2-19) where he saw two men who represented two types of ministries in the body of Christ. One was the baker, who made bread for the king's family and the other, the cupbearer, served the wine in the presence of the king. Both were being accused of putting poison in their service to the king. The baker was found guilty and put to death. The cupbearer was found innocent and was released from prison to be exalted to serve wine in the presence of the king again.

However, this releasing would not take place for ten years (sure enough, the church went through some very dark and disheartening days with a series of public scandals among Christian leadership in those ten years).

Mike Bickle admits he was deeply disappointed on two counts with Bob Jones' word. First, because he spoke of wine and not fire, and secondly because he would have to wait another ten years to see revival break out:

"Ten years? I will be almost forty years old. It will be too late. Ten years?" Bob's response was simply, "Well, ten years will be here in a minute."

---

5   http://www.mikebickle.org.edgesuite.net/MikeBickleVOD/2009/20090917A-T-The_Early_Days_
    Cairo_Egypt_and_the_Solemn_Assembly_IPH01.pdf

The Lord told Bob Jones that in ten years (1994) there would be the first of three waves of revival. The first wave would be characterized by new wine, which would release refreshment and joy and produce humility in the body of Christ. In the future, a wave of fire (conviction, passion, holiness, evangelism, signs and wonders) would come, followed by a wave of wind (significant increase of miracles and angelic activity), leading ultimately to the end of this age and the return of Christ. Each wave would build on the last wave, not replace it. And these three waves would come in reverse order of the outpouring described in Acts 2, on the day of Pentecost, which was: wind, fire, and wine.

The Lord showed Bob Jones that this first wave of wine would not only bring refreshment and healing of hearts, but that it would be used by the Lord to offend the mind to reveal the heart. God would be testing hearts. He would be seeking hungry and humble hearts. Many people would be offended by the first wave of new wine and miss out and perhaps find it very difficult to enter into the later waves of fire and wind.[6]

I, Jerry, first heard of this prophetic word in 1988, while living in Vancouver, and began to grow in faith and anticipation of what might come in 1994. I had also received a personal prophetic word around that time; it predicted that when I turned forty, it would be "a year of a perpetual birthday party". That got my attention because it lined up perfectly with the timing of the prophesied first wave of revival for 1994. Little did I know, when the Lord directed my wife and me (through words from Terry Lamb, Marc Dupont and others) to move back to the religiously conservative province of Ontario in 1990 to work with John Arnott, that we would be privileged to see this word of the first wave come to fruition in January 1994, before our very eyes.

Mike Bickle and the leadership of Metro Vineyard received further revelation in 1984 and 1985 concerning the soon coming move of God. God told them to "keep your eyes open for a great flood. When you see

---

6   Word of Bob Jones given to Mike Bickle in 1984, can be heard or read on Mike's website, Kansas City prophetic history, Joseph's dungeon: the power of the Spirit and humility, May 4, 2013. http://mikebickle.org/resources/resource/1645?return_url=http%3A%2F%2Fmikebickle. org%2Fresources%2Fseries%2F38 (accessed Aug. 20, 2013).

the Mississippi flood and even change direction, this is the signal that a mighty move of the Spirit is about to begin." [7]

Cindy Jacobs, 1986

In the January 1995 issue of *Charisma* magazine, Cindy Jacobs wrote an article entitled '1995: A Critical Year'. In it she said,

> Many of the moves of God we are seeing in the 1990s were prophesied in the 1980s. I remember two gatherings of prayer leaders held in 1986—one in Tulsa, Oklahoma, the other in Pasadena, California—in which almost identical prophecies were given about a sweeping revival that would begin in Canada. As I write, sparks of revival are already leaping into the United States from Toronto! [8]

Larry Randolph, 1986

In 1986, Larry Randolph had a powerful visitation from the Lord. As he lay on his bed, God said to him,

> As it was in the days of Noah, so shall it be in the coming of the Son of Man. I'm going to bring an unprecedented outpouring of My Spirit upon the church and the world. Just as Noah received a rain that was unprecedented in his generation, I'm bringing a rain of My Spirit unprecedented upon this generation.

When Larry asked the Lord when this outpouring of rain would come, he felt the Lord say it would be in seven years. It would start in the fall of 1993 and develop from there. [9]

James Ryle, 1989

In his 1993 book *Hippo in the Garden*, Pastor James Ryle relays a startling dream he had in the fall of 1989. He dreamed he was standing in his

---

7   Wes Campbell, Welcoming a Visitation of the Holy Spirit, Creation House, 1996, p. 42; Roger Helland, Let the River Flow, Bridge-Logos, 1996, states that Bob Jones received this word in 1984, p. 21.
8   Charisma Magazine, January 1995 issue, p. 14; cited in Richard Riss, The Awakening of 1992-1995.
9   Wesley Campbell, pp. 42-43, citing Larry's message, "Why God is moving powerfully in the Nineties", spoken and taped at New Life Vineyard, Kelowna, B.C., June 1994; also Roger Helland, p. 21

house, looking out at the English garden in his backyard. Everything was perfect—warm sunshine beaming down upon the beautiful flowers with a gentle breeze carrying the fragrance of the flowers throughout the neighbourhood. And the children's sandbox, swing set, toys, lawn chairs, hammock and lawn mower were all neat and tidy. He felt like a king surveying his peaceful, happy little kingdom.

But then he saw a man enter the garden with a pet animal following behind. It was a huge hippopotamus! James was so jolted and shocked by the intrusion and by such an outrageous sight that he immediately woke up from the dream.

James Ryle writes:

"I lay awake in my bed in the early morning hours contemplating the curious and unsettling sight. I asked, 'Lord, what was the meaning of that?' I was surprised by His answer. 'I am about to do a strange, new thing in My church,' He said. 'It will be like a man bringing hippopotamus into his garden. Think about that.' 'What is the strange thing You will do?' I asked. He answered, 'I will surely pour out a vast prophetic anointing upon My church and release My people as a prophetic voice into the earth. It will seem so strange and out of place—like a hippo in a garden—but this is what I will do.'

The 'hippo in the garden' is a fulfilment of Joel's ancient prophecy (that is, Acts 2:17), which initially occurred among the one hundred and twenty believers on the day of Pentecost (Acts 2:1-4). The people who witnessed this supernatural occurrence responded with a variety of emotions. Some wondered while others mocked (Acts 2:12-13). These are typical reactions toward a hippo in a garden...

I realize now why the dream startled me awake as it did. It was exactly what the Lord intended to happen, for the uniqueness of what the Lord is about to do will likewise jar the church from her season of slumber... We tend to think that we can dictate to God what He can and cannot do. But now, as always, God will arise and do His own bidding. He will enter into our docile kingdoms—uninvited, if necessary—and bring His pet hippo with Him!" [10]

---

10   James Ryle, Hippo in the Garden, Creation House, 1993, pp. 258-262

Wesley Campbell, in his book Welcoming a Visitation of the Holy Spirit, not only highlights this dream but gives an update:

> "Just months after the renewal began and we compared notes on how many people were being released in the prophetic during this move, James said, 'This is the dream—the hippo in the garden.' But whoever thought that it would be a shaking hippopotamus?"[11]

I would like to make a further observation. The word hippopotamus literally means, "river horse". It's interesting that James Ryle mentions that, shortly after this dream, he watched a documentary on hippopotamuses called *River of Life*. The 1994 outpouring has often been described as a river and churches that continue to soak in the river are known as "river churches."

Marc Dupont, 1992-1993

In May 1992, Marc Dupont, a prophetically gifted leader from San Diego, moved his wife, Kim, and his family to Toronto to come on staff at the Toronto Airport Vineyard Christian Fellowship. Within days, God gave him a significant vision of what was to take place soon in the Toronto area. Here is a condensed version:

> I had a vision of water falling over and onto an extremely large rock. The amount of water was similar to Niagara Falls. Toronto shall be a place where much living water will be flowing with great power, even though at the present time both the church and the city are like big rocks—cold and hard against God's love and His Spirit. The waterfall shall be so powerful that it will break the big rocks up into small stones that can be used in building the Kingdom... A new song will spring up from the heart of the church as we respond to the moving of the Holy Spirit. Not so much literally a 'new song', but a new freedom for worshipping with God's favor and presence resting on us... There will be a radical move in late 93 and throughout 94 of

---

11   Wesley Campbell, pp. 145-146.

many ordinary Christians beginning to form on their own prayer groups of intercession for the city, the nation, and the peoples.

The disciples of Jesus were gathered from many different areas of life. The leaders of the coming move of the Lord are also going to be coming from many different areas... Many of them are also not mainstream, but many will be without a lot of previous experience, but they will end up both being used by God in evangelism, signs and wonders and also in discipling new converts... many leaders will not be in leadership of what is to come, because many current leaders will disqualify themselves by not responding to what the Father will be saying...

Like Jerusalem, Toronto will end up being a sending out place. It is of God that there are so many internationals in this area. The Lord is going to be sending out many people, filled with His Spirit with strong gifting, vision, and love to the nations on all continents. There are going to be new Bible schools, training centers, and leadership schools raised up in the move that is coming. These schools will have a focus not only on Bible knowledge, but also on training in healing the broken hearts and setting the captives free and on developing intimacy with the Father.

As God's rock began to be raised up out of the stony city, it began to be shaped like a huge dam, which to some degree stored the living water. But at the same time the water began to be poured out of the dam and flow west quite strongly. I saw those waters like a strong raging river head west all the way to the Rocky Mountains. Then it ran north along the eastern edge of the mountains and back east across the plains. In essence there was like a huge circle of water that wrapped around the plains of Canada. As the waters originating from Toronto began to go into the plains areas, they began to find wells or pockets of water in many areas of the plains. I believe these wells are symbolic of remnant areas of Mennonites and other groups that experienced revival years and years ago, but like unused wells, have not been tapped into for a long time. As the waters began to mix, the wells came to life and began to become like geysers shooting water up for hundreds of feet. People began to flock to many areas of the plains, and these areas became centers of revival, which then spread to other cities and towns. I believe that there is a strong contingent of prayer warriors, who are descendants of people many years ago who have continued to seek the face of God for their country.[12]

On July 5, 1993, while Marc was in Vancouver, British Columbia, he felt the Lord give him a second part to the 1992 vision, which had a sense of urgency to it. This word was for the leaders of the body of Christ in the Toronto area:

I believe the Lord indicated that the increase in evangelism, the moving of the Holy Spirit, and the call to Christians from the Spirit for prayer is going to happen even this summer and autumn, with the pace accelerating into the new year. At the same time, the refiner's fire is going to increase on leadership. As it says in Malachi 3, 'who can stand' when the refiner's fire comes? Many leaders are going to be greatly shaken... For those that begin to catch what the Spirit is saying to them, they are going to be making radical steps that are going to be extremely radical for those in the churches who are not hearing what the Spirit is saying...

There are going to be two basic stages in this process, which are represented by the two stages in Ezekiel's vision of the valley of dry bones. The first stage of the dry bones involved receiving muscle, sinew, and flesh. This is the prophetic stage, where the church and the leaders of the stage begin to seek the Father and cry out to Him for grace, mercy, and a sovereign move of His Spirit. It is during this stage that leaders are going to come together for prayer, with a new attitude of humility as they realize that the Lord is calling us to do things which are completely beyond our abilities or past experiences... the Father is going to be speaking things to leaders that will appear as impossible in our understanding of what can happen in our time and culture.

---

12 Marc Dupont, condensed version based on the unpublished full version copy of the May 1992 Vision of water like Niagara Falls coming upon Toronto, Mantle of Praise Ministries; also Wesley Campbell, pp. 45-46 and Roger Helland, pp. 23-24.

The second stage is the apostolic stage of power and authority coming on the Church in the Toronto area. There is going to be a move of the Spirit of God on the city that is going to include powerful signs and wonders, such as in the early days of the church in Jerusalem. But also there are going to be leaders raised up in the body of Christ that are going to move in authority that will be trans-denominational. These will end up being pastors of pastors and will be recognized as spokesmen and leaders for the government of God in the body of Christ across the denominational board. It will only be when all of the five fold offices of Ephesians are in operation, and when church leaders are coming into unity in the Spirit of the Lord that there will be a powerful release of the gospel through the church to touch the cultures of southern Ontario. There will also be an increase in powerful healings and miracles.

What God is going to do in southern Ontario and Canada will be something totally unique and special. When the winds of the Spirit begin to blow there will be elements from all four corners of the earth as to what is currently happening with the body of Christ today, but the make-up of what will happen will not be like revival that has happened anywhere else in the world. I believe that Toronto will be affected by what is currently happening in Asia, South America, the Soviet countries, Britain and Europe but it will still be highly unique...[13]

In August 1993, as John Arnott, Wes Campbell and Marc Dupont walked across the parking lot at the Vineyard family camp in Stayner, Ontario, Marc received another powerful word about a coming revival and that within seven months, John and Carol Arnott would begin to visit cities of the world to be used in releasing a fresh anointing of the Spirit to thousands.[14]

---

13   Marc Dupont, condensed version of unpublished copy of part 2 Vision of July 5, 1993.
14   Ibid., p. 19, 46.

Larry Randolph, 1993

Early in 1993, Larry was invited by Fred Price to share on his radio broadcast in Los Angeles what he felt the Lord was saying about 1993. Live on radio, Larry prophesied the following:

> The Lord is bringing an unprecedented revival. The fall of 1993 is its beginning. A sign will be that the nation is going to have one of the wettest years ever in the last hundred years in this nation. It's going to rain in the Midwest, it's going to rain in California. It's going to rain, rain, rain.[15]

By February, mudslides were taking place in California and the Midwest was pounded by torrential rains in the spring, causing many to claim that it was the worst flooding in one hundred years. Even the Mississippi river reversed its flow in some areas.[16]

Stacey Campbell, October 1993

While ministering at the Toronto Airport Vineyard, Stacey prophesied,

> The Lord is going to come in a wave of miracles... with His great power and with His great celebration... For I am telling you that the day is coming when miracles will be commonplace... And it (will go) not only from this place, from the interior of this province, but it (will) go from nation to nation to nation to nation...[17]

John Wimber, 1993

In April of 1993, John Wimber was told that he had some form of cancer in his nasal area. He underwent many radiation treatments during the following months. During this time of illness and weakness, the Lord spoke to John Wimber's wife, Carol, in July 1993, and said, "John is to go to the nations." John understood this to mean that he would be going to minister to churches around the world, which meant a

---

15   Ibid., p. 43; also Roger Helland, pp. 20-21.
16   Ibid., pp. 43-44, citing Larry's taped message at New Life, June 1994.
17   Ibid., p. 19.

ministry of fresh renewal.[18]

By October 1993, God had spoken twenty-seven times, confirming again that John Wimber was to go to the nations, and seventeen times He said that it would be a "season of new beginnings."[19]

Paul Cain, December 31, 1993

Paul Cain came to visit John and Carol Wimber in Anaheim, California and prophesied to them at their December 31, 1993, New Year's Eve service. He said, "There is coming a fresh release and visitation to John and Carol... This move of the Spirit will bless the whole Vineyard." Later that evening, Paul talked to John and Carol Wimber and said that the Lord had told him, "John and Carol, not Wimber." The only other John and Carol that John Wimber knew who were in the Vineyard movement were John and Carol Arnott of Toronto, Canada.[20]

Anni Shelton, early-mid January, 1994

Anni Shelton, wife of Randy Clark's worship leader, Gary Shelton, had a vision a week or two prior to Randy's trip to Toronto. She saw a map of North America. Fire started in Toronto and the flames burned a hole through the map there, and spread throughout southern Ontario and beyond, in all directions, similar to the Ponderosa map on the old television show, Bonanza.[21]

John Wimber, January 16, 1994

On the afternoon of Sunday, January 16, 1994, the Holy Spirit spoke the word 'Pentecost' to John Wimber... He went off to the Sunday night service at the Vineyard in Anaheim. During the service, the Lord gave him a vision of young people in a certain order. During the ministry time, John asked the young people to come forward. The Lord came and consumed them with His love and power. That night began an overflow of power in the church that lasted for months.[22]

---

18 Bill Jackson, The Quest for the Radical Middle, Vineyard International Pub. 1999, p. 279; Wesley Campbell, p. 25, citing John Wimber's article in the Anaheim Vineyard publication, Vineyard Reflections (May/June 1994), pp. 2-3
19 Bill Jackson, p. 279; Wesley Campbell, p. 25.
20 Roger Helland, pp. 22-23; also Wesley Campbell, p. 25.
21 Randy Clark, Lighting Fires, p. 84; also Guy Chevreau, Catch The Fire, Harper Collins, 1994, p. 35.
22 Bill Jackson, The Quest for the Radical Middle, Vineyard International, 1999, pp. 282-283.

Conclusion

Through a string of prophetic words of encouragement, the Lord had revealed that a new season of renewal and refreshment would be coming. Some words even gave a specific time—late 1993 and 1994; a specific place—Toronto; and pin-pointed specific human vessels that He planned to use as conduits of His renewing grace—John Wimber, leader of the Vineyard movement, Randy Clark of St. Louis, Missouri, and John and Carol Arnott of Toronto, Canada.

Leonard Ravenhill, the influential revivalist, prayer warrior, evangelist and author, prayed his whole Christian life for revival. He despaired over the contrast between the New Testament church and the modern western church. Before he was promoted to glory in November 1994, he saw the beginnings of this visitation of the Spirit—and he blessed it.[23]

---

23 Wesley Campbell, p. 54; also I recall David Ruis stating, in 1995, that he visited Leonard Ravenhill shortly before he passed away and Leonard blessed David's worship music ministry as well as this move of God.

CHAPTER 2

People and Events Leading up to January 20, 1994

Throughout biblical and church history, we see how God has used individuals to impact others in their generation for the Kingdom of God. For example, we see in the Book of Acts that Stephen's martyrdom pierced a hard-hearted, zealous Pharisee, Saul, who later became Paul, a giant of the faith. Paul became an apostle who helped turn the known world upside down and who wrote a good portion of the New Testament.

We see in church history, Count Zinzendorf who was used by God to impart the DNA of Christian unity, passion for Jesus and world missions among the Moravian refugees on his estate. In 1727 when they received a fresh outpouring of the Holy Spirit in their community, they organized a 24/7 prayer chain that continued unbroken for one hundred years. They released hundreds who fearlessly travelled, many on one-way tickets, to take the gospel to the far corners of the globe.

The domino effect continued. The well-educated Anglican preacher, John Wesley, was on a ship bound for America when a violent storm broke out and he feared for his life. Yet he was even more rattled by the Moravian missionary families on-board. They joyfully sang hymns of praise, immersed in a deep peace and confidence in their Saviour's care. Deeply impacted by the Moravians, Wesley was soon confronted with his own need for a personal, heart-level encounter with the living Saviour. And of course, the leaders of the Great Awakening in Britain in the 18th century—Wesley, Whitfield, Edwards, and others— mutually influenced each other for the cause of Christ.

Let us take a look at some of the people that God has used to play a significant part in what later became "The Toronto Blessing". We want to celebrate God's goodness and wise orchestrations as well as give honour to those who have stewarded the anointing and been used by God as conduits of His reviving grace.

Rodney Howard-Browne

Rodney M. Howard-Browne was raised in a Pentecostal family in South Africa. In 1979, at the age of eighteen, Rodney experienced an ever-growing hunger for more of God. While at a youth prayer meeting, he cried out to the Lord, "God, either you come down here tonight and touch me, or I'm going to die and come up there and touch you." For twenty minutes he shouted (frightening the other youth), "God, I want your fire." Rodney described this encounter fifteen years later at one of his camp meetings (July 18, 1994). He claimed that the fire of God suddenly fell upon him and he was immersed in the liquid fire of the Holy Spirit. He found himself totally intoxicated in the Spirit, laughing, crying and speaking in tongues. After four days, the glory of God was still upon him. He asked the Lord, "God, lift it. I can't bear it any more…Lord, I'm too young to die…don't kill me now." He felt the manifest presence of God for about two weeks.

A year later, while travelling in ministry with a group of people around South Africa, he invited those who wished God to bless them to come forward and line up. He went down the row and prayed for them and they all ended up on the floor under the power of God. Rodney again felt this strong anointing of the Lord for about two weeks. He asked the Lord what he must do to get the anointing back. The Lord told him that there is no formula and that he can't do anything to get it back. He said,

I just gave you a taste of what will come later on in your ministry, if

you are faithful. If I gave it to you now, you would destroy yourself...
From now on, whenever that anointing comes, you'll know it's not you
and you'll know it's all Me and you'll have to give Me all the glory and
all the praise and all the honour.[24]

In 1981, Rodney married his wife, Adonica. In December of 1987, he
and his family emigrated to the United States. Rodney is a Pentecostal
preacher and evangelist. On his website, he describes the move this way:

In 1987, when the Lord opened the door for us to come to the United
States of America, He told us to stir up the churches, to get them on
fire for God, so they would be stirred to win the lost. God is always
calling the church back to their first love...[25]

Starting in April of 1989, the revival power of God began to fall
continuously in Rodney's meetings that he conducted throughout the
United States. People were being "slain in the Spirit", saved, healed
emotionally and physically, and breaking out in "holy laughter".

In February of 1993, Rodney Howard-Browne came to do one week
of meetings at the Carpenter's Home Church in Lakeland, Florida,
pastored by Karl Strader. The meetings went on for four weeks. During
the early part of 1993, Rodney spent a total of thirteen weeks ministering
at that church. Christian leaders and believers came from all over the
United States as well as from Africa, the UK and Argentina. Richard
Roberts, as well as Marilyn Hickey and Charles and Francis Hunter,
came to the Lakeland meetings and were freshly touched by the Lord.
In the spring of 1994, the Hunters would bring the laughing revival
to Kensington Temple, in London England, pastored by Colin Dye.[26]

A local Episcopal priest, Bud Williams, was also powerfully
touched in these meetings. Within a year, Bud Williams had ministered
before one hundred thousand people in twenty cities.[27] Other notable

---

24 Richard Riss, A History of the Awakening of 1992-1995, Ch. 3. Rodney Howard-Browne: Back-
    ground, http://www.revivallibrary.org/catalogues/pentecostal/riss.html
25 Quote from the website: rodneyhowardbrowne.net (accessed March 6, 2013)
26 Charles and Frances Hunter, Holy Laughter, Hunter Books, 1994, pp. 51-56.
27 Richard Riss, A History of the Awakening of 1992-1995, Ch. 6-7, Karl Strader and Bud Williams.

evangelists flowing in this anointing, particularly in 1994, were Jerry Gaffney of Washington State and Ray Sell, who died in December 1994.

Mona and Paul Johnian, pastors of the Christian Teaching and Worship Center in the suburbs of Boston, went to Rodney's meetings in Georgia at the end of October 1993. Soon the manifest presence of God broke out in their four hundred and fifty member church. In her book Fresh Anointing, Mona details what God has done in this revival.[28]

Randy Clark reluctantly came to the meetings held by Rodney Howard-Browne[29] at Rhema Bible Church, Tulsa, Oklahoma in August of 1993, where he received a fresh touch and impartation from the Spirit of God.

Randy Clark

Randy Clark first met John Wimber, leader of the Vineyard movement in 1984. John prayed and prophesied over Randy. One of the things he prophesied to Randy that deeply encouraged him was, "You are a prince in the Kingdom of God."

But that wasn't all the Lord had told John Wimber about Randy. Apparently God had spoken audibly to Wimber that Randy would "go around the world and lay hands upon pastors and leaders for impartation of the Holy Spirit, and to stir up and impart the gifts of the Spirit." A few days after the Toronto outpouring began, in January 1994, John Wimber called Randy to tell him that this was the fulfilment of the word God showed him about Randy's life ten years earlier.[30]

In 1993, Randy Clark was in a state of burnout and close to a nervous breakdown. A former Baptist pastor, he was pastoring a Vineyard church he'd planted in St. Louis, Missouri. Randy had been fasting and was desperate for a fresh touch from God, when he received a call at midnight from Jeff, a friend from Illinois. This friend had never

28 Mona Johnian, Fresh Anointing, Bridge Pub., 1994; also described in an article by Steven Smith in Charisma magazine, June 1994, pp. 54-58.

29 Rodney Howard-Browne presently pastors The River at Tampa Bay, a Florida church that he and his wife founded in 1996. Wikipedia website: http://en.wikipedia.org/wiki/Rodney_Howard-Browne, (accessed Mar. 6, 2013)

30 Global Awakening website, history, http://globalawakening.com/home/about-global-awakening/history-of-global-awakening (accessed August 3, 2013)

called Randy before in all the ten years they had known each other. He asked Randy how he was doing and how his church was doing. Randy lied in response to both questions, claiming that everything was fine.

Jeff told Randy about the dark place he had been in for some time, and about how he has been feeling very powerless and dry. One night, at three in the morning, he came very close to taking his own life. The next morning, a pastor called him to ask what he was doing up at three in the morning. The Lord had woken the pastor up and told him to pray for Jeff against a spirit of suicide that was oppressing him. Jeff also had an aunt call him up and challenge him to get his spiritual house in order because she was tired of the Lord waking her up at three in the morning to pray for him.

After seeing an advertisement in Charisma magazine, Randy's friend Jeff went to a seminar led by a South African man named Rodney Howard-Browne. He told Randy how he'd been powerfully refreshed and restored by God. Randy finally admitted that he too was in a desperate place and cried on the phone. His friend strongly urged Randy to go to some of Rodney Howard-Browne's meetings, and called him several times to make sure he would follow through with his promise.[31]

So Randy contacted Rodney's ministry office to find out where he would be ministering the following week. To his dismay, he learned that Rodney would be in Tulsa, Oklahoma, at the Rhema Bible Church. Randy did not want to go because he was very judgmental of the Word of Faith movement and this was ground zero of the movement. He asked the Lord if he could wait a week before going to Rodney's meetings. The Lord replied to him, "You have a denominational spirit if you think you can only drink from the well of your own group. How badly do you want to be touched afresh?" Randy, along with his associate pastor, Bill Mares, reluctantly went to the Tulsa meetings.

On the first night, Randy Clark sat in the back, up in the balcony. He was quite upset with a lady who was laughing throughout the

---

31 Randy Clark speaking at the Catch The Fire Conference in Toronto, Oct. 13, 1994, on video, also documented by Richard Riss, A History of the Awakening of 1992-1995, Chapter 14, Randy Clark.

message. He thought to himself, "She's in the flesh." And as if knowing his thoughts, Rodney Howard-Browne said, "There are others of you, who, if you get upset, that's your flesh." Randy was also skeptical of seeing people being slain in the Spirit in mass and of the hysterical laughing. But on the fourth and final day, Rodney promised to pray for all forty-five hundred people in attendance.

Up to this point, nothing had happened to Randy. Then, in his desperation, he decided to receive ministry from Rodney and got in line to be prayed for. Randy hated waiting in lines but he had told the Lord that he would not eat until the Lord touched him. After receiving prayer, Randy lay on the floor, thinking that nothing had happened to him and feeling how unfair it all was. But he found he was glued to the floor and could not get up. After finally getting off the floor some forty-five minutes later, he went to another part of the building. Hoping he wouldn't be recognized, he took his glasses off, got in line for prayer a second time. Rodney came down the line proclaiming, "Fill, fill, fill" and when he came to Randy he said, "You don't get drunk on a sip" and gently slapped him on the head.

After getting off the floor, Randy put on his glasses, went to a different part of the building, got in line, and bowed his head, hoping again he wouldn't be recognized. After prayer, Randy went down to the floor a third time. Once up, Randy followed Rodney around to watch and learn from him, until an usher told him to back off because he was a bit of a distraction for Rodney. In time, he received prayer again when Rodney's brother, Basil, asked him if he wanted prayer. Randy told him that he had already been prayed for three times but Basil gave him permission, saying that he looked "thirsty".[32]

Randy admitted that he had come to the meetings in desperation but that the Lord had dealt with his judgments towards the Word of Faith camp. He repented of his critical judgments and even went to one of the leaders of Rhema Church and humbled himself, asking for forgiveness for being "mean-spirited against the church and its members."[33]

---

32   Randy Clark, Lighting Fires, Creation House, 1998, pp. 78-80; also, Randy's talk at the Catch The Fire Conference in Toronto, Oct. 13, 1994, on video.
33   Randy Clark, Lighting Fires, p. 80.

On the way to the airport to fly home, Randy's assistant pastor, Bill, exclaimed, "Randy, I can hardly wait 'til we get home and this begins to happen at our church!"

Randy replied, "What did you say?"

Randy had been leading his church towards the "seeker-sensitive" model of church and was cautiously thinking that he needed about six months just to teach them first. But his assistant stated, "I can't wait that long!" Randy pulled rank on him by saying, "I'm the senior pastor!" Then, Clark recalls, God pulled rank on him and said to him in his spirit, "I'll do it when I want!"[34]

The church that Randy had pastored for eight years in St. Louis had never seen anyone get slain in the Spirit before. But the following Sunday, after Randy had finished the teaching, they went into a time of praise and worship. In the middle of the worship, one of the backup singers dropped to the floor, knocking a guitar stand over. This quite sophisticated young woman lay on the floor laughing and slapping her thigh. Apparently, just before she went down, she had seen the glory cloud enter the church. At the end of worship, Randy invited folks to come forward for prayer and, as he prayed a blessing over each one, they dropped to the floor. To Randy's surprise, the same thing happened in the second service. God dropped a bomb on them! [35]

Randy Clark tells how a few weeks later, at the regional meeting of Midwestern Vineyard leaders, the power of God blasted everybody, including his leaders, Happy Leman and Steve Phillips. Happy, who was nicknamed, "Mr. Control", was laughing uncontrollably! Besides getting drunk in the Spirit, Steve Phillips also received healing of a serious spinal injury. The intense pain had awakened him every morning for years.[36]

In November of 1993, at the Vineyard Board meeting in Palm Springs, California, Happy Leman shared with John Arnott about what had happened through Randy at the October regional meeting. When John Arnott got home, he called Randy and asked him to come do four

34 Ibid., p. 81.
35 Ibid., p. 82.
36 Randy Clark, pp. 82-83.

nights of meetings in Toronto in January. Randy wasn't sure he could come up with four messages and suggested he bring his youth pastor and they could each speak twice.

Randy remembered something Rodney Howard-Browne once said, "If you want to have revival, go north in the wintertime!" In his book, Lighting Fires, Randy says he might not have agreed to come to Toronto in January if it were not for this comment of Rodney's. Randy was nervous, not confident that an outpouring of the Spirit would happen if he came to Toronto. Maybe what had happened at his church and at the regional meeting was a fluke. John Arnott still wanted Randy to come.[37]

Randy was encouraged by a vision given to Anni Shelton, the wife of his worship leader, Gary Shelton, just weeks before he was to go. As previously mentioned, Anni had seen a map of Toronto and the city being set on fire, with the blaze spreading out in all directions. She felt the Lord was saying that God was going to start something in Toronto and it was going to spread all over North America.[38] This encouraging vision was reinforced when Randy's friend, Richard Holcomb, gave him a clear prophetic word the night before heading off to Toronto:

> The Lord says, 'Randy, test Me now. Test Me now. Test Me now! Do not be afraid. I will back you up! I want your eyes to be opened as [when] Elisha prayed for Gehazi, that you would see into the heavenlies and see My resources for you. Do not be anxious because when you become anxious, you can't hear Me.'[39]

This emboldened Randy to declare to his people, "We're getting ready to go on an apostolic mission out of the country, and we are going to see more of God than we have ever seen in our lifetime. God is going to show up!" [40]

---

37 Ibid., p. 83.
38 bid., p. 84.
39 Ibid., p. 85; also Randy's message October 14, 1994, Catch The Fire Conference, Toronto, Canada, on video.
40 Ibid., pp. 85-86.

John and Carol Arnott

John Goodwin Arnott was born in Toronto December 25, 1940, to John Thomas Matthews Arnott and Hazel Louise Turner. John's paternal grandfather and maternal grandparents came originally from England. He was born again in 1955, at a Billy Graham crusade.[41]

John lived for most of his life in Toronto. He was married and had two daughters, Lori and Vicki, in the early 1960s. John attended Ontario Bible College in Toronto from 1966 to 1969, then pursued several business opportunities, including a travel business.

Within six years of leaving Bible College, John experienced a very traumatic event; the tragic end of his first marriage to divorce due to irreconcilable differences. Referring to this time of depression and feeling like a failure, John states, "I ended up with my two daughters kind of looking after dad."

Four years later, John met Carol, who "loved him back to life."[42] John claims, "When my first marriage broke up, I made a vow that no woman would ever hurt me like that again. It took me quite a while, with Carol's help, to break down that vow. I thank God that Carol penetrated my defenses. It meant that I was able to be healed of judgments rooted in bitterness, and to see mercy triumphing over judgment."[43] No wonder, the message of forgiveness has become a life message of the Arnotts over the years.

Carol Sandra Bechtold was born in Milverton, Ontario, near Stratford, on May 9, 1943, to a Lutheran couple, Wilfred Bechtold and Florence Hahn. After high school, she became a secretary in a bank and later a legal secretary.

Carol married her childhood sweetheart and they had two boys, Rob and Mike. Her marriage fell apart, however, after about seven years, when her first husband left her for another woman; someone with whom Carol worked. In the midst of her pain and confusion, the

---

41 John Arnott, The Father's Blessing, Creation House, 1995, pp. 5, 42; also John Peters, The Story of Toronto, Authentic Media, 2005, pp. 57-58.
42 John Peters, The Story of Toronto, p. 60, 68.
43 Ibid., p. 98.

Lord met with Carol. One day she heard a voice speaking to her in her home. She wondered if the voice was her husband and whether she may be on the verge of a nervous breakdown. The voice, however, began to repeat the words of Psalm 23.

She got her old Bible out of the dresser and repeatedly read the Psalm. The Lord ministered deeply to her with the revelation of His extravagant love for her. Her shame and depression lifted and she was overwhelmed with the joy of the Lord and Jesus' love for her. Soon afterwards, she led her two boys through a prayer to invite Jesus to forgive them of their sins and to come into their hearts.[44]

Christian neighbours helped Carol in her newfound faith. They invited her to attend meetings conducted by Kathryn Kuhlman. At these meetings, Carol saw that Jesus was not just our Saviour, but also our healer. In seeing the supernatural healing power of God at work to heal bodies, including her own back, Carol was introduced to the person and work of the Holy Spirit.

John and Carol married in 1979. The following year, they went on a life-changing mission trip to Indonesia; two weeks in Jakarta and two weeks in West Papau. They came home with a strong sense that the Lord was calling them into full-time pastoral ministry but they struggled with feeling that they were disqualified since they were both divorced. But the Lord made it clear that He wanted them to move to Carol's hometown of Stratford and start a church. John and Carol came to Stratford in 1981, after selling their business, saying, "Lord, we're just a couple of broken pieces; if you can use us to build your Kingdom, that would be great."

Frank Damazio makes this insightful comment on brokenness in his book, *Seasons of Revival*:

> "Anything that is broken is deemed by man to be unfit, and he ends up throwing it away. But to God, only that which is broken is useful. Just as flowers yield their perfume when they are crushed and grapes produce wine when they are squashed, so the vessels of God—His

---

44 Ibid., pp. 68-71.

people—are ready for revival only when they are broken. God's vessels, the ones He uses, are broken vessels." [45] I remember John Wimber, on more than one occasion, stating that he has more trust in "leaders who walk with a limp."

So, stripped of pride and self-confidence, John and Carol obeyed the Lord and planted a "love church," called Jubilee Christian Ministries, with John leading worship on his autoharp.

John, being an apostolic catalyst and entrepreneur, established not only a church in Stratford that grew to close to three hundred members in eleven years, but also a Christian school and a forty-one-unit rent-geared-to-income townhouse, called Vineyard Village. John was also the area coordinator for the Vineyard churches in Ontario and frequently took teams from various Vineyards on mission trips, particularly to Central America.

While still pastoring the Stratford church, John and Carol felt led to plant a church in Toronto. They started by first establishing a home group (Vineyard called them kinships) in John's mother's home in Toronto in 1987. They officially launched the Toronto Vineyard in 1988. John and Carol pastored both for about four years before moving to Toronto. [46]

People, movements and events God used to prepare John and Carol Arnott

Kathryn Kuhlman and her powerful healing anointing and sensitivity to the Holy Spirit had deeply impacted the Arnotts many years earlier.

John had also been friends with Benny Hinn since the 1970s. John and Carol had Benny come to their Stratford church to minister in the 1980s, which resulted in many youth coming to Christ. Benny had

---

45 Frank Damazio, Seasons of Revival, BT Publishing, 1996, p. 155.
46 Richard Broadbent and I were assistant pastors with the Arnotts in Stratford, with Jeremy Sinnott, Paul White and Dale Bolton assisting in Toronto. Paul and Sandy White would launch out from the Airport Vineyard in the spring of 1993 to plant the Scarborough Vineyard, and Dale and Linda Bolton planted the Thornhill Vineyard in September 1993 Source:Dale Bolton, telephone interview, September 5, 2013.

lived in Toronto for years before moving to Florida and becoming well-known. The ministry of Kathryn Kuhlman had also impacted Benny. In 1993, the Arnotts went to Toronto Maple leaf Gardens to a Benny Hinn meeting. Backstage, Benny ministered to them and Carol received a fresh anointing and became drunk in the Spirit. Later, they attended other meetings of his.[47]

In the early 1980s, the Arnotts experienced a move of God in their new church. Many came to the Lord, particularly young people. It was wonderful, but John tried to tidy it up and keep it from getting too wild. Rather than properly pastor the few who were "getting off track", the Arnotts made general rules, including one that stipulated they would be the only ones who could pray and minister. It was as if the Holy Spirit said, "Fine, you run it then."[48] The Spirit soon lifted.

John repented to the Lord for putting his hand on His move. He promised the Lord that if He ever brought revival again, he would not seek to control it. Here are John's own words:

> "\We effectively killed what had begun as a definite move of the Spirit, but we determined that we would not repeat that error. We also determined that if God gave us a second chance, we would not restrict him so as to make us feel comfortable.[49]

John and Carol were also deeply impacted by the inner healing ministry of John and Paula Sandford, the Father's heart teaching and ministry of Jack Winter and learning to hear the voice of God through the ministry of Mark Virkler and his Communion with God teaching. The Arnotts invited all these gifted teachers to their Stratford and Toronto churches to teach and minister to their leaders and their congregations. By the time the renewal hit in 1994, John estimates that about one hundred and fifty of their people in each of the two churches had gone through extensive training and ministry regarding

---

47   Richard Riss, History of the Awakening 1992-1995, Ch. 16, John Arnott; also from conversations with the Arnotts over the years.
48   Interview with John Arnott, June 14, 2013.
49   Quoted in John Peter's 2005 book, The Story of Toronto p. 56; also author Jerry Steingard heard John share this story several times.

the healing of the heart, the revelation of the Father's love and learning to hear God's voice.

From the mid-1980s, John Wimber and the Vineyard movement contributed significantly to John and Carol Arnott and their ministry. John Arnott's friend, Dale Bolton, who was a leader with Youth With A Mission, in Cambridge, Ontario, had attended the Vineyard Signs and Wonders Conference in Vancouver in May 1985. Dale then said to John, "You gotta come with me next year." After attending that life-changing event in May 1986, John and Dale came home as excited as little kids in a sandbox. John wanted to disciple and equip the saints and he had now seen a practical "turn-key" model that provided training manuals and resources to do that more effectively.

John Arnott contacted Ron Allen, Vineyard area director in Fort Wayne, Indiana, to pursue the process of building a relationship and joining the Vineyard movement. [50] With support and encouragement from Ron Allen in Fort Wayne and Gary Best and his team from the Langley Vineyard in British Columbia, the Arnotts and their church joined the Association of Vineyard Churches in 1987.

John and Carol grew to deeply appreciate and seek to replicate all that this baby boomer, California-based Vineyard movement represented. This included biblically-grounded and Kingdom-centred Vineyard values of intimate worship, practical and non-religious Bible teaching, small home groups or kinships, culturally relevant church life and evangelism, as well as seeking to do only what the Father initiates. Their philosophy of Kingdom ministry revolved around making disciples, training up and reproducing leaders, team ministry and equipping the saints to heal the sick, deliver those who are oppressed, minister to the poor, evangelize and plant churches, all in the power of the Holy Spirit.

Without the Vineyard model of team ministry, the Toronto church would never have been able to continue renewal meetings six nights a week for twelve years. One of the reasons why most revivals in the past have only lasted a few years is because they have usually

---

50 Dale Bolton, telephone interview, September 5, 2013.

been personality-driven, one-man shows, which inevitably result in exhaustion and burnout. [51]

John Wimber's highly influential ministry of diplomacy and fathering had established a strong level of trust and relationship among churches and leaders throughout the western world. Wimber had served for years as a church growth consultant, in partnership with the church statesman, C. Peter Wagner. He had taught at scores of renewal conferences around the world, helping to radically transform the lives of many evangelicals to make their ministries more fruitful. Many leaders from the UK and the United States who flocked to the Toronto Vineyard when the outpouring happened, may not have been so quick to respond if it weren't for their relationship with John Wimber.

One of the many things I've grown to appreciate about John Arnott is his willingness to take risks. This is certainly true of John's willingness to invite speakers to come minister to his people. He may not know them personally, but if he trusts the person recommending them, he is very open to the idea. And it doesn't matter to John if the speaker is from another stream in the body of Christ. He loves cross-pollination. I believe the fact that John invited a plethora of apostolic and prophetic fathers and mothers from other streams to come speak and pour into the Toronto meetings and conferences over these past twenty years has contributed immeasurably to the success, depth and fruit of the Toronto outpouring.

Within a couple of months of coming on staff with John as his assistant pastor and worship leader in Stratford, in the fall of 1990, I told him about a prophetic guy whom I had met in Vancouver earlier in the year and recommended him to John. His name was Marc Dupont, of Mantle of Praise Ministries, based in San Diego, California.

Without hesitation, John suggested that I call Marc Dupont to see if he would come and minister to the Vineyard churches in Ontario sometime. I contacted Marc and he told me that he is usually booked at least a year in advance, but strangely enough, he just had a cancellation

---

51   Interview with John Arnott, June 14, 2013.

come in and now he had a two-week block of time freed up for the following month. We all sensed God was in it. So in late January of 1991, Marc came to minister in the Ontario Vineyards for the very first time

At the last meeting of the ten-day tour, Marc prophesied at the Toronto Airport Vineyard that John and Carol needed to leave Stratford and move to Toronto to give their full attention to the new church and prepare for what God had in store in the coming days. Marc was aware that it's generally not wise to prophesy directional words to church leadership in front of their congregation, but he felt the Lord telling him to do so. As it turned out, Carol had prayed to the Lord that if God clearly wanted them to move, and if Marc was indeed a prophet, then he would publicly prophesy the move to Toronto. Carol was struggling with the idea of leaving her quaint hometown and moving to the big city and she wanted clear confirmation.[52] John and Carol resigned the pastorate in Stratford on June 14, 1992, leaving the church to me to pastor, while they made the strategic move to Toronto.[53]

Another factor that helped prepare the Arnotts for the coming outpouring was a request directly from the Lord. About a year and a half before the outpouring began, John and Carol felt the Lord challenge them to give their mornings over to seeking Him in prayer, worship and studying the Word. This further prepared their hearts and created an ever-deepening passion for Jesus. They are quick to admit that revival did not come to their church because they had somehow earned it. It was simply God's mercy, grace and sovereignty. But they certainly were hungry and desperate for a fresh move of God. About a week before the renewal began, Connie Sinnott recalls Carol Arnott confessing, "Lord, we need more power, it's taking too long in counselling."[54]

The Argentina Connection

Revival broke out in Argentina in the early 1980s, shortly after Argentina's defeat in the Falklands war with Great Britain. Mass

---

52 Conversations with the Arnotts at that time.
53 Author's journal, daytimer and Jubilee elder's records.
54 Recording of Connie Sinnott, Australia, November 5, 2012.

conversions were taking place through such power evangelists as Carlos Annacondia. City church unity and cooperation greatly increased the work of God during these years. Many saw a further surge of revival break out in 1992 through the power ministry of Claudio Friedzon. This move of God was characterized by being slain in the Spirit, joy and laughter, drunkenness in the Spirit, and praise and adoration of the Lord.

Claudio Freidzon, considered by some to be South America's Benny Hinn, was born near Buenos Aires, Argentina in 1955. He came to the Lord before the age of ten. After high school, Claudio attended an Assemblies of God Bible college. Since then, Claudio has been a theology professor and an Assemblies of God pastor. In 1986, he founded the King of Kings Church in Argentina. His ministry accelerated after reading Benny Hinn's book, Good Morning Holy Spirit and receiving prayer ministry from Benny in Orlando, Florida, in 1992.

Not only Claudio, but many other Christians in Argentina, had been impacted by Benny's two books, Good Morning Holy Spirit and The Anointing and these contributed significantly to the Argentina revival.[55]

Rodney Howard-Browne also prayed for Freidzon on another occasion, in a Benny Hinn meeting.[56] Claudio Freidzon's church exploded with both anointing and numerical growth and he began to conduct miracle services in arenas throughout Argentina and South America. He also became internationally known through his own television ministry.

John and Carol Arnott, Vineyard pastors Dale and Linda Bolton, and I, flew to Buenos Aires, Argentina for the third annual Harvest Evangelism International Institute, which was held from November 4 to

---

55 According to Pablo Deiros, in the book co-edited with C. Peter Wagner, The Rising Revival. The Rising Revival, edited by C. Peter Wagner and Pablo Deiros, Renew Books, 1998, gives firsthand accounts of the Argentina revival.

56 According to Dave Roberts, in his book, The Toronto Blessing Dave Roberts, The Toronto Blessing, Kingsway, 1994, p. 15. Claudio Freidzon website: www.empowering-faithministries.org http://www.empowering-faithministries.org/claudio-freidzon.html (accessed March 6, 2013); The Rising Revival, edited by C. Peter Wagner and Pablo Deiros,, Renew Books, 1998, pp. 40-41;

the 13, 1993. This annual pastors' school was led by C. Peter Wagner and Cindy Jacobs, and sponsored by Ed Silvoso and his Harvest Evangelism, Inc. Approximately one hundred pastors and leaders from around the world gathered for this school.

In a brochure advertising this event, Ed Silvoso wrote, "What is so unique about Argentina that warrants a trip to South America? For one thing, God is at work there in an amazing and incomparable way. Have you ever read a book about revival and felt the intense desire to be there? Well, in our time, Argentina is such a place. Come and experience the hand of God as you visit churches that hold services every day of the week." In the same brochure, C. Peter Wagner wrote, "Like a burning, dry tinder, the Spirit of God has ignited an extraordinary spiritual bonfire in Argentina over the last ten years." [57]

We did, indeed, see revival up close. We attended various ministry events led by a number of Argentinian apostolic and evangelistic leaders who partnered together in impressive unity: Carlos Annacondia, Omar Cabrera, Pablo Deiros, Eduardo Lorenzo, Hector Gimenez and Claudio Freidzon. Many of our group also visited Olmos prison, the highest security prison in Argentina, where close to a thousand inmates were radically on fire for Jesus. John and Carol were overwhelmed by the presence of God as well as the passion, joy and freedom these imprisoned believers expressed in their chapel worship.

One night, during a larger pastors' conference, the pastors from our school were invited on stage to be prayed for by Claudio Freidzon. I remember seeing Peter Wagner and Cindy Jacobs on stage, getting quite intoxicated in the joy and wine of the Spirit. We lined up single file and waited our turn to receive prayer by the laying on of hands. After being prayed for, many of the pastors were overwhelmed by the Spirit, collapsing to the ground and rolling and laughing, including Carol. When it was John Arnott's turn, Claudio prayed for him but nothing much seemed to happen, though he did go down to the floor. John began to analyze the experience and was soon on his

---

57   Richard Riss, History of the Awakening of 1992- 1995, Ch. 15, Argentina as a Prelude to the 'Toronto Blessing', www.revival-library.org/catalogues/pentecostal/riss.html (accessed June 17, 2013)

feet. Claudio came over to John again and asked him, "Do you want the anointing?" John replied, "Oh yes, I want it." Claudio responded, "Then take it," and slapped John's outstretched hands. By faith John took it and something significant transpired in his heart and life.[58]

On the way back to Canada from Argentina, John and Carol Arnott had to go via Palm Springs, California, for a Vineyard Board meeting. At this meeting, Vineyard pastor, Happy Lehman shared with John about Randy Clark's recent dramatic experience with the Holy Spirit. He told John how that had released a new level of anointing in his church and at a regional Vineyard leaders' meeting the previous month. John came home and wasted no time in contacting Randy to try to get him to Toronto for some meetings in January. They made plans for four days of meetings, starting Thursday night, January 20th, 1994.

---

58 John Arnott, The Father's Blessing, Creation House, 1995, p. 58; also, author Jerry Steingard personally witnessed this event.

CHAPTER 3

On the Floor in '94

Part One: The Start and Early Days of The Outpouring
The First Four Months of 1994

How many times have you tried to bring to mind past events? There can be a tendency to embellish them, making them 'larger than life' or to trivialize them into a 'been-there-done-that-got-the-T-shirt.' But thankfully there are scenes so emblazoned on our memory that they can never be forgotten; such as the initial days of revival that began for us in 1994. Amazing how the events of one evening can expose and destroy your religious box. In one extravagant puff of joy, my concepts of what the Holy Spirit would or would not do blew out the window, and I discovered that God was no longer going to anoint my predictable and comfortable patterns of 'doing church'.[59]
—Mary Audrey Raycroft

As a fairly small and young church, the Toronto Airport Vineyard Christian Fellowship, leased two units in a small industrial plaza, at the end of an airport runway.[60] The two rooms provided space for a little over three hundred people comfortably in each. One room was used for the sanctuary and the other for children's ministry and seminar training. Mary Audrey Raycroft recalls, "There were two small offices, two washrooms and a snack bar."[61] Their neighbours were a post office,

---

59 Mary Audrey Raycroft, I Remember 94, Spread the Fire magazine, Issue 1 – 2004, article "In the River 10 Years", pp. 16-18.
60 At Dixie Road just south of Derry Road
61 Ibid.

an Italian banquet hall, a furniture store and several empty units. A small "truckers" motel, the White Knight, was close to the entrance and a cornfield beside them. Car parking was seriously limited. On Thursday night, January 20, 1994, at least one hundred and twenty people[62] showed up for the first of four meetings planned with Randy Clark and his team from St. Louis.

In John Arnott's own words, "When Randy shared his testimony that first night and gave an invitation to come forward, my recollection was that there was this incredible explosion as the Spirit of God just sort of fell on the people."[63] Elsewhere, John says,

> We were used to very limited manifestations of the Spirit... but this was suddenly 'kaboom', and eighty percent of our church was all over the floor, and laughing and rolling and totally overtaken by the Spirit of God.[64]

Mary Audrey Raycroft, who had come on the pastoral staff with the church shortly before this eventful day, had been teaching a class in the seminar room. Afterwards she peeped into the auditorium to see how the meeting was going. She was stunned to see people all over the floor and, while she was attempting to process what she was observing, the Holy Spirit hit her too. She fell backwards into the hall and was out of commission; her mouth was frozen for quite a period of time.[65]

Connie Sinnott, who was sitting in the front row while all this bedlam began to unfold, suddenly realized that her mouth and lips were frozen, as if she had been to the dentist. John Arnott was going around interviewing people to ask them what they sensed God was doing with them. When he came by Connie with the microphone and realized she couldn't open her mouth, he was quite amused and

---

62 Warren Marcus, Go Inside the Toronto Blessing video, 1997; Bill Jackson, The Quest for the Radical Middle, Vineyard International Pub. 1999, p. 283, claims about 160 people attended the first night of the renewal; according to an article in Christian Week, December 13, 1994, by Bruce Woods, there were about 150 the first night.
63 John Arnott, recorded interview with author Jerry Steingard, June 14, 2013.
64 John Arnott interviewed in article, "'Mighty Wind from Toronto' Blows Faithful Away", 1994.
65 Tenth anniversary Spread the Fire magazine article by Mary Audrey, 2004; also Connie Sinnott's email to author, August 23, 2013.

prodded her, "Say something, Connie!" With lips frozen and clamped shut, she attempted to mumble, "I can't talk."

Over the following week or two, Connie prayed and asked the Lord for understanding about her strange experience of having a frozen mouth for several hours the first night. She felt the Lord say, "This was so you would know that this was of me. You couldn't make it up."

Further confirmation to her that this was not mere hype or manipulation was watching our mother, Carol Steingard. Carol, by nature, was as shy and as quiet as a mouse. But it wasn't long before Connie saw our mother on the prayer team, praying over someone with her head shaking like a windmill; she was praying and prophesying with a fierce and holy boldness. Connie thought to herself, "My mother would never do that." Afterwards, our father, Bill Steingard often complained that he would wake up in the middle of the night because the whole bed was shaking![66]

Ten o'clock the next morning, Friday January 21, began the all-day Ontario Vineyard pastors' day with Randy Clark, which had been arranged for weeks. Randy's worship leader, Gary Shelton, started off with a song that would become a theme song of the renewal in the coming months, Fred Hammond's "Be Magnified". It starts by saying, "I have made you too small in my eyes, oh Lord, forgive me." A couple of lines later, it says, "Heal my heart and show Yourself strong." A heavy presence of the Lord came upon us while singing that song and many of us spontaneously burst out in tears of brokenness and repentance before the Lord.

After Randy spoke, he invited the pastors and their wives to come forward for prayer. Before Randy prayed for me, he discerned that I was a left-brain analytical kind of guy and wisely coached me by saying to me, "You are waiting for God to hit you with a baseball bat to be sure it is Him but it's probably not going to happen that way for you. Like a child, you need to trust Him and receive by faith. There is a catcher behind you just in case; so don't be fearful, just relax." Before I knew

---

66 Telephone conversation with Connie Sinnott, August 29, 2013.

it, I was on the floor soaking in the euphoric presence of the Lord for the first time in my life. For years I had been secretly jealous of others who had been given this experience of being "slain in the Spirit". I was both afraid of it happening to me and of it not ever happening to me.

For the first few days, the church office was not functioning very well. The receptionist could not talk. Then, after that, she could only speak in tongues. She and her husband were filled and transformed by the joy of the Lord.[67]

In his book, *Lighting Fires*, Randy tells of an incident on the first Sunday morning service, January 23. Anni Shelton, wife of Randy's worship leader, Gary Shelton, shared with Randy that the Lord had given her the names of five people and words of knowledge regarding them. Randy gave her the go ahead to share those words from the microphone. While Anni was giving out these words of knowledge, a man at the back of the auditorium stood up and began to shout:

> "Did you get my name? I'm Taz—the Tasmanian Devil!" He continued to shout and interrupt things. After he shouted, "I'll show you power," Randy Clark felt the anointing of God burst within him and countered with, "No. I'll show you power—the power of God!"

Then to the attendees, Randy said, "Pay no attention to him; focus in on Jesus. The devil has overplayed his hand this morning, and now we are going to see the power of God!" Randy requested that those who felt the anointing of the power of God upon them to come forward for prayer. The front of the auditorium was soon packed with people. Randy asked the Holy Spirit to come and fall upon them. Right away, people were falling, shaking, weeping and laughing under the power of God.

While this was going on, some of the men of the church helped "Taz" out of the service and into one of the church offices to hear his story and care for him with the compassion of Christ. They learned

---

67 Richard Riss, A History of the Awakening of 1992-1995, Ch. 16, John Arnott. http://www.revival-library.org/catalogues/pentecostal/riss.html

that just days earlier he had been stabbed multiple times and had been hospitalized and almost died. In the course of ministering to him, "Taz" committed his life to Christ.[68]

John Arnott knew that what was happening must continue in protracted meetings. He insisted that Randy stay beyond the four days, until the Lord was finished. Randy called his wife several times to say he was staying a little longer. John, at one point, even offered to fly Randy's wife, DeAnne, and their four children up to Toronto. But with the children's school commitments, it was decided not to go in that direction. Randy went home briefly a number of times to see his wife and family, but the bulk of his time was given to the renewal in Toronto. Of the first sixty days, he was in Toronto for forty-two of them.[69]

On Monday, January 24, the first night the meetings had been extended beyond the original four days, Steve and Sandra Long came to their first renewal meeting. With them came Steve's brother, Richard, a Fellowship Baptist pastor, and Steve and Sandra's senior Fellowship Baptist pastors, John and Anna Freel. John Arnott had called Steve that day and encouraged them to come.

They nervously sat in the back row. Before the meeting even began, they saw and heard Peter Jackson up in the front row laughing uncontrollably. This distraction caused red flags to go up for them. They were determined to watch and observe but not ask for prayer. Anna Freel, however, went forward for prayer at the end of the preaching. Soon she was crying and even sobbing. When she finally started walking back to her seat, she was joyfully laughing. Apparently the Lord had ministered significant healing to her hurt heart that brought great release and freedom.

When Randy Clark, a former Baptist pastor, saw this row of Baptists standing up, putting on their coats and getting ready to leave, he went back to talk with them and offered to pray for them. They reluctantly obliged and soon found themselves on the floor, feeling the wonderful peace of God.

---

68 Randy Clark, Lighting Fires, Creation House, 1998, p. 92.
69 Ibid, p. 87.

This was the beginning of a new journey for all of them. For some time, John Arnott and Steve Long had been in conversation about the possibility of Steve coming on board at Toronto Airport Vineyard (TAV) as an administrator. Starting on Monday morning, February 1, 1994, Steve was on loan to the Toronto Vineyard to work with John, Carol and their team. Steve came on their full-time staff in early June of 1994 and, two decades later, he is still working with them. Steve Long's contribution in administrating the nightly revival meetings and organizing the conferences over the years has proved to be invaluable. This partnership is another example of how God orchestrates things behind the scenes for Kingdom purposes.[70]

Connie Sinnott, TAV children's ministry pastor at the time, remembers the early days and recalls how the youth and children were impacted,

> The Holy Spirit landed heavily on the youth. They then sat all over the stage area because there were no seats available and because they wanted to be up front to get right in on the action. Then two weeks into the renewal the Holy Spirit landed on the children in their children's ministry area on Sunday morning. A number of the children fell under the power of God when they were prayed for. I spoke to two boys of around eleven or twelve years of age who were making fun of another boy who had gone down, telling them to leave him alone as this was a special moment for him. A few minutes later the same two boys were out on the floor themselves, eyes closed and shocked looks on their faces. Two year olds prayed for another two year old who was sick with an ear infection, who then got up and played happily, with no more signs of sickness. A four-year-old girl laid on the floor having visions for four hours while her Mom and I stayed after the service until she sat up again and told us of her visions.[71]

---

70 Steve's brother, Richard, eventually gave leadership to the Greater Toronto Area pastors' network and helped facilitate citywide pastoral unity, cooperation and intercession across Canada. The Lord used John Freel, not only as a pastor, but also as an international itinerant renewal minister over the following years. Steve Long interview with author Jerry Steingard, June 3, 2013.
71 Connie Sinnott, email, October 23, 2013.

A few days into the revival, John Arnott tried cancelling a healing seminar that was scheduled at Hamilton Christian Fellowship for January 28, 1994. However, pastor Bruce Woods, who had already been to the Airport Fellowship to see what was happening, would not let John off the hook. John remembers this as a test, thinking, "Would the Holy Spirit show up with Carol and me when we were on our own? The amazing thing is that he did, for as we preached, the whole thing broke out again. The same thing happened in February when we went to Hungary. In fact, we saw even greater signs and wonders with healings and conversions."[72]

The first folks to come from outside of Ontario were primarily from Vineyard churches. Ron Allen, Vineyard regional overseer and pastor from Fort Wayne, Indiana, first planned to come check out the events and evaluate them. But the Lord stopped him in his tracks and said, "If you go to criticize, I will lift my anointing. You go to receive." Ron came up to receive and was powerfully hit. He was left incapacitated for days, hardly able to speak or move.[73]

Guy Chevreau, in his book, Pray with Fire, recalls watching Ron Allen attempt to give a testimony of what God was doing in his life:

> Ron Allen was introduced and invited to testify. He was helped up to the microphone and with a dumb-drunk look on his face, Ron slowly panned the congregation. His mouth dropped open—and for perhaps a minute, he made several attempts to speak. Then, without warning, he fell over sideways. I could not suppress my cynicism. I muttered, 'God doesn't do that to people.' A short time later, I came across Ezekiel 3:26-27. There the Lord says to His prophet: 'I shall make your tongue cleave to the roof of your mouth and you will be unable to speak...But when I have something to say to you, I shall give you back the power of speech.'[74]

72 Christian Week, December 13, 1994, article adapted from a transcript by Bruce Woods, called "We say, 'Holy Spirit, let it come!'"
73 Author witnessed Ron Allen telling this story on more than one occasion, during his testimony; also, Wes Campbell, Welcoming a Visitation of the Holy Spirit, Creation House, 1996, p. 23.
74 Guy Chevreau, Pray with Fire, Harper Perennial, 1995, p. 4.

Two weekends into this outpouring, John and Carol, Randy Clark, and Ron Allen came to Stratford, Ontario, to the Arnott's first church that they had planted and pastored, Jubilee Vineyard Christian Fellowship. They held revival meetings on the Saturday night, February 5, and Sunday morning and evening, February 6. Some of us from Stratford had already been going down to the Toronto meetings and had been powerfully touched. But this weekend felt like a Holy Spirit bomb went off in the Stratford Vineyard.

On the Saturday night, Ron Allen prayed for me and I went down, finding myself getting quite intoxicated in the Spirit. This was a first for me. As I was lying on the floor, the Lord brought to my mind Psalm 23, *"The Lord is my Shepherd, I shall not want. He makes me to lie down…"*

The whole weekend, Ron, a very intelligent and educated man of God, continued to be overwhelmed by the Spirit and was often struck speechless. John Arnott recalls Ron falling off the platform numerous times in those early days, both in Toronto and Stratford, and was amazed at "how he didn't break his nose or neck or whatever."[75] Ron spent much of the days "doing carpet time." We all found it quite amusing, including the time at the Swiss Chalet restaurant, after the Sunday morning meeting. John, with his mischievous smile and twinkle in his eye, asked Ron to pray for the food. I think he got one word out and that was it. In the midst of the laughter, someone else finished the prayer before the food got cold.

On Sunday evening, after preaching from the Parable of the Prodigal Son on how we don't need to live in the bunkhouse, but were invited to live in the Father's house, Randy Clark invited the Holy Spirit to come and minister. The auditorium looked like a battlefield, with at least two hundred of the almost three hundred attendees down on the floor, sometimes two or three bodies deep! I had read, dreamed and preached about and prayed for revival for years. But as the pastor, I must confess that I was quite stressed out that evening as I tried to process what my eyes were seeing and my ears were hearing. It was overwhelming, trying to make sense of it all. It was one thing to go to

---

75   John Arnott, recorded interview, June 14, 2013.

Toronto and see all the glorious chaos. It was another thing when I felt pastorally responsible for what was happening on my turf.

At eleven-thirty, I went to Randy to share how stressed and overwhelmed I felt. Randy prayed for me and I was out on the floor until one-thirty in the morning, laughing, crying, and experiencing pins and needles, with my hands raised into the air, fingers and hands as cold as ice, while the rest of me was burning up and shaking. Ron Allen came up to me afterwards and said that he saw Jesus walking around the room and that he stopped, stood over me and talked to me. He asked me if Jesus had said anything to me and I admitted that he had, from Matthew 11, *"Come to me, those who are weary and I will give you rest. Take my yoke."* The Lord showed me that I had taken my eyes off of Him and onto the religious, the flesh, the demonic, the skeptical and those not pressing in to the Lord.

I recall as well that, for about fifteen minutes, my mouth was cranked wide open. I heard the words from Psalm 81, *"Open wide your mouth and I will fill it."* Ron Allen wept that night. He said he had never seen Jesus before.

On the Monday morning, I dropped in to visit John and Carol, Randy and Ron, before they were to head back to Toronto. They had been staying for the weekend at Bill and Eleanor Kaethler's Bed and Breakfast home. We were all as excited as little kids in a candy shop! It was really starting to dawn on us that this anointing of God really was extremely contagious and transferable. They started to make even more phone calls to pastor friends throughout North America, telling them that this was what we all had been longing and praying for and urging them to get to Toronto ASAP.

Like many weary and empty Christians and church leaders, Fred Wright, a burned out Vineyard pastor from Denver, Colorado came to Toronto in early March to be refreshed. Fred had called Ron Allen in February to ask what was going on in Canada. Ron replied, "Sell the farm if you have to, but get up here to Toronto fast. God is here!"[76]

When his wife, Sharon, dropped him off at the Denver airport, she

---

76 Fred Wright, The World's Greatest Revivals, Destiny Image, 2007, p. 33.

said to him, "Fred, you are so dry and so crotchety, I don't care what they ask for, even if it is for women who want prayer to get pregnant, you go forward for prayer." The presence of God was so strong when Fred first came in the door that he could hardly stand and it took much effort just to find his way to a seat. At the end of the first meeting, an invitation was given for pastors to come for prayer. God certainly met Fred and his four elders that week and, the next Sunday at their Denver Vineyard, with one of the elders giving their testimony, all heaven broke loose.[77] Fred and Sharon Wright would later come on staff in Toronto.

After that first weekend, we held nightly renewal meetings in Stratford for three weeks and then cut back to Thursday nights only. This continued for over a year and a half, with people coming from within an hour's drive. Although we had sub-zero temperatures outside, the auditorium was extremely hot and reminded me of a gymnasium. Night after night, we had to prop all the doors open for cool, fresh air and some of the ladies put out cups and large jugs of ice water. Aside from the wonderful refreshing from the presence of the Lord that we were experiencing, many were violently shaking and experiencing fire. Many were receiving prophetic and intercessory gifts, children were having visions of angels, and physical healings were spontaneously and sovereignly taking place.

One older woman, Gloria Forbes, was looking at the words on the screen during worship when, all of a sudden, everything went blurry. She took off her glasses and could see perfectly. Another woman, Judy, got prayer for her right shoulder, which had been a problem for six months. After the meeting, she walked out to the parking lot to get into her car, slipped on the ice and wrenched her right shoulder. The next morning, she called Florence Kehl, one of our lay leaders, to report, "I'm completely healed. God has quite a sense of humour!"

It's interesting to note that various people who have been mentored by the Arnotts at the Jubilee church in Stratford have gone on to make

---

77   Fred Wright, interview in Toronto, June 14, 2013; also in The World's Greatest Revivals, pp. 33-34

an impact beyond Stratford since the renewal began.[78] Many musicians have come out of the Stratford Jubilee Christian Fellowship over the years as well. Let me just mention one—the young YouTube sensation, Justin Bieber. Justin's mother, Pattie Mallette, came to the Lord through John and Susan Brown and their downtown, youth, drop-in centre ministry, The Bunker, in the early 1990s. She gave birth to Justin weeks after the renewal had broken out. As a very young and energetic little boy, he would often sit in the front row, play a little guitar, and watch the worship team musicians closely. On occasion, at the end of a service, Justin would ask if he could go up on stage to play the drums.

Ron Allen and his wife, Carolyn, made frequent visits from Indiana to Toronto in the following weeks and months. It wasn't long before their Vineyard church in Fort Wayne was also blasted by the power of God. They conducted renewal meetings nightly for nine weeks. During the seventh week, they felt directed to acquire a large tent that could house one thousand people. They pitched the tent in a rough and dangerous part of the city. One night, a ten-year-old black boy, whose friend had recently been killed by a drive-by shooting, asked if he might give his testimony from the microphone. With his heart burdened for the lost, he urged people to repent and come to faith in Christ. There were gang members in attendance that night and fifteen of them came forward to give their lives to Jesus. Within a week, a total of fifty-five gang members found Christ.[79]

Within weeks of the outpouring in Toronto, it was obvious that the little church at the end of the runway could not handle the massive crowds, nor could they handle the parking of so many vehicles. It was a logistical nightmare. They had to find a larger venue. John Arnott

---

78 Al and Helen MacDonald came on staff at the Toronto church for several years, starting in the spring of 1995, to establish the Prayer and Care counseling ministry. A month later, John and Patricia Bootsma also came on staff at TACF. Ivan and Isabel Allum became church planters in Stratford and London, Ontario. They also became prophetic ministers and trainers at the Toronto leadership schools and around the world. John and Susan Brown went on to plant a church in Stratford, initially with the Allums. David and Charmaine Hicks became directors of the TACF School of Ministry for several years, in the mid-1990s, before launching into pastoral and worship ministries in Indiana and California and then returning to Stratford. Roger and Anne Markle planted a church in Woodstock, Ontario. And my wife and I, Pam and Jerry Steingard, pastored in Stratford until November 1998. Then, after running a retreat centre for three years, we oversaw a network of house churches and a downtown storefront ministry in Barrie, Ontario, until 2012. As of October 20, 2013, I am interim pastor back at Jubilee in Stratford.

79 Wesley Campbell, Welcoming a Visitation of the Holy Spirit, Creation House, 1996, pp. 24-25.

found a larger rental facility farther down on Dixie Road, called Capital Convention Hall, which could nicely accommodate a crowd of a thousand or so. This rental hall had a ballroom bar area that became affectionately known as "Joel's Bar".

Wes and Stacey Campbell, who had experienced a powerful visitation from the Lord in their church in Kelowna, British Columbia back in 1987, came to see for themselves. The American prophetic minister, Larry Randolph, who had accurately prophesied about this coming move of God, was there as well.

Wes Campbell had received a call from John Arnott about a week or two into the renewal. In his book, Welcoming a Visitation of the Holy Spirit, Wes recalls that pivotal telephone call, when John excitedly asked, "Wes, Wes! Where are you, Wes?" Wes thought, "What a dumb question...I'm right here at home, in bed, where I should be at six-forty-five in the morning?"[80] John blurted out, "I've been trying to track you down for days. It's all happened, Wes. Everything that was prophesied, it's all happened."

He was referring to the prophecies from Marc Dupont and Wes' wife, Stacey, a few months earlier. After Randy Clark talked to Wes on the telephone, John came back on the line and said, "All that stuff you were telling me about last summer is happening here, now! The filling, the laughing, the falling, the violent shaking, and the prophecy—it's all breaking out. You've got to come and help us, Wesley. Can you come immediately?"

Within a week, Stacey and Wes headed for Toronto and came to the rental facility where the meetings were taking place. Wesley recalls that, at the end of one of the meetings, around two in the morning, after much ministry of prayer and prophecy, and after seeing a Muslim come to Christ, John turned to him saying, "Oh Wesley, isn't this wonderful? What do you think?" Wes had to acknowledge that the manifest presence of the Lord was the thickest and heaviest he had ever experienced.[81]

---

80 Kelowna, B. C., has a three hour time difference to Toronto
81 Ibid, p. 18-22.

The Barrie Vineyard, with Peter and Heather Jackson, the Cambridge Vineyard, with Steve and Christina Stewart, and the Stratford Vineyard, were already being hit by the powerful presence of God and Wesley Campbell, Larry Randolph, the Arnotts, Randy Clark, and Ron Allen were rotating around to these and other locations to fan the flames.

By May 1994, a handful of churches and pastors in Victoria, BC, were meeting together in the four hundred and fifty seat Leonardo da Vinci hall. David Hixson, pastor of the Victoria Vineyard, and Bob Brasset of Victoria's East Gate Church were a part of the leadership of these renewal gatherings. Hixson was quoted in a newspaper saying, "The church has been too serious. We've taken ourselves too seriously. We build our lives around dryness. We need to drink."[82]

Christian Week[83] featured the revival on its front page in an article entitled "Holy Laughter Lifting Spirits," by Doug Koop, who wrote:

> Since the outbreak of joy began in mid-January, the Airport Vineyard has been holding services six nights a week, some in rented facilities to accommodate crowds of up to a thousand people. In mid-February, they reported a nightly average attendance of 800... The phenomenon has spread throughout southern Ontario and more meetings were being held in cities including Cambridge (a reported average nightly attendance of 600), Stratford (300), Barrie (250) and Hamilton (250).[84]

On Friday February 11, Stacey Campbell prophesied at the pastors' meeting in Toronto. With her head shaking back and forth and arms spinning, Stacey declared,

> "The Lord would say this movement is from the Spirit of God... give it freely away, this thing is not for yourself, it is not to be contained and held onto. If you don't give it away, it will turn to ashes and dust

---

82 Laughing Revival, by Casey Korstanje, The Spectator, Hamilton, August 1994.
83 According to the March 15, 1994 issue of Christian Week, published bi-weekly in Winnipeg, Manitoba
84 Richard Riss, A History of the Awakening of 1992-1995, Chapter: Vineyard.

in your hands. The only way it will continue is if you continually give it away...[85]

The following Sunday morning, February 13, Wes Campbell and Larry Randolph came to Stratford to minister. Wes spoke from 2 Kings 4 and 13. Chapter 4 speaks of filling jars with oil. The oil would continue to flow as long as there were jars to fill. 2 Kings 13 tells the story of the king who was told to take the arrows and strike the ground. He only struck the ground three times when he should have been much more aggressive and should have struck it five or six times for total defeat of the enemy.

John and Carol Arnott, though shocked and overwhelmed by the intensity of both the presence of God and the physical reactions or manifestations, knew that this was what they had prayed and believed for over the years. John told his staff, "Guys, we gotta keep going."[86]

With extremely cold, sub-zero, Canadian winter temperatures and after weeks of going back and forth between the Dixie Road building and the Capital Banquet and Convention Hall (which was not available on weekends), and the occasional use of the Canada Christian College, the meetings returned to the Dixie Road church auditorium. Closed-circuit TV was provided for the crowds in the overflow room. But as the year progressed, the numbers began to swell again. We felt helpless as we watched the police come by from time to time and gleefully write up and slap parking tickets on countless vehicles, many from out of province or car rental companies.

Very early in the renewal, Jeremy Sinnott, worship pastor of the church, was not feeling anything or experiencing any outward manifestations. So he spoke to John Arnott and said, "I don't want to get in the way of what God is doing here. I'm willing to hand in a resignation letter." John looked at him, laughed and told him to "Go read Acts chapter two." When Jeremy said he knew what that

---

85 A cassette tape-recorded and transcribed into author Jerry Steingard's personal journal, February 11, 1994
86 John Arnott, recorded interview, June 14, 2013.

entailed, John said, "Read on, read further in the chapter. The Apostle Peter got up and spoke to the crowds with great clarity. He too was full of the Holy Spirit. John's point was that Peter was 'the designated driver' among those drunk in the Spirit. Jeremy's wife, Connie, told Jeremy, "You are changing; becoming more patient and gentler." These responses helped reassure him that he was not "getting in the way" of what God was doing.[87]

Carol Arnott's First Vision

In February, John and Carol Arnott went to Hungary for two and half weeks and were thrilled to find that the anointing continued to be highly contagious and transferable.

But before they headed to Hungary, Marc Dupont prayed for John and Carol. While Marc was preaching, Carol was out in the Holy Spirit, on the floor, beside the pulpit, having what turned out to be a forty-five minute vision in Technicolor. In this vision, Carol found herself in a gorgeous meadow. The colours were vibrant and stunning. Beyond the meadow, she could see a city in the background. She saw Jesus walk up to her and give her a bouquet of Lily of the Valley flowers.[88]

Within this vision, Carol and Jesus shared heart to heart. They danced and walked through the meadow with arms crossed and made circles like kids. It was a time of intimacy, friendship, laughter and joy. Then Jesus said to her, "Carol, can I have the bouquet back?" Though disappointed at His request, she gave Jesus the bouquet. Jesus took the bouquet and then went to gather different coloured and wild flowers from the meadow and made them into a wreath. Jesus placed the lilies among the flowers in the wreath. He then placed the wreath on her head. Out of nowhere came a long white wedding veil that Jesus attached to the back of the wreath.

---

87 Conversations with Connie and Jeremy Sinnott in 1994 and August 2013.
88 Years earlier, during an emotionally difficult time, and before they were married, John had given Carol a bouquet of Lily of the Valley flowers. Driving home to Stratford, Carol was crying while smelling the fragrance of the flowers. At that time, the Lord had said to her, "Carol, lilies do not grow on the mountain tops. They only grow in the valleys. And whenever you are in a valley, I will have my lilies there for you. You will be able to find them by their fragrance."

At this point the scene changed and Carol was walking along a street with her arm in His, looking at the building and thinking, "Where are we? I don't know this place." Her attention then went to all the people on both sides of the road who were cheering. All of a sudden, Carol looked down and was stunned to find that they were walking on streets of gold! "I've married Jesus! I'm walking on streets of gold!"

The scene changed once again. Carol found herself in a massive banquet hall, the end of which was nowhere in sight. She realized that everything was prepared; tables were set with flowers, candlesticks, crystal glasses and plates. She thought to herself, "I've been invited to the wedding feast of the Lamb. This is the banquet. Where is everybody?" She felt to turn around and look behind her and, as she did, she saw the most beautiful people. Their faces were radiant with the glory of God and they were dressed in wedding attire. "Lord, who are these people?" Jesus replied, "They are the broken, the outcasts and the downtrodden; the ones that nobody has loved. And I have bid them to come to my wedding feast."

Then Jesus walked up to Carol and said, "Carol, can I have the first dance?" When Jesus wanted to dance with Carol, she knew it was an answer to her heart's cry.[89] She then realized that she couldn't dance with Jesus because her wedding veil was too long. Suddenly, little birds came and picked up her wedding veil, allowing her to dance with Jesus.

When Carol came out of the vision, she asked the Lord, "What should I do with this? It is so incredible. Is this just for me?" Jesus said,

No, I want you to get up and ask Jeremy to sing the song 'So Come', and then tell them the vision. When you are finished telling the vision, I want you to say, 'The banquet feast is almost prepared. Be like the five wise virgins… The foolish did not have extra oil. The oil of the Spirit is now being poured out. The cost is vulnerability and humility. This is a place to buy oil so that we are ready at all times, should He tarry. Buy oil.'

---

89 When Carol was first saved, as a single mom, she was kneeling by her bed and felt the glorious presence of the Lord. She had just read in her Bible about getting crowns as a reward. She said, "Lord, the only reward I want is a long big hug from You."

Even though Carol's feet were up in the air and she was running, shouting and waving her arms around, John did not stop the vision that Carol was having on the platform, nor did he let anyone else interfere with what God was doing. They believe that if he or anyone else had, the flow of God's oil and wine may have been short-lived. This dramatic vision has significantly impacted John and Carol over the twenty years of this outpouring. They interpret it like a prophetic blueprint, feeling an urgency to encourage people to be like the five wise virgins who kept their lamps full of oil of the Holy Spirit.[90]

---

90   Interview with John and Carol Arnott at Catch The Fire, September 27, 2013.

CHAPTER 4

On the Floor in '94

Part Two: The Fire Spreads to the UK

In the UK, the manifest presence of God broke out in late May of 1994 at an Anglican Church called Holy Trinity Brompton (HTB) when Eleanor Mumford[91] shared a testimony of her time in Toronto. In her own words, Eleanor said, she had visited Toronto "because I have never been slow to go to a party. I also went because I felt that I was spiritually bankrupt, and I went with tremendous expectancy."[92]

While in Toronto, Eleanor Mumford and her friends, Penny Fulton and Carolyn Allen,[93] visited the Arnott's home one morning.[94] Wesley Campbell and two prophetic friends, Cathy Graham, and Jan Steffen,[95] were there to join in praying for the three friends.

The first to be prayed for was Carolyn Allen. As Cathy Graham prayed and prophesied that she would be released in the prophetic, Carolyn shook violently, marched like a soldier, and shouted like a warrior would when running towards enemy lines. She prophesied, "I told you to get ready, but I'm coming anyways!"[96]

Next it was Eleanor's turn. While the others were gathering around her, Eleanor began praying out a burden for Great Britain. Then Cathy Graham began to pray and prophesy over Eleanor. In a loud voice,

91 Eleanor is the wife of John Mumford, who at the time was Southwest London Vineyard's pastor
92 Wallace Boulton, editor, The Impact of Toronto, Monarch Pub., 1995, p. 17. Carolyn Allen, wife of Fort Wayne Vineyard pastor, Ron Allen
93 The three women were all friends and Vineyard pastors' wives,
94 It was either May 18 or 19
95 Cathy Graham and Jan Steffen were from Wes Campbell's Kelowna B. C. church
96 I was in attendance and noted this in my personal journal, May 18 or 19, 1994.

she proclaimed, "It's not 'Great Britain'; it's 'God's Britain.' It won't be 'Great Britain.' It will be 'God's Britain.'" All of us in the room sensed the sacredness of the moment. Eleanor spent much of her time over the next several days on the floor, getting freshly filled by God, as well as praying for her country. She could not have imagined how God was about to use her to be part of the answer to her prayers.[97]

After getting back to her home in South London, Eleanor and her husband John, invited some of their friends and staff, to hear Eleanor's testimony of how God met her in a powerful way in Toronto.[98] With fresh faith in the room, they prayed and everyone was touched by the immediate presence of the Lord.

Nicky Gumbel,[99] curate at Holy Trinity Brompton Church (HTB) and his wife, Pippa, were at the meeting, which went on into the lunch hour. Suddenly Nicky realized he was missing his church's staff lunch meeting. Leaving the meeting, he rushed back and arrived close to the end of the HTB staff meeting. After he briefly shared about Eleanor's testimony, he was asked to close the meeting in prayer. As he prayed all heaven came down. People fell to the floor under the power of God. Even people walking past the room were affected.

At 4 PM, the church secretary, Glenda, managed to make an emergency telephone call to Sandy Millar, the vicar of HTB, who was in an important meeting of the Evangelical Alliance. She apologized for the interruption but said she felt he should know that all his church staff were on the floor and unable to work. He asked her if this was a good thing. She replied that it was. He then asked her, "What are you doing on the telephone then?" She admitted that she had to crawl on her hands and knees to the telephone.

Sandy Millar invited Eleanor to come and speak the following Sunday, May 29, at both the morning and evening services. The Holy Spirit faithfully showed up, touching most people present, including children. Sandy and his pastoral director, Jeremy Jennings, decided to

---

97 Wesley Campbell, pp. 26-27; also author was present to witness.
98 This happened on Tuesday morning, May 24, 1994
99 Nickey Gumbel was the leader responsible for the world-famous Alpha courses

head off to Toronto that week for a three-day visit.[100]

From this point on, long line-ups of people could be seen waiting to get in to the renewal meetings at Holy Trinity Brompton. These meetings continued for many months and would be used by the Lord to revolutionize thousands, including many pastors and leaders. Those touched by God at HTB include Pastor Ken Gott of Sunderland, England, who held protracted revival meetings in his city for over three years. Also impacted was evangelist Steve Hill, who would become the catalyst for the Pensacola, Florida revival.

Not only was Holy Trinity Brompton greatly impacted, but there were also reports of renewal breaking out in other places in the UK due to Eleanor's testimony.

> Just as Florrie Evans' heartfelt declaration of her love for Jesus in a New Quay youth meeting helped ignite the Welsh revival of 1904, Elli Mumford's unadorned and heartfelt testimony was to be like a spark to dry grass in many churches, some of which played the cassette over the church PA system and then witnessed astonishing scenes as pastors fell off platforms and keeled over in the choir stalls.[101]

Ken and Lois Gott

Ken Gott, a Pentecostal pastor from Sunderland in northern England went to the renewal meetings at London's Holy Trinity Brompton and had his life revolutionized by God. He then travelled to the Toronto meetings.

Ken went back to his church, Sunderland Christian Centre, only to see God pour out His Spirit upon his people. Ken and Lois Gott and their leadership team began protracted renewal meetings in August, 1994, which became a focal point for the outpouring for over three years. They became a renewal centre not only for their own city but

---

100 Wallace Boulton, editor, The Impact of Toronto, pp. 20-21; also, Bill Jackson, The Quest for the Radical Middle, Vineyard International Pub., 1999, p. 295; and Wesley Campbell, Welcoming a Visitation of the Holy Spirit, pp. 27-28.
101 Dave Roberts, The Toronto Blessing, Kingsway, 1994, pp. 12, 30-31.

also for many people from nations around the world, and held meetings six nights a week.

In 1995, Jim Richardson was a gang member involved in organized crime, prostitution and drugs. His girlfriend came to Christ resulting in Richardson being extremely angry at the church and at Ken Gott. He attended a renewal meeting in order to punch Gott out. Before he could do that, he came under deep conviction and the power of the Holy Spirit and had a radical "Saul of Tarsus" type conversion.[102]

Jim Richardson became a bridge between the church and the community, opening up a club for street kids four nights a week. His first convert, ironically, was an eleven-year-old boy by the name of John Arnott. Sunderland was known for its high rate of auto theft. But mysteriously, it was reported that auto theft and other crimes had noticeably decreased in the city over the subsequent months.[103]

After planting several churches and turning their church over to others, Ken and Lois Gott travelled the world and brought the fire to thousands. In 1998, they wound down their travels and began to focus on building cell-based churches through the "G12" vision. The cell model of discipleship also included "encounter weekends" for repentance, cleansing and deliverance, and discipling people to pursue the lost. Recently they have also established 24/7 prayer and intercession.

The Widespread Outpouring in the UK

Within weeks, the 'Blessing' had spread to hundreds of churches across the British Isles and, by the end of 1994, estimates were suggesting that between 2000 and 4000 congregations had embraced it. It became one of the biggest stories covered by the British Christian media in recent times, and remained so through 1995 and into early 1996.[104]

---

102 Ken Gott, speaking at TACF; James A. Beverley, Revival Wars, Evangelical Research Ministries, 1997, pp. 16-17.
103 Spread the Fire magazine, August 1996, pp. 4-5; also Andy and Jane Fitz-Gibbon, Something Extraordinary is Happening, Monarch Pub. 1995.
104 Taken from David Hilborn's document, "Introduction: Evangelicalism, the Evangelical Alliance and the Toronto Blessing", Evangelical Alliance, UK, internet page 2.

This fresh downpour of God's Spirit came to Kensington Temple in London, England, through Charles and Frances Hunter of Texas during Easter 1994.[105] In April 1994 Dave Holden from New Frontiers International was visiting Terry Virgo's church in Columbia, Missouri, where Rodney Howard-Browne had recently ministered and returned home to see laughing and falling down start to happen. Another leader from New Frontiers, Alan Preston,[106] had just returned from Toronto and the phenomena broke out in the Brighton church on Sunday May 1.

Gerald Coates, leader of the Pioneer group of churches, would also begin to see some manifestations break out in meetings in mid-May. And while Norman Moss, pastor of Queen's Road Baptist in Wimbledon, was in Toronto the weekend of May 15, things were beginning to percolate at his church back home. Many were touched by a fresh sense of the power of God just days earlier at an Ichthus conference held at his Baptist church. On Tuesday May 17, roughly two hundred New Frontier leaders met with Terry Virgo and Dave Holden with many being freshly touched by the presence of God.[107]

Various summer Bible Weeks, such as Stoneleigh, organized by New Frontiers, reported that many of the fourteen thousand people were affected by manifestations. New Wine Bible week, as well as Ichthus 'Revival Camp' and Grapevine Bible week all saw many of their people impacted. Gerald Coates and his Pioneer network were also receiving this fresh outpouring of God's love and joy.[108]

Word got around and soon not only scores of Canadians and Americans were making a pilgrimage to the Toronto Vineyard meetings but also the Brits. Within months, it was estimated that forty percent of daily visitors to Toronto were from Great Britain.[109] It became quite challenging for businessmen to get a flight between London and Toronto. Airlines needed to add additional flights between these two cities due to this British invasion.

---

105 Charles and Francis Hunter, Holy Laughter, Hunter Books, 1994, pp. 51-57; Richard Riss, History of the Awakening of 1992-1995.
106 Dave Roberts, The Toronto Blessing, Kingsway, 1994, p. 23.
107 Patrick Dixon, Sings of Revival, Kingsway, 1994, pp. 18-21.
108 Patrick Dixon, Signs of Revival, Kingsway, 1994, pp. 47-59.
109 Spread the Fire magazine, Toronto, January 1995, pp. 4-5.

John Wimber's teaching and conference ministry in the UK over the previous decade had established relationship and trust with leaders and people in many Church of England, Free Church networks and para-church ministries. So the fact it was a Vineyard church experiencing this fresh and powerful move of God, helped many British believers take it seriously. The fact that this outpouring was emanating out of Canada, a British Commonwealth country, rather than the United States, may have also contributed to the openness and willingness of many from the UK to make the trek across the Atlantic and drink from this refreshing river of life.

Roger Mitchell, a British church leader from Ichthus Fellowship,[110] sent John a fax asking him about what was going on in Toronto and whether he should come. John took the fax and wrote, "Roger, God is moving. Get over here as soon as you can" and sent it back. Roger read the fax and promptly fell to the floor.[111]

Other British leaders such as Dave Markee, Steve Hepden, David Campbell and Trevor Baker soon attended meetings in Toronto.[112]

David and Ze Markee were pastors of Folley's End in Croydon. With the outpouring hitting their church, they conducted renewal meetings and conferences for years. They also established a school of ministry, a program to restore creative arts in the church, called King David Kompany, and planted churches. David has been a professional bassist and has recorded with musicians such as Eric Clapton, Bing Crosby, and Joan Armatrading.[113] Renewal and revival meetings and conferences also began in 1994 with Trevor and Sharon Baker, in the Midlands. In 1998, they planted the Revival Fires Church in Dudley.[114]

The expression "Toronto Blessing" made its first public appearance in an article by London Times journalist Ruth Gledhill. In her article, "Spread of Hysteria Fad Worries Church"[115] Gledhill reported that it

---

110 Roger Mitchell first met John Arnott in Argentina in the fall of 1993
111 John Arnott recorded interview, June 14, 2013; author also remembers John Arnott telling that story in 1994 when it happened.
112 Apostolic leaders of British movements, such as Gerald Coates and Terry Virgo, would later be speakers at conferences in Toronto.
113 Dave Markee, By Their Fruits, Word Publishing, 2001, p. 89.
114 Trevor and Sharon Baker website: www.revivalfires.org.uk/church/index.html
115 The article was printed on Saturday June 18, 1994

was becoming popular as a nickname for a "religious craze" of "mass fainting" which had "crossed the Atlantic and was becoming a cause for concern in the Church of England."[116]

David Hilborn, writing for the Evangelical Alliance makes these comments about the name "Toronto Blessing":

As we have seen, the phrase 'Toronto Blessing' was first popularized by a London journalist. It does not appear to have been used by Toronto Airport Vineyard (TAV) in the six months between Randy Clark's historic visit on 20th January 1994 and The Times' circulation of it in mid-June. From an early stage, TAV in fact preferred more explicitly biblical descriptions, most notably the phrase 'times of refreshing', which was borrowed from Acts 3:19… In due course, however, 'Toronto' became an affectionate shorthand, especially among British supporters of the movement…

Despite all this, there remained certain unease within the Airport church and AVC leadership about its use as a definition of what was taking place. Indeed, by February 1996, John Arnott was insisting, 'It isn't the Toronto Blessing; it's the Father's Blessing', and was encouraging people to read a book he had just written under the preferred title… and despite the best efforts of Arnott and others, the 'Toronto Blessing' moniker not only stuck, but also flourished. Today, at a distance of years, it looks to have established itself as the standard term by which the movement is known, and by which it will be referenced in textbooks on the late twentieth century Church.[117]

It is worth noting, as a matter of interest, that, according to the historian Vinson Synan, the Azusa Street Revival was originally called the "Los Angeles Blessing".[118]

---

116 Gledhill, Ruth, "Spread of Hysteria Fad Worries Church"', The Times, June 18, 1994, p.12; cited in David Hilborn's document, "Introduction: Evangelicalism, the Evangelical Alliance and the Toronto Blessing", Evangelical Alliance, UK, internet page 2.

117 David Hilborn, Internet document, "Introduction: Evangelicalism, the Evangelical Alliance and the Toronto Blessing", Evangelical Alliance, UK, internet pages 4, 7–8. http://anb.eauk.org/resources/publications/upload/torontointro.pdf

118 Interview with Randy Clark, September 26, 2013, citing Vinson Synan speaking in 1994 or 1995 in St. Louis, Missouri.

CHAPTER 5

On the Floor in '94

Part Three: Second Half of the Year

By the sixth month of the outpouring, the Toronto church had doubled, from 350 to 700 people and renewal meetings had gone every night (except Mondays) for 175 days. Total attendance had been 70,000 with 30,000 different attendees including 2,500 pastors. There had been 2,500 rededications to Christ, 300 accepted Christ for the first time, 3,000 people ministered to weekly, and hundreds of pastors had "taken it home" and were now affecting hundreds and thousands in churches and cities around the world.[119]

In his summer '94 newsletter, John Arnott gave his answer to the often-asked question:

> Why Toronto? Frankly, I do not know. Carol and I and the Toronto Airport Vineyard folks know that we did not pray this down, earn it or deserve it in any way. It is a sovereign work of God. Carol and I concluded last year that, without a powerful anointing of the Holy Spirit, our ministry would be mundane, ineffective, and far from reaching our desired goals of impacting our community and city, let alone the nations of the world. We now have much more faith for this, thanks to the Holy Spirit, as we have seen more people saved, healed, refreshed, and empowered in the last six months, than all our years

---

119 Statistics taken from "John & Carol's 'Vineyard Family' News, Toronto Airport Vineyard,", vol. 1., issue 1, mid-July 1994 "The Fire Keeps Falling, July is our Sixth Month".

of pastoral ministry.

How long will it last? At first I was afraid that it might not continue. 'It happened last night Lord, but will it happen again tonight?' Someone told me early in this renewal that the Azusa St. revival continued for 3½ years and continues to impact the world to this day. As we keep watching what began in Toronto rapidly spreading throughout the whole world, our prayer is, 'Oh Lord, may it never stop, but just get better!' May the earth be filled with the knowledge of the glory of the Lord as the waters cover the sea (Habakkuk 2:14).

When Steve Long was asked how long he thought the revival would last, this was the answer he gave: "We have no idea how long this will continue. We've decided that as long as God is continuing to do what He's doing, we'll keep making service time available."[120]

In the second half of 1994, God continued to revive and refresh his weary ones, especially the pastors. Here are a just a few stories of what God was doing:

Che Ahn

Che Ahn, pastor of Harvest Rock Vineyard, in Pasadena, California, told Spread the Fire, that:

1993 was the worst year of my life. I said, 'Lord, take me home.' I was ready to quit the ministry. Then I went to the Vineyard conference…
I got hit with laughter, shaking, falling—the whole thing. And from that point on it's been a bullet train ride! They too, launched renewal meetings six days a week.[121]

Che Ahn, and his friend and co-worker, Lou Engle, were initially hit by the Spirit at the annual Anaheim Vineyard conference at the end of January 1994.[122] Che's depression was gone, his love for Jesus was

---

120 Steve Long quoted in "'Toronto Blessing' garnering worldwide attention", article in Christian Week, Aug. 23, 1994).
121 Spread the Fire magazine, October 1995, p. 25.
122 The guest healing evangelists at the conference were Francis MacNutt and Mahesh Chavda.

renewed and a fresh impartation for ministry was released in his life.[123]

Though they recognized that Toronto was the new "Azusa Street" for this fresh wave of the Holy Spirit, Che Ahn and Lou Engle were not able to get there until the October 1994 Catch The Fire Conference. They were hungry and desperate for more of the Lord and they were not disappointed. It was another life-changing experience with God.

While on the floor in Toronto, Che asked God to show him what He wanted him to receive that first night. Immediately the Lord showed him bitterness in his heart toward someone. Lying on the floor, Che began to sob and repent for the sin in his heart. Meanwhile his friends were on the floor nearby being filled with joy and laughter. The Lord helped him come to terms with the hurt, bitterness and rejection in his own heart and began the process of bringing deep healing and restoration on the inside. Che recalls how this was the beginning of months and months of God's renewing and sanctifying work in his wounded heart and the restoration of his relationship with his father and his wife, Sue.

Che writes:

The Scriptures say that God will turn the hearts of the fathers to the children and the children to the father before Christ comes back (see Malachi 4:6). That is exactly what I have experienced and what many others are experiencing during this current move of the Spirit. I believe this is surely a sign of the end-time revival. That is why I get so perturbed when people criticize this revival as a laughing revival. Yes, God is pouring out His joy... My experience and my observation is that he is also doing a deep work of convicting us of our sin so we can resolve root issues that have not been addressed and can defile many if left to grow (see Hebrews 12:15; 1 John 1:10). That is bringing tremendous freedom and sanctification to many.[124]

---

123 Source: Che Ahn's 1998 book, Into the Fire
124 Che Ahn, Into the Fire, Renew Books, 1998, p. 35-37, 123-127.

Once a pastor on the verge of quitting the ministry, Che Ahn became a new man, revived by the outpouring of God's Spirit. He went on to found a new apostolic network of churches, birthed on the wings of revival, and called Harvest International Ministries (HIM).

Darrell Stott and Michael Thompson

Darrell Stott, pastor of the Seattle Revival Centre and Michael Thompson of The Tabernacle in Melbourne, Florida, both attended the 1994 conference with Che Ahn and all three said their lives were significantly changed. A year later, in October 1995, all three pastors were leading "watering holes" of the Holy Spirit in their respective cities. Thompson claimed that not only did he experience a radical change in his own life, but, "It's re-written the DNA of our church." The Tabernacle held renewal services six nights a week for nine months. Now services are two nights a week with two outreach ministries operating as a direct result of the renewal.[125]

Bill and Melinda Fish

It was at one of the Wednesday pastors' sessions, led by Guy Chevreau[126] at the old industrial warehouse, that Bill and Melinda Fish had their first exposure to a renewal meeting in Toronto.

During the eighteen years they'd been pastoring near Pittsburgh, Pennsylvania Melinda and Bill had received numerous prophecies that they would experience a coming revival. The prophecies described the revival in terms of a river flowing and bringing "the blessing". By the time they heard of something happening in Toronto in 1994, they were spiritually dry, disheartened and desperately hungry for God.

After Guy's teaching, the ministry team began praying for those who came forward for prayer. Guy came to Bill and Melinda and asked them their name. Melinda replied, "We're the Fishes. And we are really

---

125 Source: a letter that Darrell Stott wrote to John Arnott
126 Guy Chevreau (Th.D.) first came out to the renewal meetings in early February of 1994. Guy had served in the Convention Baptist denomination for years as a pastor., Having studied in the area of the history of theology, Guy was very instrumental in the early years of the revival, teaching regularly at the pastor's sessions on Wednesday afternoons, giving historical context to revival and particularly to the manifestations. Guy also travelled extensively as part of the renewal team, teaching and ministering in the anointing of this revival.

dry." Guy then prayed, "Well, then, let the river flow." Suddenly the river that had been prophetically promised to them all these years began to trickle into their dry souls, bringing needed refreshment and new hope. In the following months and years, Bill and Melinda drove to Toronto dozens and dozens of times. Not only has their church been powerfully transformed and renewed, but they have also taken ministry teams all over the world.[127]

Melinda, a very gifted and humorous communicator, has spoken frequently at the Toronto meetings and conferences. This energetic and delightful woman has also written half a dozen books and was the editor of Toronto's Spread the Fire magazine for a number of years.

David Ruis

David Ruis led worship at the first Annual Catch The Fire Conference,[128] October 12-15, 1994. Five thousand were in attendance during the day and at night the place was packed out.[129]

On Sunday night, October 16, after David Ruis finished leading the worship, a Spirit of prophecy came upon David and with arms flailing, he prophesied a very serious and sobering word:

> I am here. I am here. I am here. Am I not He who sits in the heavens and laughs at the plans of man? Has it not already been established from time of old that My King would be established on His holy mountain? I say to you, you thought My movement has begun. I tell you it has yet to begin. You have seen nothing. You have seen nothing. You have seen nothing yet.
>
> This is just a preparation. You thought the seed is going out to the nations of the earth. I tell you it hasn't even begun. I'm just growing up a plant. My rains are coming to grow up a plant that will grow and grow and grow and then, and then, come to the place of seed. You thought you felt wind. It has been nothing. My wind shames the

---

127 Melinda Fish, Keep Coming Holy Spirit, Chosen Books, 2001, pp. 11-16.
128 The conference was held at the Regal Constellation Hotel, which was on the opposite side of the airport from the Dixie church building. The main convention room could accommodate three thousand and the second room about twenty-five hundred.
129 Steve Long interview, June 3, 2013.

greatest hurricanes. My wind shames the greatest tornadoes. My rain and My wind reap greater, greater, greater havoc and destruction on the realms of the enemy than any natural thing that you have seen. And My wind will blow on this plant and the seeds will go forth to the nations of the earth and bring forth the greatest harvest written page or oral tongue has ever declared in the nations. Give Me glory!

The holy fear of the Lord came upon us during this intense prophetic message and afterwards, the leaders put on hold the agenda of the meeting as they sought to have us all respond appropriately to the Lord, in faith, reverence and humility. We sang together, "Let Your Glory Fall in this place. Let it go from here, to the nations..."[130]

Revival Anthems

In every move of God, He releases fresh creativity among His people in the arts, worship and evangelism. Most of the great hymns of the church were birthed out of waves of God's reviving mercy and grace. Within the first few years of this move of God, a plethora of worship songs came forth to express our love and worship to the Lord and to give testimony to what He was doing.

At the very outset of the outpouring, the song, *Be Magnified* (I have made You too small in my eyes...), written by Fred Hammond, became a powerful vehicle for people to express their hearts to the Lord. A number of songs written by David Ruis became iconic in this season of refreshing. These included songs such as *Let Your Glory Fall*, *Sweet Wind, Mercy is Falling* and *We will Dance*. Andy Park's song, *The River is Here* became another favourite among many as we danced and celebrated God's goodness to us.

Many songs came out of the musicians at the Toronto church as well—songs such as *Great Big God, Keep Coming, Holy Spirit* and *God of the Breakthrough* by Rob Critchley; *Do it Again, Lord, Lift Your Name,*

---

130 David Ruis, video recording, Catch The Fire Conference, Sunday night, October 16, 1994.

The Father Loves You and *Son of Man Appears* by Jeremy and Connie Sinnott; and *Jesus, Name Above All Names* by Owen Hurter.[131]

Meanwhile, with such an influx of people from around the world flocking to Toronto to experience a fresh encounter with the Living God, it was not surprising to hear that, in the December, 1994 edition of the *Toronto Life* magazine, titled 'Best and Worst: A Year in the Life of the City', the Toronto Airport Vineyard was declared as Toronto's "most notable" tourist attraction for the year.[132]

---

131 Email conversation with Jeremy Sinnott, September 5, 2013.
132 Toronto Life magazine, December, 1994, "Best and Worst: A Year in the life of the city", cited by John Arnott and staff; and Guy Chevreau, Pray with Fire, Harper Perennial, 1995, p. 20.

CHAPTER 6

Coming Alive in 1995

The church worldwide came alive in '95. Reports came out that there were literally thousands upon thousands of churches throughout the world that have been experiencing the laughing revival. In fact, according to Charisma magazine, May 1995, "an estimated four thousand churches in England had been impacted and at least seven thousand churches in North America."[133]

Aside from the move of God flowing out of the Toronto church, in 1995 God sovereignly released an extraordinary season of visitation in other nations, church streams and parachurch ministries.

Randy Clark tells of meeting an American missionary to China, Dennis Balcombe. Dennis told Randy that while we were experiencing revival in Toronto in 1994, he witnessed an outpouring of the Spirit in a house church movement in the province of Shantung. Dennis saw thousands of Chinese believers falling down, crying and laughing under the power of the Spirit.[134]

Another American missionary, David Hogan also claimed that the manifestations of "laughing, rolling on the floor and praising the Lord" broke out sovereignly among thirty of his indigenous leaders in rural Mexico, shortly after revival broke out in Toronto.[135]

Canadian evangelist, Bill Prankard of Ottawa, and a ministry team

---

133 Stephen Strang, "More, Lord!", Charisma magazine, May 1995.
134 Source: Randy Clark, Supernatural Missions, Global Awakening, 2012
135 Randy Clark, Supernatural Missions, Global Awakening, 2012, pp. 25-26.

of Canadian Inuit, travelled in 1994 to the Russian Arctic. Their aim was to take the gospel to the Russian Inuit; one of the world's unreached people groups. According to Prankard, "They had never heard of Jesus or the gospel." The team arrived by helicopter to these isolated and poverty-stricken villages with clothing and supplies, and ministered the love of Jesus to them. By the time they had left, most of them had invited Jesus into their lives and were given Bibles.

When Bill Prankard and his team returned a year later, in 1995, they were shocked. When they landed by helicopter, about one hundred and fifty Russian Inuit were there to greet them, shouting, "Hallelujah!" These baby Christians had devoured the Bible. When they read the book of Acts and realized there was another experience with the Holy Spirit, they invited the Spirit to come and fill them. Without anyone modeling it to them, the manifest presence of God came and they spoke in tongues and experienced all the physical manifestations that can accompany an outpouring of God's love and power. Prankard stated:

> They are at the ends of the earth but you'd think they have been to Toronto! We barely started the meeting and wave after wave of laughter hit the people who had never laughed... They were jerking, crunching, bouncing, falling, groaning and birthing... They weren't copying. This was a very fresh move of God. If I had had any doubts about what God was doing (in Toronto), they would have been dispelled by what I saw there.

These new believers were reliving the events of the book of Acts, complete with miracles, signs, and wonders— and persecution from Russian authorities. They soon began travelling to other villages as missionaries and saw others come to Christ. One new convert told Prankard, "They can threaten us, they can beat us, they can even kill us, but we will never stop loving Jesus."[136]

---

136 Bill Prankard's story, Russian Arctic, Spread the Fire magazine, December, 1996, Source: p. 32 and also documented on "Go Inside the Toronto Blessing" Part 2, video, by Marcus Warren, 2002. Bill Prankard's evangelistic ministry then raised funds for Inuit leaders to attend Bible College and to establish a place of worship.

On January 1, 1995, God showed up big time in Melbourne, Florida. A network of pastors in the area had been meeting for some time to build relationships of trust and friendship, as well as pray for God to move in their city and region. Randy Clark was invited to come to speak and minister. Randy usually only commits to four days in a location but he scheduled himself for fifteen days in Melbourne, believing this place had great potential to experience a major revival. The meetings were held at the largest church in the area; Tabernacle Church, formerly pastored by Jamie Buckingham and pastored, at that time, by Michael Thompson, who had been to the Toronto Catch The Fire Conference months earlier.

One of the most outstanding stories from the Melbourne outpouring took place on Friday, January 6, 1995 when Fred Grewe[137] and Randy Clark drove an hour south to a Christian radio station in Vero Beach, to be interviewed. When the morning interview was finished, Randy and Fred briefly prayed for the radio staff, which was normal procedure after having a pastor on the air. The Lord was obviously touching a few individuals but Randy and Fred needed to leave for another commitment.

As they continued to pray for each other, the majority of the radio staff, mostly non-Charismatic Christians, collapsed to the floor under the power of God. The radio manager, Jon Hamilton, managed to make it to the microphone and informed the radio audience of what was going on and invited them down to the station for prayer. Some people were healed while listening to the broadcast and others reported that the presence of God was so strong in their car that they had to pull over. Some came under conviction and drove to the station to give their lives to Christ. Before long, the radio station was inundated with people hungry for God and the floor was strewn with bodies, out under the power of God.

As the day went on, they had to use the space in the church auditorium next to the radio station and that too became filled with

---

137 With all that God was doing in Melbourne, the local Vineyard pastor, Fred Grewe, soon resigned from his church and became the administrator for the renewal meetings that would continue for much of 1995.

people who had fallen under the Spirit onto the floor. Soon several local pastors dropped in and, at first cautious, recognized this was God and joined in. Eventually, word got back to Randy Clark and Fred and they drove back to see what God was sovereignly doing.[138]

Bill Johnson

In February of 1995, a pastor from California came to the Toronto meetings for the very first time. The Holy Spirit had significantly impacted Bill Johnson while attending two Anaheim Vineyard conferences with John Wimber in 1987. This resulted in an outpouring of the Spirit in his church in Weaverville, but it was sporadic. When Bill heard about Toronto, he promised God, "Lord, if you'll touch me again, I'll never change the subject."

In visiting the Toronto Airport Vineyard, Bill Johnson was eager for more of God and received prayer at every opportunity. Though Bill did not experience any dramatic encounters with God at that time (though he did months later, during the night, while in bed), he claimed, "I knew I had just seen what I was going to give my life to... Toronto took it all to another level; all that fire and passion. Every week, since February 1995, with no exceptions, that's all we do. We are just interested in the presence of the Lord; learning to host that presence, learning to take risks."[139]

In February of 1996, after pastoring seventeen years in Weaverville, California, Bill Johnson and family were asked to move to Redding to pastor the mother church, Bethel Church. Bill made it clear that he was born for revival and that if they did not want that, then they would not want him. The leadership was totally on the same page. But when the power of God came, almost half of the more than two thousand people in their church chose to leave. Bill and his wife, Beni, did not apologize for the presence of God nor were they rattled by the price tag. They were

---

138 Richard Riss, A History of the Awakening of 1992-1995, which includes a letter written by the radio manager, Jon Hamilton; Bill Jackson, Quest for the Radical Middle, Vineyard International Pub. 1999, pp. 296-297; Further details of these events were later recorded in a report by J. Lee Grady in the March 1995 issue of Charisma (vol. 20, no. 8, pp. 56-57).

139 Bill Johnson, testimony on Catch The Fire TV, YouTube, uploaded May 16, 2011.

thrilled that the Lord's precious presence was coming and salvations, healings and miracles began to take place.[140]

Bill and Beni Johnson are now two of John and Carol Arnott's dearest friends and source of inspiration. Bill speaks frequently in Toronto as well as around the world. On occasion, he would start his message in Toronto by saying, "It's good to be back on the mother ship." Bethel church, with its team of gifted leaders, musicians and Supernatural School of Ministry, has become a major, cutting edge, apostolic resource centre to the body of Christ worldwide.

In June of 1995, John and Carol travelled to Australia and New Zealand to conduct Catch The Fire Down Under Conferences to packed out crowds.

In one of the sessions in Auckland, New Zealand, at Victory Church, the Holy Spirit sovereignly fell, hijacking the meeting, which the Arnotts love to see. Halfway through a worship song, the worship leader collapsed to the floor. Someone took their place but soon they were out on the floor as well. A third worship leader was soon down and out, followed by the bass player and drummer. Max Legg, the pastor, went up to the microphone but he crashed to the floor, followed by his assistant pastor.

The elders asked John to go up to the platform and urged him not to forget the offering! John was thinking, "Lord, what are you doing?" He said, "Because you are honouring Me. I am honouring you with My presence." In an interview, John said, "I will never forget that. I realized that, to have the Holy Spirit come in a meeting that we are in, is probably the greatest honour that you can ever imagine. I felt I got hit by a two by four. Bong. Hello! Of course. This is great. But when you go in and the controversy is raging and the radio and media are there and it's a circus. It's a zoo. We want them to like us and in the midst of that, God said that. My goodness. What a night it was. Stuart and Lynley Allan were there and they got wrecked. The room had theatre seats and Bill Subritzky, a lawyer, Bible teacher and healing-deliverance

---

140 Bill Johnson's talks in Toronto as well as Wikipedia website: http://en.wikipedia.org/wiki/Bill_Johnson_(pastor)

evangelist, who is known all over New Zealand, was wedged in the theatre seats. John got Bill up on the platform that night and he said, "I got the lot," meaning he got everything.[141]

The Pensacola Outpouring
Father's Day, June 18, 1995

One of the most significant events of 1995 was when the Holy Spirit fell upon the Brownsville Assemblies of God church in Pensacola, Florida, on Father's Day, June 18.

God had previously spoken about his intentions for Pensacola to Pastor David Yongi Cho, of Seoul Korea. In 1991, Pastor Cho was conducting a meeting in Seattle, Washington. While praying for revival in America, he asked God if He planned to send revival to the United States or was it destined for judgment. The Lord asked him to get out a map of America. He then instructed the Korean pastor to point his finger at the map. As he did, he felt his finger drawn to Pensacola Florida. The Lord said to him, "I am going to send revival to the seaside city of Pensacola, and it will spread like fire until all of America has been consumed by it." Dr. Cho shared this prophetic vision with others and it spread to pastors in the Pensacola area.[142]

Prior to the fresh outpouring at the Brownsville Assembly of God church in Pensacola, Florida, which began on Father's Day, June 18, 1995, Pastor John Kilpatrick had felt prompted by the Lord to turn the Sunday night service into a prayer meeting, a house of prayer, which included prayer for revival.

They created about a dozen large banners that were hung up around the sanctuary; groups of people could rally around these. Each banner represented a category that needed prayer. There was a banner for the family, another for souls, schools, the peace of Jerusalem, political leaders, pastors and, of course, a banner for revival.

John Kilpatrick admits that he felt the devil hassling him,

---

141 John Arnott, recorded interview with author Jerry Steingard, June 14, 2013.
142 John Kilpatrick, Feast of Fire, 1995, in Foreword, p. vii.

whispering, "You're going to lose your crowd if you keep this prayer stuff up... You are crazy." The attendance Sunday nights, however, actually increased by twenty percent. For about two and a half years, they were knocking on heaven's door calling out for God to move among them. These Sunday evenings gave priority to worship, intercession, taking communion together and closed with the pastor giving a priestly blessing over the people. They believed this was foundational to preparing the soil for revival.[143]

John's wife, Brenda, had gone with a friend, Shirl, to the revival meetings in Toronto for a few days in February 1995.[144] While at the meetings in Toronto, Brenda was not only refreshed and overwhelmed by the Spirit, but also healed of back problems. She found greater intimacy with Jesus and was healed of past hurts, a sense of unworthiness, guilt and shame. In Brownsville the following Sunday, John Kilpatrick had Brenda and her friend share of their experience in Toronto. This intensified everyone's hunger for revival, and the power of God landed on a few individuals while John was preaching.

During the following months, Brenda's walk with the Lord became sweeter and sweeter. Waves of God's glory would wash over her. Her Bible came alive again for her. John would see the changes in her, which increased his hunger for God and for revival to come to their church. Their church staff was also growing more desperate for a visitation from God. John released most of them to make a trip to Toronto in April 1995, including the new worship leader he had just hired, Lindell Cooley. John had taken ill and was not able to go with them.[145]

Lindell Cooley found the services in Toronto extremely laid-back and less polished than he was accustomed to. He struggled with offense and pride. Despite this, he and his father volunteered as catchers for a prayer ministry person and soon they were feeling the presence of God and couldn't stop weeping. Lindell cried for the next two weeks as movers transferred his furniture from Nashville to Pensacola, as he

---

143 Brenda shared her testimony in the book, Experience the Blessing, edited by John Arnott.
144 Brenda Kilpatrick's testimony in Experience the Blessing, edited by John Arnott, Renew Books, 2000, pp. 88-96.
145 Brenda Kilpatrick's testimony in Experience the Blessing, edited by John Arnott, Renew Books, 2000, pp. 88-96.

soaked up the worship music CDs he purchased in Toronto, and as God performed a deep work in his heart, dealing with spiritual arrogance and religiosity.[146]

Once he arrived in Pensacola, he discovered that all the staff that had gone to Toronto had come away with "an experience that would change them for years to come. We knew that God had kissed our souls and refreshed us in ways we didn't completely understand. Our hunger continued to grow. We would find ourselves at Pastor Kilpatrick's house, sitting on the screened porch. One by one we would share the story of what God had done for us in Toronto. Like those on the road to Emmaus, we found our hearts stirring within us. We would well up with tears and His Spirit would visit us. We prayed for one another, fell under God's power and experienced His glorious presence."

> Ironically, the refreshing that was happening on the pastor's back porch wasn't yet happening in the church. John recognized this but spoke very directly. He told us we couldn't manufacture what was happening; we had to wait until God sovereignly did it.[147]

Pastor Kilpatrick asked Assembly of God missionary evangelist, Steve Hill of Texas, to speak in the Sunday morning service on Father's Day. Steve Hill, who had been a missionary in Argentina for seven years, had been mentored by such men as David Wilkerson, Nicky Cruz, and Leonard Ravenhill, and prayed for by Argentina's Carlos Annacondia.[148]

During his message, Steve Hill shared with the congregation about his recent encounter with the Holy Spirit at Holy Trinity Brompton. He was on his way back from Russia and stopped to rest in England. Sandy Millar, the Anglican vicar whose church was flowing in a fresh outpouring of the Spirit, prayed for Steve. He was powerfully touched and experienced personal renewal. This Sunday morning in Pensacola,

---

146 Lindell Cooley's testimony, Experience the Blessing, pp. 120-128.
147 Ibid
148 An Interview with Evangelist Steve Hill www.thunderstruck.org/hill.htm December 21, 1996.

Steve could hardly get through his sermon, he was so excited about the altar call. He believed God was going to move powerfully that morning. John Kilpatrick, who was feeling very tired, discouraged and still grieving the recent loss of his mother, wasn't as confident as the evangelist. But when Steve Hill gave an altar call, about one thousand came forward for prayer.[149]

John Kilpatrick then declared from the platform, "'Folks, this is it! Get in – this is what we have been praying for!' Then, with no one touching him, he fell to the platform in the Spirit, where he remained for four hours. God kissed John and said, 'Now, rest!'"[150]

John Kilpatrick recalls Steve Hill walking past him, waving his hand in his direction, and simply saying, "More, Lord." With that, John said, "I hit that marble floor like a ton of bricks... it felt like I weighed ten thousand pounds, I knew something supernatural was happening. God was visiting us... Many families never did make it to celebrate Father's Day dinners with their earthly fathers that afternoon. We had a different kind of Father's Day celebration that lasted throughout the day and then picked up again that evening."[151]

God poured out His Holy Spirit upon them and the astounding visitation of God began. Steve Hill cancelled his plans to go to Russia and ended up staying to conduct revival meetings in Brownsville, from Wednesday to Saturday nights, for the next five years. Service after service, Steve Hill preached the gospel uncompromisingly and threw out the nets to bring in a great harvest of souls. Sinners and backslidden believers alike came running to the altar to repent of their sins and to be forgiven, cleansed and filled with the grace and love of God. Within the first two years of revival meetings, it was reported that over one hundred thousand people made either first-time commitments to Christ or rededications. People flocked from around the nation and around the world.

In January 1997, they established the Brownsville Revival School of Ministry to further equip and train new converts as well as those

---

149 John Kilpatrick, pp. 73-76.
150 Brenda Kilpatrick, Experience the Blessing, p. 94.
151 John Kilpatrick, pp. 75-78.

simply hungry to advance in their relationship with Christ and to be used by Him. [152] In the same year, Steve Hill, John Kilpatrick and worship leader, Lindell Cooley, travelled to various American cities conducting revival gatherings called "Awake America".

In 2000, Steve Hill moved on from Pensacola to do other ministry work. In 2003 worship leader, Lindell Cooley, also moved on. [153] However, the Pensacola church continued holding Friday night revival meetings until 2006.

More than four million people are believed to have visited the revival meetings between 1995 and the year 2000, producing somewhere between one hundred and two hundred thousand commitments to Christ. Thousands of pastors also visited the revival, causing mini-revivals to break out in their respective churches, many of which were Assembly of God and Pentecostal churches.

I visited the Brownsville church in March, 1996. Though the style was different than what I was accustomed to in Toronto, it was obviously the same wonderful presence of the Lord and there was a genuine hunger for God. It was wonderful too, to listen to the powerful preaching of an anointed and passionate evangelist and watch sinners and backsliders alike run to the altar to do business with God.

Of all the hot spots of revival that have broken out since 1994, the Toronto and the Brownsville outpourings seemed to have experienced what has been called a "tipping point." The right ingredients came together to create critical mass. Toronto and Brownsville have attracted the most attention worldwide and the greatest number of people to their meetings.[154]

---

152 The first class had one hundred and twenty-five students. Dr. Michael L. Brown initially directed this training school.

153 In October 2003, although people continued to visit the revival, John Kilpatrick resigned as pastor, after twenty-two years, to answer an apostolic call of God upon his life. Randy and Suzann Feldschau became the pastors of the Brownsville church and remained for three years. In 2006, Dr. Evon G. Horton, former pastor of Mississauga Gospel Temple in Canada and President of Master's College and Seminary in Toronto, became the new pastor at Brownsville Assembly of God. Pastor Evon is on the Canadian and U.S. Board for Benny Hinn Ministries and also Bill Hybels Ministries.

154 For at least one conference, the Pensacola worship leader, Lindell Cooley, came and ministered in Toronto as well. Furthermore, John Arnott spoke twice in Florida and John Kilpatrick ministered at the Partners in Harvest Conference in Toronto. And Brenda Kilpatrick came to speak at the women's Releasers of Life Conference in Toronto.

With the Brownsville meetings being led by an evangelist (Steve Hill), the primary focus of their meetings was to boldly preach the gospel and to see sinners come to faith in Christ and walk in holiness of life. Many believers were also renewed and revived, of course, in the process.

With the Toronto revival meetings being overseen by a pastoral/apostolic father (John Arnott), the primary focus of their meetings, in contrast, was to see believers in the body of Christ refreshed, healed, empowered and restored in heart, mind, body and relationships. As they often provided altar calls, a good number of people also gave their lives to Christ, of course, in the process.

In July 1997 Rick Stivers wrote an insightful article comparing the Toronto and Brownsville outpourings. [155] Rick begins by contrasting Toronto with Pensacola in terms of climate and terrain; one with lots of sunshine and beaches, the other a frozen ice field in the middle of winter. He then contrasts their church buildings; Toronto meets in an industrial warehouse with stacking chairs while Pensacola meets in a beautiful sanctuary complete with stained-glass windows and wooden pews. He also compares their attire; in Toronto the dress is quite casual while in Brownsville it is more suit and tie.

Rick continues:

So much for the variety of adornment, what about the substance? I've met men and women who have made the pilgrimage to Toronto and others who have taken the southern route to Pensacola. They all seem to come back the same! A renewed love for Jesus; an insatiable thirst for more of the Lord in their lives; a revived life of prayer and Bible reading; a broken and repentant heart; and a desire to share their renewed life with everyone they meet. From the fruit it would appear that the trees are more alike than they are different. So what's the scoop? Simple: Same olives, different jars.

---

155 It is called Same Olives Different Jars – Toronto Airport Christian Fellowship and Brownsville AOG, by Rick Stivers.

Rick recalls a friend of his who visited an olive factory. He watched the complex process that ended with the olives going into jars and labels being placed on the jars. At one point, however, the factory whistle blew and the whole system came to a stop. Employees then replaced the jars and labels with much fancier jars and "designer" labels. The assembly then picked up speed and the same olives were now going into these upgraded jars. His friend enquired of the supervisor regarding this change up. His explanation was simple, "Different packaging appeals to different consumers. We want to reach as many buyers as we can."

> Our Heavenly Father has obviously pulled the old jar switch on us for the same purpose; He wants to reach everyone. I'm sure some folks would not even consider buying those 'other' olives, as theirs consistently tasted just right. A pastor I met recently in Texas, who had been revived in Pensacola, said, 'We don't want any of that Toronto stuff around here.'
>
> I, on the other hand, sat for the first two days of my recent trip to Pensacola in my own puddle of critical comparison-shopping. 'Man!' I thought, 'All this hollerin' about gettin' the sin out. Where's the love of the Lord?' Sometime during day three at BAOG, God finally cracked the thick crust of my heart to reveal a peek at His own...
>
> In my opinion... neither stream is greater than the other... It's just different labels. Whether it is the goodness of God in Toronto, which leads a person to repentance, or the repentance of God in Pensacola, which leads a person to His goodness, the results are the same. We want more of the Lord...[156]

The Miracle of Modesto

1995 was also a year when the Holy Spirit breathed on evangelistic ventures, such as the Heaven's Gates, Hell's Flames drama production

---

156 Rick Stivers' article, Same Olives Different Jars – Toronto Airport Christian Fellowship and Brownsville AOG; also: http://www.shekinah.blessedbereans.org/pensacola/kilpatrick/olives.html (accessed June 2, 2013)

performed in Modesto, California. What's been called, "The Miracle of Modesto," saw thirty-three thousand people come to the altar at Calvary Temple to receive Christ in just a twenty-eight day period, which began January 15, 1995. Over eighty thousand attended the twenty-eight nightly performances, causing serious traffic jams in the neighbourhood. Churches in the city had their hands full, scrambling to baptize and disciple the newly converted. The leaders produced a one-hour documentary video called The Miracle of Modesto and they have seen many people come to salvation just through watching it.

Bethany World Prayer Center, of Baton Rouge, Louisiana, pastored by Larry Stockstill also hosted the Heaven's Gates, Hell's Flames drama in 1995. They were believing and praying for a thousand to fifteen hundred salvations. What was originally scheduled to be four nights lasted five weeks, with eighteen thousand people making a public profession of faith in Christ.[157]

College Revivals

On Sunday, January 22, 1995, a fresh move of God began at Coggin Avenue Baptist Church in Brownwood, Texas, as well as at a few other churches in the area. By Thursday, January 26, it spread to the Howard Payne University campus, a Baptist school with about fourteen hundred students.

This revival was characterized by testimonies, increased prayer, healing of brokenness, repentance, public confession of sins and reconciliation of relationships. Fresh winds of revival began to blow to various churches and college campuses around the nation in the following months, including Southwestern Seminary in Fort Worth, Beeson Divinity School in Birmingham, Alabama, and Wheaton College in Illinois. Dozens of other American schools were impacted in some measure throughout the year.[158]

---

157 Mission Frontiers website, from the September/October 1995 issue, Bethany World Prayer Center: One Church pays off its building While Giving $ 7 Million to Missions, September 1, 1995, by Luis Bush http://www.missionfrontiers.org/issue/article/bethany-world-prayer-center-one-church-pays-off-its-building-while-giving-7 (accessed August 23, 2013).

158 Pastor John Avant of Coggin Avenue Baptist Church and Henry T. Blackaby were instrumental leaders in this move of God. Henry Blackaby, a Canadian, was involved in a similar revival in Saskatchewan, Canada, in the early 1970s, while pastoring in Saskatoon. He is the director of the

By 1995, the annual March For Jesus, which was birthed out of Great Britain in the late 1980s and which had God's fingerprints all over it, was exploding among the cities and nations of the world. Throughout the early to mid-1990s, the numbers participating in dancing, praying and praising Jesus on the streets with great joy and abandonment, grew into the millions.

During this decade, the 10-40 Window prayer movement also gained momentum. Tens of millions of intercessors were committed to praying for the Kingdom of God to break into the cities and nations within the geographical window between ten degrees latitude north of the equator to forty degrees north. This included the most resistant nations to the gospel of Christ where missionaries are generally not free to minister. Since the decade of the 1990s, we have heard many credible and inspiring reports of major breakthroughs with signs and wonders and salvations of millions.

The ten-week Alpha course, a thoughtful introduction to the Christian faith, originating with Nicky Gumbel and the Holy Trinity Brompton Anglican Church in England several years earlier, had begun to gain astounding momentum and spread throughout churches of all kinds in all parts of the world. Scores of seekers have been making commitments to Christ and getting established in their new faith. One session in the course focuses on the person and work of the Holy Spirit and many have received a fresh infilling of the Holy Spirit through Alpha.

The Promise Keepers ministry has challenged men to follow Christ and be the husbands and fathers that Christ has called them to be. This North American-based ministry has been another phenomenal God-breathed movement that has further extended the Kingdom of God in this decade of the 1990s.

Office of Prayer and Spiritual Awakenings for the Home Mission Board of the Southern Baptist Convention. Perhaps his greatest contribution to preparing hearts and churches for revival has been through his books Experiencing God and Fresh Encounters, which were co-written with Claude King. More than a million copies have been sold.

CHAPTER 7

Toronto's Separation from the Vineyard
December 1995

… Nearly immediately I began to question how institutional forces were interacting with charismatic fires. Is it possible for these two actors—charisma and organization—to work together in a long-term revival? Or would strong institutional forces shear the wings of the soaring charismatic spirit?"

True charisma remains a fragile and illusive gift that cannot be manufactured. Once given, however, it can be either nurtured or stifled by institutional norms and structures. How long the Toronto Airport Vineyard and other benefactors of the Toronto Blessing are able to stay the forces of institutionalization remains to be seen.[159]

I recall standing in John Arnott's office in Stratford in 1991. I was his assistant pastor and worship leader at the time. We both were sharing how we simply loved the Vineyard movement and felt like this was our home, our tribe. We both agreed that we hoped that we would live and die as Vineyard pastors. But we both also agreed that history shows that movements tend to institutionalize over time; the vehicle, or the means, can become an end in itself. Our loyalty and devotion must

---

159 Sociologist, Margaret M. Poloma wrote an insightful paper called, Charisma and Institutions: A Sociological Account of the 'Toronto Blessing', which was updated October 25, 1995, less than two months before the separation between the Association of Vineyard Churches (AVC) and Toronto Airport Vineyard Christian Fellowship (TAV). http://www.evanwiggs.com/revival/manifest/soc97.html

first be to Jesus and His Kingdom, and only secondly to a particular movement or an association.

In this chapter, we'll look at the disfellowshipping of the Toronto Airport Vineyard from the Vineyard movement in December 1995. I recognize that seeking to pastor and steward a move of God for optimal Kingdom advancement is no "walk in the park" for anyone. I believe these next pages will show that John Wimber and the leaders of the Association of Vineyard Churches desired to see the charisma nurtured rather than stifled. Yet differences of perspective as to where the fine line between nurturing and stifling is to be found created an ever-increasing tension with the leaders of Toronto Airport Vineyard (TAV) that finally led to a parting of the ways.

John Wimber Visits Toronto
late June 1994

Five months after the start of the outpouring in Toronto exploded, John Wimber, leader of the Association of Vineyard Churches (AVC), came to "ground zero" to spend a couple of days with the Toronto Airport Vineyard leadership. He came to observe what God was doing in and through the church, as well as to bring his fatherly wisdom and years of experience to support, guide and encourage.

On Wednesday, June 22, after Dr. Guy Chevreau gave a brief teaching on historical revival, John Wimber gave a very biblical and pastoral talk to a room full of pastors of all denominations. It was a historic moment for us to draw from the wealth of practical experience and wisdom of this seasoned man of God.

In response to a pastor's question, Wimber stated, in his laid-back, Californian, non-religious style:

> To coin a phrase, 'Die sucker!' It's a matter of who's boss and He can do it any way He wants to, anytime He wants to, by any means He wants to employ... Bottom line is that God is not like we think He is,

and He employs means that we wouldn't employ, to do things that we don't understand, to accomplish things that we do understand. And the bottom line is simply that this is not controllable and ought not be. This really is God. You have to give place to it. You don't have to give over everything to it. You don't have to quit getting up and bathing, going to the bathroom, taking care of your children and cleaning your house and going to work. There's a lot of routine things that can, by and large, stay in place. And I think it's good that we keep on taking the offerings and that we teach the Bible and counsel those who need counselling. There ought to be an ongoing routine relating it to, for instance, the issue of sanctification.

John Wimber went on to tell the story of how the Spirit had fallen dramatically on his church on Mother's Day, 1980.[160] Of the seven hundred in attendance in a gymnasium, half came forward for prayer and the guest speaker, Lonnie Frisbee, prayed, "Come Holy Spirit". John Wimber described what followed:

"Bodies fell out on the floor, many gobbling like turkeys, one guy for one and a half hours, with the microphone in his face, and no one could get over the bodies to get the mic!" Wimber then shared how he was up most of the night reading through his books on Wesley and Edwards as well as the Bible. At six in the morning, he asked, "Lord, is this really you?" At that moment the telephone rang. It was Tom Stipe, a pastor friend from Denver. He apologized for calling so early but said that the Lord told him to call Wimber and tell him that, "The Lord says this is Me!"[161]

John Wimber brought us comfort and reassurance regarding the power of God in a visitation and the phenomenon that seems to usually

---

160 Kevin Springer, editor, Power Encounters, Harper & Row, 1988, pp. 12-13, Carol Wimber tells this story and claims the occasion was Mother's Day, 1981; Bill Jackson, The Quest for the Radical Middle, Vineyard International Pub., 1999, p. 77, claims that 1979 has often been given as the date but research has now shown it was 1980.
161 Video tape, John Wimber speaking at TAV, June 22, 1994; also, Kevin Springer, editor, Power Encounters, pp. 12-13.

accompany it. He told us that he had seen close to seventeen years of the manifestations with times of ebb and flow. He stated that this outpouring in Toronto had a greater intensity than what they were experiencing in Anaheim at that time. He felt that on a scale of one to ten, Anaheim was at about a four and Toronto was at a seven. He shared with us that he had recently been to Brisbane, Australia, where they momentarily experienced about a nine.

> The laughter started—in fifteen minutes three thousand out of the four thousand people were gripped by the Spirit; many on the floor, laughing, crying, howling, shaking and thirty-five or forty other manifestations. There's a whole range of things that you have seen and a whole range of things that you haven't seen yet. But it's all coming folks. It's all part of the package.[162]

That night the evening renewal meeting was in a different location (Attwell Drive). Perhaps because of that, as well as having John Wimber present, things seemed to be a bit subdued. John Arnott likens it to when kids are playing in the family room and when the father steps into the room, everyone gets a bit quiet. In his message, however, John Wimber declared that he came, "not to put a lid on things, but to take the lid off".[163]

Critics of the Vineyard and Toronto

In John Wimber's July/August 1994 article in Vineyard Reflections, he stated that over one hundred thousand people in the Vineyard movement alone had been touched by this visitation that was only six months old. Two thirds of all the Vineyard churches had been impacted due to the outpourings in both the Anaheim and Toronto Vineyards.[164]

---

162 Video tape, John Wimber speaking at TAV, Dixie building, June 22, 1994.
163 Video tape, John Wimber speaking at Attwell building, June 22, 1994; also John Arnott interview, June 14, 2013.
164 John Wimber, Vineyard Reflections, July/August 1994, p. 7; also Wesley Campbell, Welcoming a Visitation of the Holy Spirit, Creation House, 1996, p. 26.

With any fresh move of the Spirit within biblical and church history, the critics—the "orthodox watchdogs"—are not far away. The Toronto Blessing and the Vineyard movement certainly received their share of criticism. Some would even say that they received more favourable and fair treatment from the secular media than from segments of the evangelical community.

John Wimber, was under increasingly intense criticism from people like Hank Hanegraaff, of southern California. Through his books and daily radio talk show, Hanegraaff, "The Bible Answer Man", relentlessly attacked and accused John Wimber, the Vineyard movement and the Toronto Airport Vineyard of cult-like deception and demonization. The Pensacola outpouring would later have their share of grief from this critic as well. This blast of accusations struck fear in many people, including folks within various California Vineyard churches. Soon a noticeable number began leaving Vineyard churches and migrating to safer and more conservative church circles.

Hardest hit was John McClure's Vineyard in Newport Beach, California. He lost forty percent of his congregation, many of whom went down the street to Chuck Smith's Calvary Chapel, because they were being scared by the comments of Hank Hanegraaff, a member of Chuck Smith's Calvary Chapel.[165]

Vineyard Tensions with the Kansas City Prophetic Movement

Unfortunately, John Wimber was no stranger to criticism. Just a few years earlier (1989-1991), John Wimber and the AVC had expended considerable time and energy wrestling with controversial issues, tensions, and criticisms related to their involvement with the Kansas City prophets.

With the introduction of the prophetic movement (with Paul Cain, Mike Bickle, Bob Jones, John Paul Jackson, Jim Goll and others) to the Vineyard in 1989, John Wimber and many in the Vineyard received

---

165 Source: Bill Jackson, The Quest for the Radical Middle, Vineyard International Pub. 1999, p. 313.

fresh vision, encouragement and blessing. For instance, one of Wimber's sons, Sean, repented, came back to the Lord and was reconciled to the family through the prophetic ministry of Bob Jones.[166]

Paul Cain and the prophets claimed that God was offering to launch the "last days" ministry through the Vineyard movement. But that they needed to repent for seeking God's power (His hand) and not God's presence (His face), for immorality in the movement that was not dealt with by leadership ("unsanctified mercy"), and for their prayerlessness as a movement. It was stated that God was in the business of "offending the mind to reveal the heart" and through reproach and rejection, would be preparing and raising up a "faceless generation", "Joel's Army" for an end-time revival. Worldwide movements of 24/7 prayer and intercession would be established, deep humility and extravagant giving to the poor would be required and the foundational ministries of prophet and apostle were being restored to the church.[167]

Former Dallas seminary professor of Old Testament, Dr. Jack Deere, became good friends of both Paul Cain and John Wimber and came on staff at the Anaheim Vineyard. Dr. Jack Deere and Dr. Wayne Grudem, former professor of Biblical and Systematic Theology at Trinity Evangelical Divinity School[168] would become extremely helpful apologists in support of the biblical foundations for the prophetic gift and ministry of the prophetic as well as biblical guidelines for its use.

Mike Bickle's Kansas City Fellowship joined the Vineyard movement on May 12, 1990.[169] They believed the Lord was calling them, with their core values of intercession, holiness, offerings to the poor and prophecy, to cross-pollinate with the values of worship and compassion in the Vineyard.

Many Vineyard leaders found themselves full of faith and anticipation about Vineyard's merging with the prophetic movement, which brought them a new sense of calling and direction towards an

166 Ibid., pp. 204-211.
167 Ibid., pp. 206-207.
168 Wayne Grudem is also author of the 1988 book The Gift of Prophecy in the New Testament and Today
169 Ibid., p. 217.

end-time revival. Many other Vineyard leaders, however, were having very serious concerns that the Vineyard movement was getting off track.

These concerns would soon intensify with Paul Cain prophesying that tokens of revival would break out in London and throughout England in October of 1990. Though the meetings and conferences held in England in October by John Wimber and his team (which included Paul Cain and Mike Bickle) were very powerful, John Wimber and many other Vineyard leaders were quite disappointed that revival had not broken out. The whole matter created disillusionment for many, believing that the emphasis on the word "token" was an attempt to back-peddle and justify a prophetic word rather than admitting it was wrong.[170]

The painful polarization within the Vineyard camp would ultimately result in some Vineyard leaders and churches leaving the movement and returning to a more conservative evangelical position, such as Calvary Chapel.[171]

By May 1991, the AVC council decided to make a shift away from the prophetic emphasis and get back to their original mandate as well as be more intentional about planting churches. John Wimber admitted that he had been intimidated by the gifting of the prophets and failed to use his authority to weigh prophecy and pastor them. He now realized "that in the same way that the Vineyard had met the prophetic, it was now time for the prophetic to meet the Vineyard.[172]

The prophetic emphasis had shifted the movement momentarily to a much more Arminian emphasis on fasting, intercession and holiness in order to usher in a coming revival. But soon afterwards the Vineyard went back to its more conservative evangelical roots, with its emphasis on a more reformed theology, pastors and teachers, the historical-grammatical interpretation of Scripture and the process (versus crisis of revival) of seeing the Kingdom expand by evangelism, ministry to the poor, healing the sick, the pursuit of wholeness, church planting, and missions. Vineyard pastors Rich Nathan and Ken Wilson wrote the

---

170 Ibid., pp. 224-226.
171 Some Vineyard leaders, including John Wimber, used to be a part of the Calvary Chapel movement
172 Ibid., p. 230.

1995 book, *Empowered Evangelicals*, to convey this attempt to blend the best of the evangelical theological world with the best of the charismatic world, including the power and ministry of the Holy Spirit.[173]

At the Vineyard pastors' conference, in the summer of 1995, John Wimber expressed regret and apologized for leading the Vineyard movement into the prophetic movement. In the end, no merger took place between the two streams and very little cross-pollination occurred. Mike Bickle and his Metro Vineyard in Kansas City would officially leave the Vineyard in the summer of 1996 to uncompromisingly pursue the course God had originally called them to: intercession, holiness, offerings to the poor and prophecy; making the acrostic IHOP. They remain deeply thankful to the Lord for John Wimber and the Vineyard movement and recognize that they have benefitted tremendously from their association with them.[174]

Vineyard Frustration with Toronto's Methodology of Pastoring The Outpouring

With this recent history of controversy and criticism weighing heavily on them, John Wimber and a growing number of Vineyard pastors, were getting worn down from the relentless verbal assaults from the critics of the Toronto Blessing. They were disheartened by the exodus of some of their members, and increasingly frustrated with some of the methodology employed by the Toronto church. This methodology seemed, in their estimation, to be incompatible with the Vineyard philosophy of ministry.

Using catchers, drawing lines on the floor,[175] giving testimonies on stage,[176] seeking to give explanation to some of the manifestations—particularly the rare ones, such as roaring—placing this move of God in the context of a possible end-time revival scenario, and other issues

---

173 ich Nathan and Ken Wilson, Vine Books, 1995.
174 Bill Jackson, pp. 220-223; 234.
175 To indicate where those who wanted to receive ministry should stand for prayer
176 Though the TAV team wanted testimonies to focus on what God was doing in the heart, they often inadvertently resulted in giving manifestations a high profile, as those giving testimony started manifesting, coming under the power of God again as they spoke of what He had done for them.

created an ever growing tension between the AVC's senior leadership and the delightfully naïve and playful Vineyard leaders in Toronto.

The AVC leadership board felt caught between a rock and hard place. I can empathize with the leadership of a movement of worldwide influence when it sees a church within its ranks become high profile and inadvertently change the flavour of "renewal", which, they believe, does not sufficiently or accurately represent the movement at large. When some people in parts of the world began to think that real Vineyard ministry has to look like Toronto renewal ministry, it created quite the conundrum. It was like the tail wagging the dog.

By September 1995, a list of fifteen concerns about the Toronto church had been compiled and circulated among Vineyard leaders. John Arnott received a copy of the list and was quite shocked. Vineyard leader, Fred Wright, who had just spent five weeks at the Toronto meetings,[177] concluded that only two concerns seemed to really mirror the situation. As Fred Wright was living near the Vineyard headquarters in California, he dropped in to see if he could talk with someone about this matter. He ended up talking with the editor of the Vineyard International Newsletter who had been working on the list. The editor had spent two hours attempting to correct the misconceptions that he believed had been included in the list.

While they were talking, John Wimber came into the editor's office to finalize the list before releasing it for distribution to the churches. John Wimber took Fred Wright up to his office and they went through the fifteen points over the next two hours. John kept saying to Fred, "I see it differently." Fred then realized that the situation had clearly gone beyond an "easy fix".[178]

John Wimber was taking a middle of the road approach to Toronto by neither endorsing nor condemning the Toronto renewal. He sought to make a careful distinction between the renewal of the Spirit, which he deeply loved and valued, and how that renewal was being pastorally administered and dispensed by the Toronto Vineyard. However, many

---

177 Fred Wright moved to Toronto to be on staff several months later.
178 Fred Wright, Prophetic History of Partners in Harvest, September 2007, pp. 12-13.

within the Christian community at large would not be discerning enough to see that important distinction.

The Toronto Airport Vineyard was determined to remain committed to not quenching renewal fires. And they believed that meant not terminating the nightly renewal meetings, the use of testimonies in the meetings, the use of catchers and lines on the floor, nor the extensive travelling to take the fire to other locations.

With most revivals of the past, there are typically a few new "innovations" that are implemented and that create controversy. Some leaders, especially leaders of a previous move of God, can get threatened and upset over new methods of administration. Richard Riss, in his book, *Images of Revival*, gives us this example;

> Asahel Nettleton accused Finney of introducing 'new measures' that were changing previous evangelistic practices. It was not unusual for Finney to pray for people by name. He also allowed women to pray and testify, he encouraged people to come forward to an 'anxious seat', he would mobilize an entire community through groups of workers visiting homes, and he would arrange for church meetings on every night of the week, rather than only on Sundays. Finney also employed the 'new measure' of gathering around himself a group of like-minded friends and associates for the promotion of the revival.
>
> These so-called 'new measures' brought about a great deal of controversy. Lyman Beecher, a pastor in Boston, called a meeting of concerned evangelical leaders on July 18, 1827, at New Lebanon, New York, in order to do something about Finney's 'unorthodox' practices...[179]

In the same book, Kathryn Riss writes:

> Debates are often aroused by the other 'new methods' that revivals invariably develop. The 'anxious seats' provided for spiritual seekers by

---

179 Richard Riss and Kathyrn Riss, Images of Revival, Revival Press, 1997, p. 76.

Finney and the Holiness preachers; open-air preaching utilized by the Quakers and later by George Whitefield; tent meetings; the practice of the altar call and salvation decisions; public testimonies, especially by women; singing by the laity; use of Bible translations from Latin into common languages; new hymns set to popular tunes; the use of organs and other musical instruments during worship; laying on of hands in prayer or for healing; falling on the ground under the influence of the Holy Spirit; prayer lines, overhead projectors, and carpet tape have all come under attack during the various revivals of church history by those who opposed such 'new methods' as objectionable for one reason or another. Most of the above practices, once considered radical perversions of proper Church order, have since been quietly absorbed into common practice as their effectiveness outlived their detractors. But in their day, each aroused much criticism and controversy.[180]

There are always two sides to a story, however. The Vineyard leaders' concerns over administrative issues like the use of testimonies on stage, catchers, and tape on the floor are understandable. They perceived that such methodology can be manipulative, placing undue focus on manifestations and unfair pressure and expectation on people that they are supposed to fall, otherwise they may feel like second class Christians.

On the other hand, the Arnotts and their leadership team greatly appreciated the value and power of testimony. They believed that allowing several people to tell their fresh and up-to-the-minute story of what God had been doing in their hearts gave honour to the Lord, diminished fear and released child-like faith in the people. For many people, this was the highlight of the meeting.

Regarding the use of catchers, the leaders desired to create a safe place for people to meet with God. They didn't want to see anyone get hurt going down and they certainly didn't want those already on the floor to get hurt by someone falling on them. This value outweighed the other value about not setting people up or manipulating them.

---

180 Ibid., p. 138.

The Toronto leaders felt that to not have catchers would be pastorally irresponsible of them, since the majority of people did tend to lose their bodily strength and collapse to the floor.

In the early 1990s, someone who had been injured had taken an American ministry to court. The courts favoured the plaintiff based on the fact that, since that ministry often saw people fall down, they were negligent in not taking reasonable measures to protect the safety of those receiving prayer. Even with the use of catchers, the threat of a possible lawsuit materialized more than once for the Toronto itinerant team.

The rationale for the taped lines on the floor was also to protect people from physical harm. Lines were taped at least eight feet apart, which allowed ample space and a reasonable margin of safety, for people laid out horizontally doing "carpet time". It was not only an issue of safety but also of efficient crowd control. The taped lines helped to minimize distractions for both the ministry team member and the one receiving prayer, giving maximum focus on the Lord. This also resulted in better time management by not having to waste time assessing each situation to see if there was adequate space behind a person, in case they happened to end up on the floor. These were merely logistical and practical administration issues that the Toronto leadership felt could help minimize chaos and bring greater order.

The Toronto leaders had also come to realize that, for individuals to encounter the Lord in a fresh, deep and dynamic way, they needed to be encouraged to take time to "soak" in the presence of the Lord and not be too quick to get up off the floor. They picked up the term "soaking" from Francis MacNutt who had coined the phrase "soaking prayer". [181] What the Lord desires to accomplish during an encounter with someone may take time—maybe an hour or longer. To be able to have that opportunity with the Lord requires that the person feels they have permission to stay and that they are in a setting that is safe, worshipful and conducive to fostering intimacy with God.

Not only the physical surroundings needed to feel as safe and orderly as possible, but also the ministry team had to feel safe to the

---

181 John Arnott, Manifestations and Prophetic Symbolism, Wine Press, 2008, p.19.

people receiving prayer. The prayer ministry team was, and still is, made up of ordinary folks who are extraordinary servants. Each team member had to go through considerable training and healing before they could minister. Materials such as the book, Search for Significance, by Robert S. McGee, was required reading for the prayer team and they had to work through personal issues of acceptance, forgiveness, and significance. The team members also needed to be trusted Christians who were in relationship and accountability with others in their fellowship. And they could only give away what they had received so they too needed to be prayed for by others and continually soak in the presence of the Lord. They were then more able to minister out of the overflow of God's grace and anointing. Since the earliest days of the renewal, the prayer ministry team has tirelessly prayed, night after night, with kindness, gentleness and grace.

These values and practices, I believe, were actually a natural outgrowth of embracing Vineyard values and philosophy of ministry, such as the priesthood of all believers, ministering out of compassion for others, seeking to do what the Father is doing, equipping the saints to minister salvation, healing and deliverance in the power of the Holy Spirit, and promoting intimacy with Jesus through prayer, worship and meditation on the Word.

Unfortunately, both John Arnott and John Wimber kept very fast-paced schedules and the times they did try to contact each other they were like two ships passing in the night. John Arnott regrets not making a greater effort to having better communication with John Wimber. He also wishes that John Wimber had come to Toronto and just hung out for a leisurely period of time, rather than facilitating the teaching and ministry when he came. If they had logged more time together and knew each other's heart more deeply, perhaps a separation could have been averted or, at the very least, there could have been a less painful parting of the ways with a resounding blessing attached.

Another factor that would contribute to the eventual separation was the fact that, for some time, John Wimber had battled with serious health challenges. In April 1993, doctors found a small (3.2 centimeters) undifferentiated carcinomatous tumor located in the left side of John's nasal pharynx. He began X-ray and proton radiation immediately. As a result of the treatments, he lost tons of weight and the ability to produce saliva in his mouth. From then on, he had to use 'spray spit' when he spoke and, as usual, showed us how to laugh in the face of tragedy. He never had the same stamina after that and began to slowly fade into the background as he gave more and more authority to the international board.[182]

Larry Randolph, in an interview with Randy Clark, stated that, during the years he was connected to the Anaheim Vineyard, he grew to deeply appreciate John Wimber's heart. And Wimber would affectionately say to Randolph, "You are my token Pentecostal!" Larry Randolph believes that due to John's sickness (he also suffered a stroke in January 1995) and due to his son, Chris, being diagnosed with a brain tumour in 1994, John Wimber was not himself during this period of time.[183]

During the last week of November 1995, the Vineyard U.S. national board had their annual meeting in Anaheim, California. At that meeting, they discussed their massive and mounting concerns with the leadership of the Toronto Vineyard. John Arnott's book, *The Father's Blessing*, had just been published. In it, a chapter was devoted to explaining the manifestations, particularly the animal sounds. The title of the chapter was, 'The Prophetic: Animal sounds and Insights.' John Arnott, in the Question and Answer time of many pastors' meetings, had been asked over and over again for even some preliminary explanation for the animal sounds and so he felt a pastoral obligation to attempt to address this pressing question. Stephen Strang, publisher of the book, also encouraged John Arnott to address that subject in his book. John Wimber had given an endorsement to Arnott's book, but apparently had not read the whole manuscript. Later he was not pleased to find out that this chapter was included in the book.[184]

---

182 Bill Jackson, pp. 275-276.
183 Larry Randolph, interviewed by Randy Clark, Podcast # 67, posted July 10, 2009, Global Awakening website.
184 John Wimber admitted this in the meeting of December 5, 1995 in Toronto.

Randy Clark describes it this way, "When Wimber disfellowshipped Toronto, he did not reject the move of God or deny the move of God in Toronto. Instead, Wimber dismissed the church because he felt John Arnott had not followed his directive not to give meaning to the prophetic acts that were manifesting in the meetings. In his defence, Arnott had provided Wimber with a copy of the draft of the book, *The Father's Blessing*, including a chapter in which he tried to explain the possible meanings of the phenomena. Wimber failed to read this chapter and, when he saw the chapter in the published book, he thought Arnott had ignored his directives and was unwilling to submit to his authority. This was not actually the case; it was a terrible misunderstanding. The main point to see here is that the disfellowshipping was not a rejection of the visitation of the Spirit on Wimber's part."[185]

What seemed to be the straw that broke the camel's back, was Toronto's *Spread the Fire* magazine of October 1995, which featured an article called 'Ox in the Nursery', by Vineyard pastor, Steve Witt, of New Brunswick,[186] and an article by TAV administrator, Steve Long, called 'What About Animal Noises?'[187]

All along, John Wimber had urged people not to try to explain the exotic manifestations or draw attention to them. Aside from potentially giving the critics more ammunition against us and being on thin ice biblically, he felt that giving any attention to it would be like asking people to be present in the delivery room during the birthing process. In the July/August 1994 issue of *Vineyard Reflections*, in John Wimber's letter to Vineyard leaders, he writes:

> Most people love babies, but they don't necessarily like the details of the birthing process. The birthing of a child is a messy experience at best. Not many people want to hear about that part... In my opinion, it's not necessary to explain everything connected with revival any more than a young mother needs to share in detail the travail of the

---

185 Randy Clark, Global Awakening website, A response to the critic Andrew Strom, http://globala-wakening.com/home/about-global-awakening/a-response-to-critics)
186 Steve Witt is presently pastor of Bethel Cleveland in Ohio
187 Bill Jackson agrees with this point, p. 327.

birthing process. All she has to do is hold that baby up and everyone shares in the joy.[188]

That makes very good sense. However, there is one problem: God doesn't seem to mind having these manifestations that "push the envelope" take place in very public settings. It is very difficult to keep it contained and behind closed doors. In interviewing Randy Clark recently, he recalled what a South African pastor had said a little over a decade ago, after the power of God hit his large Baptist congregation: "We may invite the Holy Spirit to come as if we are saying 'Here kitty kitty' and He may respond by roaring. When the Holy Spirit comes, we may prefer to tell Him to sit in the back and behave."[189]

The differences between TAV and AVC didn't end with methodology and the explaining of manifestations; it also included some issues of theology and practice. The first issue was the very legitimate pastoral concern of not allowing the outpouring of the Spirit to distract or overshadow the biblical mandate to equip the saints, teach the Word, evangelize, minister to the poor and plant churches. Wimber exhorted the Vineyard to not let this renewal simply become a "bless-me" club. We are to "take it to the streets".[190]

In the summer of 1994, the Lord gave John Wimber a powerful vision of a magnificent mountain lake in which the sparkling water spilled over a dam and cascaded into a river down in a large plain where there were many acres of vineyards and men working the fields and digging irrigation ditches. Wimber felt the Lord was saying that this blessing was being poured out onto the church first, but if this blessing only stayed in the church, we may have some wonderful meetings, but they would eventually end. With this fresh outpouring that we are blessed with, we need to co-labour with Christ and go to the highways and by-ways to bless and evangelize others as well as plant churches.[191]

John Arnott and his team also believed in Christians not hoarding

188 John Wimber, Vineyard Reflections, July/August 1994, p. 1.
189 Randy Clark, interview at Catch The Fire Toronto, September 26, 2013.
190 Bill Jackson, pp. 309-311.
191 Ibid., pp. 302-303.

the blessings of the Kingdom but in giving it away to the marketplaces of the world. But for us, it was a matter of timing. We needed permission to take the time to cultivate intimacy with the Lord and to seek His face— not just His hand of power—keeping in mind that lovers are ultimately more productive for the Kingdom than workers.

A second theological issue creating tension was the matter of eschatology. In a letter, Todd Hunter wrote: "There is a difference in understanding of eschatology. The leadership of TAV has tended to tie this current outpouring with an expectation of a final last days revival... "[192]

AVC also had trouble with the issue of ecstatic prophecy (prophesying with physical manifestations such as shaking) being endorsed and encouraged as well as the degree of emphasis given to the prophetic dimension.[193]

They wanted every Vineyard church, including Toronto, to focus on "the main and plain" things of Scripture such as evangelism, daily discipleship, praying for the sick, ministry to the poor, church planting and missions.

In an article in *Christianity Today* magazine, in January 1996, John Wimber stated,

> I believe that there has been an authentic visitation of the Spirit there.
> However, I am unable because of my own scriptural and theological
> convictions to any longer give an answer for, or defend the way this
> particular move is being pastored and/or explained.[194]

On Monday, December 4, 1995, John Wimber, Bob Fulton, Todd Hunter and Gary Best met in Vancouver with Wesley Campbell and his leadership of the New Life Kelowna Vineyard. John Wimber came to express extreme concern with the Toronto Airport and with Wes and his Kelowna Church. Wes and his pastors were to discontinue

---

192 Todd Hunter, letter addressed to Vineyard pastors, December 13, 1995.
193 Ibid.
194 James A. Beverley, Christianity Today, Vineyard Severs Ties with Toronto Blessing Church, January 8, 1996.

their ministering with John Arnott and the Toronto Airport, distance themselves from them, as well as cut back their travelling ministry within this renewal.

On the evening of Tuesday, December 5, 1995, John Wimber and his delegation came to the Toronto Airport Vineyard and met with John Arnott, some of his pastoral staff, including Steve Long, Jeremy Sinnott, Al MacDonald, and Fred Wright, as well as friends Budd Williams and Paul Yuke, spiritual fathers from the city of Toronto, Dwayne Heppner, a lawyer, and me, Jerry Steingard.

On December 8, 1995,[195] the leaders of Harvest Rock Vineyard, Che Ahn, Rick Wright and Lou Engle drove down from Pasadena, California, to Anaheim to meet with the leaders of the Vineyard movement. The Pasadena Vineyard had been hosting protracted renewal meetings five nights a week since March 1995.

In his book, *Into the Fire*, Che Ahn points out that they were not asked to leave the Vineyard but one Vineyard leader said that "perhaps 'a happy parting of the ways' might indeed be the best solution for everyone." They agreed and, from that point on, they were no longer part of the Vineyard. Che shares in his book how the Lord had sovereignly led them into the Vineyard nine months earlier and now He was sovereignly leading them out. Jim Goll, a prophetic friend, had called Che in April of 1995 and had shared a vision pertaining to Che and his church. He heard a cork popping and saw Che holding a rose wine bottle. On the front of the bottle was written "nine months". The bottle had been shaken, the cork had popped, and the wine in the bottle had changed to another substance. The Lord had given Jim Goll the interpretation of the vision but was told not to share it yet with Che. A week after Che and his Pasadena church left the Vineyard, Jim called Che and reminded him of the vision and shared the interpretation.[196]

At the meeting in Toronto on Tuesday December 5, John Wimber began by announcing that the Toronto Airport Vineyard church was

---

195 Che Ahn, Into the Fire, Renew Books, 1998, p. 63, says December 8, 1995 but Che Ahn's press release/letter to Todd Hunter on December 15, 1995 states the meeting between Pasadena leaders and the AVC leaders was on December 7.
196 Che Ahn, Into the Fire, Renew Books, 1998, pp. 62-64.

being "disengaged" from the Vineyard movement. They had not come to discuss or negotiate, but simply to communicate the withdrawal of their endorsement of the leadership of the Toronto Airport Vineyard.

We were shocked and stunned, feeling that on a scale of one to ten, we were probably at a four or five in terms of trouble with Anaheim. As it turns out, we were at a ten. In the midst of all the excitement of hosting the presence of God for almost two years, we had not fully realized the speed and extent of the Vineyard movement evolving into a denomination. What we had interpreted as counsel and advice from our leaders in an association of independent churches, were really directives that must be adhered to or risk being considered insubordinate.

For instance, the AVC board met in September 1994 to discuss many of the controversial issues and concerns related to the renewal and came out with a Board Report. In the introduction it states:

> The guidelines that follow represent the majority consensus of the board… It is, therefore, important to remember that this statement is subject to the autonomy of the local church and its pastor. All of this must be worked through in a way that does not violate one's faith or conscience.[197]

The AVC leaders felt that it was obvious that they were no longer our leaders since they saw us not responding to their requests. We were told that we should have interpreted John Wimber's whispers as shouts. Rather than come to clearly spell out their concerns and request our compliance, they said that a decision had been made at the AVC–US board meeting (with Canadian director, Gary Best, present) a week or so earlier to withdraw their endorsement of the Toronto church and separate from us.

As the meeting progressed, however, it got more cordial. We thanked them for taking the heat from the critics on our behalf, particularly the ones from southern California. The meeting ended

---

197 Board Report, Association of Vineyard Churches, September/October 1994, p. 1.

with John Wimber saying it was remotely possible for the board's decision to be "undone", if we complied with certain conditions. After about three hours, we closed the meeting and Steve Long drove them to their hotel.

We stayed at the church to talk and hammered out a letter of response. Realizing that we could not comply with the restrictions being asked of us without compromising our ability to fully steward this outpouring, we sent them a letter within two hours. In it, John Arnott apologized for the stress and hurt that we had caused them and for not being fully aware of the extent of their concerns. John also agreed that John Wimber and the Vineyard should not have to continue answering for what was happening in Toronto. The letter stated that we would accept their decision to be disengaged from the Vineyard, asked for their blessing, and thanked them for their "years of ministry that provided such a wonderful environment for this current move of God."[198]

We had a follow-up meeting with Canadian Vineyard leader, Gary Best, the next morning. We raised our concern that the communication process had not been as clear as we would have wished. Gary Best acknowledged our complaint, in some measure, was valid. Nevertheless, he reminded John Arnott and the leaders that there had been considerable communication that had been quite clear. Gary asked, "Do we not both recognize that ultimately we are going in different directions?" We affirmed that a parting of ways at some point was probably inevitable.[199] Among other things, Gary shared with us that John Wimber was so weary and exhausted from all the pressures of recent months that he, Bob Fulton and Todd Hunter had to assist him into bed the night before.

John Arnott was leaving for the west coast by midday for renewal meetings. Just after John left, Ted Haggard of Colorado Springs, walked into the Toronto church office. Ted had felt the Lord prompt him a couple of days earlier to go to Toronto because something was stirring

---

198 John Arnott, letter to John Wimber, December 5, 1995.
199 Gary Best, letter to John and Carol Arnott, December 15, 1995.

and that maybe he could be of assistance. When he heard the news of what had happened the night before, he flew to the west coast to catch up with John Arnott, to spend some time with him, and to see if he could be of help.

Both Ted Haggard and Jack Hayford were involved in seeking some kind of reconciliation during the following weeks, but they were unsuccessful. Ted Haggard also attempted to see that some kind of interdenominational mechanism be established to ensure a healthier and less painful outcome when addressing future conflict and differences between a denomination and one of its congregations that is experiencing an outpouring of the Spirit.

Randy Clark, in his book, *Lighting Fires*, tells us that, the night of the separation, when he talked with John Arnott and got the news, he could hardly believe what he was hearing:

> I was upset and hurt by this action. I was also in such pain from a physical condition related to the stress of this event that I was forced to stay in bed for the next three days. I rose only at night to preach, then returned to bed immediately afterward. Friends contacted me from both the Vineyard and from Toronto, and I felt caught in the middle... much as if I were a child caught in the crossfire of a divorce. I was grieved by the entire matter—grieved by the decision of the Vineyard's leadership, grieved at the reasons given for the decision, grieved at the way the entire matter had been handled, grieved over the ramifications of the decision on the renewal as it continued in Toronto and elsewhere, and grieved over the ramifications of the decision upon the Association of Vineyard Churches...[200]
>
> The waters of outpouring, which had at first seemed a glorious and unmistakable blessing, were now churned with the whitecaps of controversy and discontent. Not everyone, it seems, was as pleased as I had been at what God had been doing. While it is not my wish to disparage or call into question anyone else's motives, it was now

---

200 Randy Clark, Lighting Fires, Creation House, 1998, p. 100.

painfully apparent to me that this new move of God would not be embraced by everyone.[201]

On January 3, 1996, John Wimber faxed a gracious letter to John Arnott. Reflecting on the meeting in Toronto weeks earlier and the process they had been through together over the last two years, as well as on feedback from others, he wrote:

> All this has led me to believe I owe you an apology for the mixed messages I have given and for the weak/flawed process we used near the end as we tried to separate in a manner that agreed to disagree agreeably... I now can see how you were surprised by our announcement on December 5, 1995, and that it seemed to you to be without due process. In my mind, John, we had been in 'due process' for sixteen months. Please forgive me for any harm or hurt I have caused you. I have tried to do my best for you and the movement the last two years. I pray God's blessing on you for this new year.

On January 20, 1996, the second anniversary of the renewal, the Toronto church would change its name from the Toronto Airport Vineyard (TAV) to the Toronto Airport Christian Fellowship (TACF).

Although Carol Arnott admits she was personally devastated by the separation, John was resolved to keep going and not lose his equilibrium.[202] They were both determined to stay sweet, thankful and honouring of John Wimber and the Vineyard. John Arnott soon sought to form an International Renewal Network of dozens of high-level international Christian leaders who were involved in the current renewal to help facilitate and give direction to it.

So in January 1996, John, Carol and their Toronto Airport church found themselves with a new name as well as a renewed zeal and determination to keep giving away this precious gift of fresh grace, anointing and empowerment to all hungry and thirsty souls.

---

201 Ibid., p. 101.
202 John Peters, The Story of Toronto, Authentic Media, 2005, p. 47.

After the January 1996 Pastors' Conference in Toronto, with RT Kendall, Randy Clark and others, Randy headed off to Anaheim, California for the Let the River Flow Conference in which he, Gary Best and John Wimber were the speakers. The separation with the Toronto Vineyard was clearly not a denial or rejection of this outpouring of the Spirit, merely a difference over pastoral and administrative concerns.

John Wimber, spiritual father and leader to the seven hundred and fifty Vineyard churches worldwide (currently it is fifteen hundred), suffered a massive brain hemorrhage on November 16, 1997 and was taken to Western Medical Center, Santa Ana, California. He passed away peacefully at 8:00 AM Monday, November 17, 1997, in the presence of his family. He was sixty-three years old. Two months earlier, Wimber had triple bypass surgery and three years earlier, he had suffered a mild stroke but had won a battle with cancer.

This man of God changed the landscape of the church and impacted scores of evangelical Christian leaders in areas such as healing, signs and wonders, worship, church growth, and renewal of the Holy Spirit and the Kingdom of God. He was a great leader and a great father to many. John Wimber may go down in history as one of the most influential American evangelical leaders of the late twentieth century.

Terry Virgo, leader of one of Britain's largest charismatic church networks, New Frontiers, was a close friend of John Wimber. Terry Virgo stated, "I would say that only Billy Graham has had more impact in England, as an American preacher."[203] Theologian, J. I. Packer said of John Wimber, "He raised the level of expectation of divine action in the life of the church." Packer also said that he was "a good gift of God to the church."[204]

The week before John Wimber died, three men came separately to visit and to pray for him: Larry Randolph, John Paul Jackson and Paul Cain. When John Paul Jackson came, John Wimber shared with him that he had two regrets: 1) how he handled the prophetic movement

---

203 Billy Bruce, Charisma Magazine, "Vineyard Founder John Wimber Remembered for Legacy", January 1998, p. 17.
204 J. I. Packer, quoted in "Editorial: Wimber's Wonders", Christianity Today, posted February 9, 1998. http://www.christianitytoday.com/ct/1998/february9/8t2015.html

and 2) how he handled the Toronto church. He added that, if he had the strength to get out of bed, he would want to make them right.[205]

In 2011, Christy Wimber arranged time for John and Carol Arnott to meet with John's widow, Carol Wimber, over lunch. They spent several hours together in a precious time of reconciliation and fellowship.[206]

Unity Service at TACF
Sunday night, September 21, 1997, with Canadian Vineyard directors, Gary and Joy Best and other Canadian Vineyard leaders

Canadian Vineyard leader, Gary Best, contacted Toronto Airport Christian Fellowship in early September of 1997 with hopes of seeing a unity service take place. The night of September 21 began with a powerful time of worship, led by Winnipeg Vineyard pastor, David Ruis, with fifteen hundred people in attendance. Gary Best spoke on the subject of unity and forgiveness. The TACF leadership came up on the platform, along with Gary Best and several Vineyard pastors and area leaders.

Gary affirmed four statements, which he and other Canadian Vineyard leaders had agreed upon:

1. It truly has been the Spirit of God that visited you and has\raised you up and has produced that which others have called the Toronto Blessing, but which is really the Lord's blessing.

2. We have been wonderfully blessed and served by the Lord's visitation and your part in it. We appreciate your service to the body of Christ and to us… You have given a hundred and ten percent of your hearts and your lives to the Lord in serving Him in this.

---

205 Larry Randolph in interview with Randy Clark, released July 10, 2009, Podcast #66, Global Awakening, Link: https://s3.amazonaws.com/GA-Podcast/testimonyPodcast/Episode67_Larry_Randolph_Part_1.mp4 Also, according to John Arnott, John Paul Jackson shared this in an interview with Catch The Fire TV about ten years ago. Also, a conversation with John Paul Jackson and John Arnott in Belgium, November 2013.
206 John Arnott, recorded interview, June 14, 2013.

3. Our prayers are for you, not against you. God has given you a difficult call, but we're praying He'll give you wisdom, protect you and allow you to see His blessing to the second, third and fourth generation. If one of us is weak, we're all weak.

4. "We covenant to speak well of you and assume the best of you." He then assured that, "if we have any offense, we shall come to you."

Gary Best prayed,

"Let this huge place be a storehouse for the harvest... As a Vineyard leader in Canada, we bless this house... and [pray] that God would bring strengths and gifts to them... [and] bring others to give them wisdom and encouragement."

The staff of TACF then responded. Marc Dupont took the microphone first.

"We thank God for the whole Vineyard movement and what the Holy Spirit has birthed through John Wimber. We are all indebted to the freedom poured out to the whole world through the Vineyard. Lord, thank you that your cross is so much greater than our petty peripheral differences." He asked the Lord to "bless all the Vineyard churches across Canada, and let it be multiplied across Canada, in the name of Jesus, from this day on."

John Arnott thanked Gary Best for coming and called it "a precious moment for all of us." He added, "We want to join hands and hearts and let love strengthen the bonds we already have." Hugs and tears erupted on the platform and the entire crowd rose in a spontaneous one-minute ovation of cheers and applause.

It was estimated that one quarter of the audience came from local Vineyard churches while another quarter or so represented the Partners in Harvest group, established by TACF after the separation.

The night ended with an hour of exhilarating music, dance, praise and celebration, led by Rob Critchley.[207]

While the separation from the Vineyard caused a good number of evangelical Christians and churches to pull back from their participation with the Toronto outpouring, for others it opened up some opportunities that might not have otherwise. Some pastors and leaders from various denominations and independent charismatic streams saw that this heavenly visitation was no longer just a Vineyard thing, but something that could be experienced by the whole body of Christ.

The truth that "most associations and denominations are birthed on the wings of revival" would prove true once again. Che Ahn's new apostolic network of churches called Harvest International Ministries (HIM) and Toronto's Partners in Harvest (PIH) family of churches would soon be born.

Like Paul and Barnabas, who had a sharp disagreement and parted company (Acts 15:36-41), our merciful Lord can take the division the enemy intends to create and transform it into multiplication of ministry as we choose to walk in forgiveness and grace.

---

207 Email letter from Richard Riss, September 29, 1997, to the "Awakening List", with a few adjustments based on author watching the video of the event.

CHAPTER 8

The Creation of Partners in Harvest

*"An affiliation for local autonomous churches pursuing renewal
and revival"*
—from the "preliminary draft" for Partners in Harvest, 1996

*"Partners in Harvest is a family of churches, a network of people
who are united in their passion for Jesus in a no-holds-barred
pursuit of Him."*
—partnersinharvest.org

With Toronto's separation from the Vineyard movement in December
of 1995, a number of Vineyard pastors and churches that were closely
connected with Toronto were feeling like they had to choose between
two parents in a divorce. It was a painful and confusing time for many.
The night before the December 5 meeting in Toronto, which I was asked
to attend, the Lord spoke to me and said, "Whatever happens at the
meeting tomorrow night, you are to follow John Arnott."

In the following month or two, several Ontario pastors—Vineyard
and independent—were asking John Arnott if he would form a network
of churches so that they might have a sense of belonging to a father and
a family for mutual encouragement and accountability. At the Pastors'
Conference in January 1996, many of us signed our names to a letter to
John requesting he prayerfully consider this.

Che Ahn, of Harvest Rock Church in Pasadena, California, was at the conference. In John's office, Che shared with John and me that he would not be joining this new network of churches out of Toronto. Cindy Jacobs had recently prophesied to Che Ahn that he was not to make any alliance with any other network because the Lord was going to have him form a new apostolic network of churches. This was indeed what happened. According to their website, Che Ahn's worldwide network of churches and ministries, called Harvest International Ministries (HIM), currently consists of over twenty thousand churches and ministries in over fifty nations and on five continents.[208]

An apostolic leader conveyed to John Arnott that history shows that any move of God that results in seeing new networks of churches birthed tends to see greater fruit and fruit that remains. But John knew that his hands were already full. He therefore approached Fred Wright, who had just come on staff, to work with him in establishing a new association. A two-day retreat was held on March 1 and 2, 1996, at the Delta Inn, located at the corner of Attwell Drive and Dixon Road. Most of the three or four dozen pastors and wives who attended were from southern Ontario, including Fred Wright from TAV. A number also came from quite a distance, such as Jim Curtis of Tulsa, Oklahoma.[209]

This retreat involved a wonderful time worshipping the Lord, soaking in His presence, praying for each other, as well as seeking the Lord for what we were to do in light of the changes in our relationship to the Vineyard that we so loved. We were encouraged by a number of significant and reassuring prophetic words that were given—some pertaining to a new family network.

At one point, Fred Wright was radically shaken and thrown over his chair while delivering a prophetic word that called us to wait on instructions about the structure of this new association. Jim Paul recalls Dennis Wiedrick of Hamilton giving this word:

---

208 HIM website: www.harvestim.org.
209 Jim Curtis' church was the first to submit an application to join the new association, beating Toronto Airport Christian Fellowship and TACF's mother church, Jubilee Christian Fellowship of Stratford

People of God look, look at the name of the hotel in which you have gathered for this meeting. We have been gathered at the Delta. It's a place where a river or even rivers spread out to the sea. We are in God's purposes in the timing of this, to allow the river of the[210] Father's presence to touch the nations—the sea of humanity.

The first name that we seriously considered for this new family of churches was ARC (Association of Renewal Churches). But the Lord directed us to wait for a destiny name.

By April or early May of 1996, a small task group, comprised of John Arnott, Fred Wright, Steve Cummings, Jerry Steingard and Jim Paul, had been prayerfully working on ideas regarding values, goals, strategy, and beliefs for this new association.

By this time, the name "Partners in Harvest" had been chosen. "It was arrived upon through prayer, prophetic word and some special insight from John Arnott as he returned from England, bubbling over with input from a week there with the pastors and leaders of Pioneers with Gerald Coates."[211]

In a more formal letter sent out weeks later to a wider circle of friends, John Arnott and the Toronto church office gave an update of developments of this new affiliation:

"A few weeks ago, a new fellowship of churches came into being that is to be called Partners in Harvest. Partners speaks of the type of relationship those involved want to have and Harvest identifies the goal, of seeing a great harvest of souls come into the Kingdom of God. This new affiliation of churches is strongly linked with the renewal that has been touching thousands of churches throughout the world since 1994. It wants to encourage and concentrate on intensifying loving relationship with the Father and with each other, on co-operating in equipping for ministry and seeing the renewal build toward revival

---

210 Jim Paul, recalling the retreat at the Delta Inn, March 1-2, 1996; the author, Jerry Steingard, was there to witness as well.
211 John Arnott and Fred Wright, letter sent out to pastors who had shown interest in a new affiliation, April 1996.

and the harvest, (including local church planting and world missions) and on working toward being spiritually accountable to each other.

This desire was first born in the hearts and minds of several pastors and leaders who met together as they came to celebrate the Lord's goodness at the second anniversary of the renewal in Toronto in January of this year. Five weeks later, they met again to seek the Lord for the details of what form this new movement would take. At the second meeting, pastors and leaders from many Canadian provinces and several US States came, even though it had not been publicized or announced in any way. The proverbial grapevine was enough to bring in many who have been touched by the renewal and who have hungered after a closer bond of friendship and co-operation.

The question has been asked, 'Has this come as a reaction to what happened last December with the separation of Toronto Airport Christian Fellowship and the Vineyard Movement?' The answer to this question is simple. This movement would not have come into existence, more than likely, if Toronto and its daughter churches were still part of Vineyard, but it has not come as a knee jerk reaction to this separation. It was more a knowing that, since they were out, they now needed to be in something where accountability and closer co-operation can happen.

What has been happening is that now many non-affiliated churches, or churches which have been forced to withdraw from their movements as a result of the effects of the renewal, are now being drawn toward each other in a new affiliation. In practice, it will function along with the International Renewal Network and be led by John and Carol Arnott and a council of key pastors. A two and a half day conference for pastors interested in Partners in Harvest is planned for the Monday through Wednesday, October 7-9, 1996, prior to the Catch The Fire Conference. Pastors interested in receiving detailed information about the goals, values, and beliefs that currently stand may write to: Fred Wright, Toronto Airport Christian Fellowship...[212]

---

212 One page letter, spring of 1996, kept in Jerry Steingard's file.

By this time, John Arnott had appointed Fred Wright to be the contact person and soon afterwards Fred and his wife, Sharon, would become the founding International Coordinators for Partners in Harvest. This new family or network sought to offer resources, support, encouragement and relational accountability.

CHAPTER 9

Academic Supporters and Critics

Every revival throughout church history has created controversy, resulting in a mix of both supporters and critics. In his book, *When the Spirit Comes with Power*, the late Dr. John White insightfully points out:

> From a safe distance of several hundred years or several thousand miles, revival clearly looks invigorating. What could be more glorious than a mighty work of God in our midst, renewing thousands and converting tens of thousands... And if we find ourselves in the midst of revival, rather than being invigorated, we may be filled with skepticism, disgust, anger or even fear... Why is revival sometimes so messy? One reason is that revival is war, and war is never tidy. It is an intensifying of the age-old conflict between Christ and the powers of darkness...[213]
>
> The irony of revivals is that, while they are so longed for in times of barrenness, they are commonly opposed and feared when they arrive... Opposition to revival comes not just from sinners but also from Christian leaders, some of them godly and respected leaders. And in this sense, revival causes division. The hostility is never to the idea of revival, which is ardently prayed for, but to God's answer to our prayers and the unexpected form it may take.

---

213 John White, When the Spirit Comes with Power, IVP, 1988, pp. 34-35.

The more articulate the leaders were, the more colorful their language became. Some leaders changed their views in time, for time makes issues clearer... Earlier in the twentieth century, the fear of Pentecostalism gave rise to verbal firecrackers. One leader called Pentecostals the 'rulers of spiritual Sodom', their tongues 'this satanic gibberish', and their services 'the climax of demon worship'... G. Campbell Morgan referred to Pentecostals as 'the last vomit of Satan.'[214]

Aside from resenting new leadership, John White, a Christian psychiatrist, gives this explanation for much of the angry opposition:

We grow angry when we are scared. We fear what we cannot understand. True revival has commonly been opposed because it came dressed outlandishly, a wild and uncouth invader. Each revival had its own style, its own novelty...[215]

John White also gives this warning:

If we insist that revival must be 'decent and orderly' (as we define those terms) we automatically blind ourselves to most revivals. Like the dwarfs in C. S. Lewis's children's story The Last Battle, we may spit out heavenly food, for to us it looks like, smells like, tastes like dung and straw.[216]

Before we mention several critics of this revival, let me point out a number of friendly and very supportive academic leaders who have been a great source of encouragement to the Arnotts and those involved in stewarding this visitation.

---

214 Ibid., pp. 39-41
215 Ibid., p. 41.
216 Ibid., p. 45.

Academic Supporters

As we were all quite overwhelmed and seeking to process all that we were seeing and experiencing in 1994, church historians such as Guy Chevreau of Oakville, Ontario, and Richard Riss of New Jersey provided much needed support and historical context, especially to the Toronto leadership and to pastors and leaders who started coming to Toronto.

Guy Chevreau, a Canadian Baptist with a Th.D. in historical theology, from Wycliffe College in Toronto, has not only written several books, including Catch The Fire, Share the Fire and Pray the Fire, but has taught in the renewal meetings, the Wednesday pastors' sessions, and various Toronto conferences. In addition, he has gone out to many cities and nations to teach and minister the renewing grace and anointing that God has been pouring out in this season.

Richard Riss and his wife, Kathryn, have written the book *Images of Revival: Another Wave Rolls In,* which also gives historical context to this outpouring in Toronto. Richard taught at the Toronto Catch The Fire conferences in 1994 and 1995 as well as the Catch The Fire Conference in St. Louis in 1995.

Other academic scholars would soon risk their reputations by publically embracing and supporting this outpouring as a true move of God in our day.

Dr. RT Kendall, who was pastor of Westminster Chapel at that time, admits:

> If you had put me on a lie detector when I first heard about it, and asked me if I thought this was of God, I would have said no. Two weeks later, I changed my mind. I saw one of my closest friends, who wasn't all that open to it, fall flat on his face for ten or fifteen minutes when he was prayed for in my vestry...[217]

---

217 "Humbled by the Holy Spirit" article.

In the book *Experience the Blessing*, RT Kendall confesses:

I feared that I might be moving toward the wrong camp, all because of my pride and my anger that this could happen at Holy Trinity and not at Westminster Chapel. I felt, in fact, that God had betrayed me and let me down. But it was obvious that something was happening at HTB... The following Sunday morning, I went into the pulpit and reminded the people of the statement I had previously made about what was happening at HTB. Then I said to them, 'I'm afraid that I was wrong. Today I have to climb down: I believe that what is going on there is of God.' I reminded them of what I had said so many times before: 'What if revival came to All Souls Langham Place or Kensington Temple but not to Westminster—would we affirm it?' I realized now that God was doing something elsewhere and that He had bypassed Westminster Chapel, and I was beginning to be very, very scared that we could miss it entirely.[218]

He went on to give permission to his parishioners to go over to Holy Trinity Brompton and check it out. They then bowed their heads and prayed for HTB and for their vicar, Sandy Millar.

A few days later, R.T. Kendall wrote a letter to Sandy Millar asking him if he and a handful of his people would come over one evening to pray for him and his deacons and their wives. They did and the Lord touched a number of them. The following year, R. T. Kendall and his wife, Louise, met Rodney and Adonica Howard-Browne. They ministered to Louise and she was healed of a serious chronic cough and from a three-year depression.

The following Sunday night, at Westminster Chapel, Kendall invited those who had gone to the Rodney Howard-Brown meetings to give testimony and then pray for those who desired prayer. Again, some were touched and that night marked the beginning of the prayer ministry at Westminister Chapel. A year later, R. T. Kendall invited John Arnott to come speak and minister at this prestigious chapel.

---

218 R. T. Kendall, editor, John Arnott, Experience the Blessing, Renew, 2000, p. 42.

Since that time, Dr. R. T. Kendall has come a number of times to speak at the Toronto meetings and conferences.[219]

The late Clark H. Pinnock, former theology professor at McMaster Divinity College in Hamilton, Ontario, attended the Toronto meetings, particularly in the early years of 1994 and 1995—not just to observe, but also to receive from the Lord. I remember several times seeing the very tall Dr. Pinnock (who was one of my theology professors in the early 1980s at Regent College in Vancouver) in line, patiently waiting to receive prayer from the ministry team.

In an article in *Christian Week*, December 13, 1994, called 'Pinnock's Pointers,' Clark Pinnock described what was happening with the Toronto Airport Vineyard as "reminiscent of what God has done in history." He outlined three broad criteria for discerning this outpouring. First, one needs to be willing to listen to how God is touching people's lives. Spiritual experience is a testimony affair. Secondly, we need to put these testimonies into a biblical and historical revival context. He urged people to take an open stance and ask lots of questions, including:

> Is God throwing a party, blessing his people? Is it a wake-up call? Are we too rationalistic? Does our Christianity have too much head and not enough heart?" Thirdly, Pinnock urged people to "try to evaluate it in the realm of Christian truth.[220]

In his foreword to the book, *Experience the Blessing*, edited by John Arnott, Dr. Pinnock states:

> The essential contribution of the Toronto Blessing lies in its spirituality of playful celebration. The Day of Pentecost (let us not forget) was a festival in the Jewish calendar, and its festive character is evident in the Toronto meetings—in the joy and laughter of God's children playing in the presence of God. When the music sounds, the people burst into joyful praise and abandon themselves to the love of God being poured out. Different images are used of this abandon to the Holy Spirit's

---

219 Ibid., pp. 43-45; By Their Fruits, pp. 71ff; video when Kendall spoke at TACF, January 17, 1996.
220 Doug Koop, "Pinnock's Pointers", Christian Week, December 13, 1994, p. 15.

Presence—catch the fire, enter the river, come to the party, soak in the Spirit—because there is much to be experienced...

It seems as if God has pitched His tent on Attwell Drive so that, when you enter the place, expectancy rises and anticipation builds. The people come wanting more of God... And they cry, 'More, Lord! More of you!' which is a prayer God loves to hear... Nowadays 'play' is reserved for the sports field. The fun has gone out of religion, making it boring and rigid. The Toronto Blessing says this does not have to be. Christianity can be alive and energizing.

What do the people come to celebrate? Not raw experience or contentless mysticism, but the Father's love...[221]

Dr. Jack Taylor, former vice president of the Southern Baptist denomination, and his wife, Barbara, were both drawn to go see what was going on in Toronto in August of 1994. For the first time in their lives, they had to stand in line to go to church. Once in the doors, Jack sensed the presence of the Lord as he had felt it twenty-five years earlier during a move of God in his own church in Texas. They felt the Toronto church was a safe place in which the Holy Spirit could renew hearts and lives.

While on the floor and resting in the Spirit, Jack Taylor testified to the Lord delivering him from roots of religion and Pharisaism. He had been critical of anything he could not understand by reason. He was easily offended. Jack claims,

Looking back on that episode, I now realize that, for the first time in forty-seven years of ministry and fifty-one years of being a Christian, I had given God the right to do anything He wanted, in any way He wanted to do it, without offending me.[222]

Jack Taylor reported receiving both a physical and spiritual healing with a marked increase in joy and anointing in ministry. He has

---

221 Clark Pinnock, editor, John Arnott, Experience the Blessing, foreword by Clark Pinnock, pp. 4-5.
222 Jack Taylor, editor, John Arnott, Experience the Blessing, p. 132.

preached on many occasions at the Toronto church as well as worked with John and Carol Arnott in conferences around the United States.[223] With the death of his wife, Barbara, Jack married Friede in December of 2004. Jack has written thirteen books and is President of Dimension Ministries, based in Melbourne, Florida. From time to time, he has also travelled, taught and ministered as a tag team with spiritual fathers such as R. T. Kendall and Charles Carrin.

Ralph A. Beisner, a New York State Supreme Court judge, reluctantly came to the meetings in Toronto in August 1995. His wife, Inger, had been touched by the Holy Spirit at a friend's church in Vermont months earlier. The combination of her testimony and her urging him to read Guy Chevreau's book, Catch The Fire, tipped the scales enough for him to make the trek north to Canada with some men from their Bible study group to check it out. Each one had an encounter with the Lord.

When Ralph Beisner went to work the next Monday, his law clerk said to him, "What happened to you?" He replied, "Nothing happened to me." She said, "Something happened to you! You look like a Christian." He didn't think he had visibly changed.[224]

Ralph and Inger Beisner returned to Toronto for the 1995 Catch The Fire Conference. At one point, John Arnott invited the couple to come to the front to give a testimony. Afterwards, they were prayed for and Ralph, who normally would receive prayer and remain standing like an oak, hit the ground like a rock. Ralph and Inger's lives changed dramatically. Ralph was re-elected to a second fourteen-year term in office by a larger margin than during the first election. He testified to a deeper and richer relationship with his wife, children and grandchildren than ever. He has also found that he has greater compassion for and understanding of those who come before him in court.[225]

Rolland and Heidi Baker, American missionaries in Mozambique, Africa, play a crucial role in the unfolding story of what God has done

---

223 With the death of his wife, Barbara, Jack married Friede in December of 2004. Jack has written thirteen books and is President of Dimension Ministries, based in Melbourne, Florida. From time to time, he has also travelled and ministered as a tag team with spiritual fathers such as R. T. Kendall and Charles Carrin.
224 Ralph A. Beisner, editor, John Arnott, Experience the blessing, pp. 62-66.
225 Ibid., pp. 68-69.   Ralph and Inger Beisner, for a number of years now, have been Partners in Harvest Regional Coordinators for the USA East Coast.

through the Toronto Blessing. They both have PHDS in theology from King's College, University of London.

However, let me say that revival has been in their DNA all along. Rolland grew up as a child hearing stories of the revival that took place at his grandfather's orphanage in China—visions, angels, and heavenly encounters, which are written about in H. A. Baker's book, *Visions Beyond the Veil*. When Rolland and Heidi were married, in 1980, Rolland's best man was Mel Tari, author, chronicler and evangelist of the Indonesian revival of the 1960s. Once married, they became missionaries in Asia, preached in Indonesia and elsewhere with Mel Tari, and also ministered in Hong Kong for four years, where they were influenced by Jackie Pullinger-To's ministry to the poor. In the fall of 1991, Rolland and Heidi moved to London, England, to study theology by day and minister to the poor and homeless at night.[226]

Many other academic scholars have, in varying degrees, participated in and been supportive of this outpouring. These include names such as: New Testament scholar-pastor, Dr. Don Williams, a California Vineyard pastor, theologian-pastor, Dr. Mark Stibbe of England, Dr. Scott McDermott and sociologist, Dr. Margaret M. Poloma.

A "Friendly" Critic

Some leaders strongly disagreed with this outpouring being described as "The Father's Blessing" or as the "Toronto Blessing." Rather, they proclaimed that it should be called "The Toronto Mixed Blessing." Some would go so far as to brand it as "The Toronto Blasphemy."

James Beverley, professor of theology and ethics at Tyndale Seminary in Toronto (formerly called Ontario Theological Seminary), wrote a book in 1995, *Holy Laughter and the Toronto Blessing*. In this "investigative report," Beverley articulated five schools of interpretation in regards to the Toronto Blessing:

---

226 Heidi Baker, There is Always Enough, Sovereign World, 2003, pp. 29-35.

1. This is the most positive view. The TB is prophetic in significance and is closely tied to God's work of preparing a bride before the return of Christ.

2. The TB is definitely a great renewing move of God, an authentic outpouring of the Spirit of God, but it should not be interpreted as having eschatological significance.

3. This interpretation uses the phrase "mixed blessings" to describe the TB. It considers this renewal as having some wonderful and good aspects, but also as having some negative, dangerous and harmful aspects to it.

4. The TB is seen as a fundamentally negative reality. It is not in keeping with authentic historical revivals and its weaknesses are so significant that Christians are advised to stay clear of it.

5. This is the most negative interpretation. Like the first interpretation, it is rooted in a prophetic and eschatological understanding. It sees this as a demonically-inspired work of the Antichrist to bring about world apostasy and a one-world church under satanic delusion. [227]

Dr. James Beverley would place himself in school number three, believing that this is indeed a work of God that has some wonderful aspects to it, but it is mixed with some dangerous and harmful elements that need to be discerned and corrected.

Extreme Critics

Extreme Critics would find themselves in either school number four or numbers four and five. However, in their concern to protect the body of Christ, some, at times, may actually have been committing character

---

227 James A. Beverley, Holy Laughter and the Toronto Blessing, Zondervan, 1995, pp. 22-24.

defamation and conducting a smear campaign. This has resulted in many believers and churches, out of a spirit of fear, to missing out on all that God is offering in this fresh outpouring.

Hank Hanegraaff, who assumed the roles as President of the Christian Research Institute and as host of *The Bible Answer Man* radio talk show after the death of Walter Martin, in 1989, is one of the most vocal critics of the ministry of Rodney Howard-Browne, the Vineyard movement, the Toronto Blessing and the Brownsville Revival.

According to *Christian Week*, May 13, 1997, and an article titled, "Hanegraaff takes on 'renewal' movement", Hank Hanegraaff sees the phenomena as "spiritual cyanide." "Hypnotic seduction" is considered to be at the core of ministries such as the "Toronto Blessing" and the "Pensacola Outpouring", as well as the phenomena of "holy laughter" and "being slain in the Spirit." His book, Counterfeit Revival, was published in April 1997. He believes "socio-psychological manipulation is not only happening in cults; it's now becoming commonplace within evangelical Christian churches." We are "aping the practices of pagan spirituality" and renewal leaders are like eastern gurus, "They work their devotees into an altered state of consciousness."

Counterfeit Revival was criticized in *Christianity Today* magazine's review of the book. In the review, written by James A. Beverley, he claims that

Counterfeit Revival "exposes some real excesses and imbalances" in the Toronto Blessing, but he also states that Counterfeit Revival is a "misleading, simplistic, and harmful book, marred by faulty logic, outdated and limited researc.".[228]

In 1997, James A. Beverley, a friend of Hanegraaff, also wrote a book called *Revival Wars: A Critique of Counterfeit Revival*, to challenge Hanegraaff's book. In his Introduction, Dr. Beverley states:

...To my dismay, when I received an advance copy, it was obvious that Hanegraaff's work was much inferior to what I would have predicted. I

---

228 James A. Beverley, Books: Counterfeit Critique, Christianity Today, September 1, 1997.

saw immediately that much of his research was outdated and that large portions of his analysis were rooted in faulty logic, selective use of evidence and an inexplicable failure to examine data that was contrary to his own position."[229]

Dr. Don Williams,[230] who became good friends with John and Carol Arnott and who taught several times in Toronto, in 1994 and 1995, wrote a rebuttal to Hanegraaff's attack of Rodney Howard-Browne and the Toronto Blessing. Don Williams' 1995 booklet, *Revival the Real Thing* came out prior to Hanegraaff's book being published. Williams was addressing Hanegraaff's verbal attacks and lectures. This well-researched work walks through both biblical and historical material pertaining to issues of revival, including manifestations, and demonstrates the weaknesses and inaccuracies of Hanegraaff's arguments.[231]

Among the many other strong critics out there, let me mention just a few of the more high profile names:

Dr. John MacArthur is a prolific writer (including the book *Charismatic Chaos*), host of *Grace to You* radio program and an evangelical pastor of Grace Community Church of Sun Valley, California. Being a cessationist (one who believes the gifts of the Spirit described in the New Testament came to an end after the death of the apostles and the completion of the canon of Scripture), he would have a problem right at the outset in believing in the authenticity and divine source of contemporary healings, miracles and the gift of prophecy. John MacArthur recently republished some of his cessationist works under the title *Strange Fire*, sparking much controversy in evangelic and charismatic circles. John MacArthur, however, is a very gifted Bible teacher and communicator and has been a great blessing to the body of Christ worldwide.

---

229 James A. Beverley, Revival Wars: A Critique of Counterfeit Revival, Evangelical Research Ministries, 1997, pp. 7-8.
230 Don Williams is Pastor Emeritus (2002) and founder of Coast Vineyard in La Jolla, California and holds a Ph.D. from Columbia University. He was formerly a lecturer in religion at Claremont McKenna College, an Adjunct Professor of New Testament at Fuller Theological Seminary and, as of 1995, the author of eleven books. In recent years, he has helped David Ruis minister to the entertainment industry in Hollywood, in a Vineyard church plant called Basileia. This unique church plant has also sought to befriend and minister to the poor and the homeless.
231 Don Williams, Revival the Real Thing, 1995.

Pastor Alan Morrison of the UK, refers to the Toronto Blessing as "the Toronto Delusion", "a plague on the land", "a different gospel" and a "heresy" that finds its roots back in the early church under the name of Montanism.[232]

Andrew Strom of New Zealand, a tongue-speaking Pentecostal, claims that the drunkenness and laughter that is invading the church is from false spirits, not the Holy Spirit. He believes it is eastern mysticism and paganism, not unlike the Kondolina charismatics of India.[233]

In response to all this, I like to point out that whenever you find a counterfeit, you know the real exists. Satan is not a creator, only a distorter, a mimicker, a counterfeiter. In a move of God, do we kiss our brains goodbye? Of course not; but neither are we to worship at the altar of the intellect. In times of heightened spiritual activity, we need the spiritual gift of discernment (which is not the gift of suspicion nor is it limited to man's natural understanding) and our Bibles even more.

While the Holy Spirit is at work, we also have the flesh and the devil in the equation. Regarding the demonic, we need to ask questions like, "Is it coming or going?" And while asking and wrestling with the tough questions in a season of visitation, while testing everything, we are to be careful not to despise prophecy nor to quench the Spirit's fire and we must be sure to hold on to what is good. (1 Thessalonians 5:19-22)

Relevant questions should also be asked of critics. Questions such as:

Have you spent time directly and personally at these meetings or are you going on hearsay?[234]

If you have personally been there, was it more than one or two meetings?

232 Alan Morrison, The Plague on the Land, 1995, YouTube, http://www.youtube.com/watch?v=83fg4eBLUfM
233 Andrew Strom, Shocking Documentary, 3 parts, YouTube http://www.youtube.com/watch?v=2X1HC-3s3uI
234 James A. Beverley, Revival Wars, p. 8. Hanegraaff attended meetings in Toronto one weekend in January 1996

Did you come for the whole meeting: for the worship, the testimonies, the teaching of the Word? Or did you come at the end to narrowly focus on manifestations after people were prayed for?

How open and hungry were you for more of God and His love and grace in your personal life?

And have you interviewed people who have been there to see the results, the fruit in their lives, as Jonathan Edwards advises us to do?

In Acts 11:22-25, we see that Barnabas was sent down to Antioch to check out the controversial events reported. It is said that when Barnabas, a man full of the Holy Spirit and faith, arrived, "he saw the evidence of the grace of God and rejoiced."

May we all seek to walk continually in a spirit of teachability and repentance, praying Jack Taylor's prayer, "Lord, change my mind on every issue in which You and I do not see eye to eye."

CHAPTER 10

The Manifestations of God's Presence

"We always thought the Holy Spirit was a gentleman. He wouldn't make you do anything that you didn't want to do—wrong. He's God, the Holy Spirit. When the weighty presence of the Holy Spirit comes upon you, the miracle is that you live through it!"[235]
—John Arnott

We have seen many unusual and dramatic manifestations, particularly in the first few years of the renewal. When the Holy Spirit came in power some people lost all bodily strength, fell down and rested peacefully on the floor. Others started to weep as God convicted them of sin or ministered healing into their heart. Many broke out in laughter, many started to tremble and shake, and many found themselves burning up, as God physically healed them or empowered them. Some became totally intoxicated in the euphoric presence of God and couldn't stand or walk. These and a score of other physical reactions or manifestations happened as a greater degree of God's power and presence came upon us.

Critics may simply write it all off as either emotional hysteria or demonic manifestations, believing that God would never be responsible for any of this strange stuff that makes them feel uncomfortable. It's worth noting in response to this, that the Arnotts, their leadership team and many of the Ontario Vineyard pastors, myself included, were well

---

235 John Arnott, recorded interview, June 14, 2013.

informed and experienced with discerning demonic manifestations. We had received half a dozen years of balanced, biblical and practical training on deliverance ministry and spiritual warfare from the Vineyard movement.

Just prior to the outpouring, we spent two years receiving intensive training and experience in deliverance ministry from the anointed deliverance minister, Graham Powell, as well as through Ellel Ministries of England. Aside from the training and experience in deliverance ministry we received prior to the renewal breaking out, many of those in the leadership also have a background in the evangelical community and Bible College, in which they have received a solid grounding in the Scriptures. So the claim that the leaders in Toronto were simply ignorant and naïve about the demonic and undiscerning about the manifestations, I believe, lacks substantiation.

We soon recognized that the demonic gets agitated when the glory of God is present, as when Jesus came into the synagogue (Luke 4:31-35). John Arnott would wisely encourage us to ask the question, "Are they coming or going?" At times, God was sovereignly doing deliverance ministry with people. Other times, the demonic was making a fuss and seeking attention; we would discern this and pray accordingly. Often our response was to "pray peace" on the person manifesting demonically; thereby not allowing the demonic to set the terms and agenda. We would then encourage that visitor to seek pastoral counseling and deliverance ministry when they got home to their church.

There are many books and materials already available that give biblical and example from church history for why and how our bodies may react to the raw power of God in revival.[236] So I won't go into any lengthy discussion in this book.

However, let me provide a chart from Bob Sorge's book, *Glory: When Heaven Invades Earth*[237] that I believe gives a helpful visual. This diagram shows that once the presence of God intensifies and we enter into the manifest presence or glory of God, we have actually stepped

---

236 I wrote a short booklet on this called Preparing for Revival Fire in 1994, which can be accessed on the Internet or found within my book, The Overcomer's Handbook
237 Bob Sorge, Glory: When Heaven Invades Earth, Oasis House, 2000, p. 57, www.oasishouse.net

Degrees of God's Presence (a continuum)

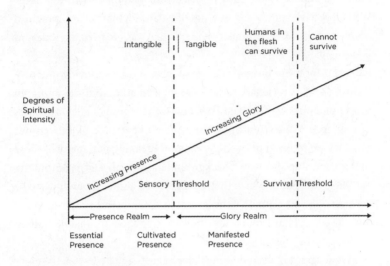

God's essential presence refers to His omnipresence. He is everywhere. Psalm 139 speaks to this fact. But believers, whether privately or corporately, have experienced times of God's cultivated presence; that is, He feels nearer and dearer. This is often during times of worship, prayer and meditation on the Word.

Jesus promised that where two or three gather together in His name, He would be in their midst (Matthew 18:20). That statement would be rather redundant if it did not mean that He would be present in a fuller, more intense way. We also see in Scripture times when God's manifest presence or glory would come and a person or group would be touched or impacted in at least one of their five senses. In Exodus 33, Moses had an audible conversation with God. We find that Moses had the audacity to ask God to show him more of His glory. The Lord warns him that no man can see God face-to-face and live but provides a creative solution to Moses' request to see and experience more of God and His goodness.

In Acts 2, on the day of Pentecost, when the Spirit was poured out, the people felt the wind, they saw tongues of fire on their heads, and heard the praises of God in foreign languages. So why would we be surprised when the raw power of God's glory comes and our physical frames are affected in some way? The miracle is that we don't turn to jelly. It is no wonder we are going to need our glorified, resurrected bodies in eternity because we will be in the midst of the full-on presence, power and glory of Almighty God.

The physical manifestations of laughing, falling, jerking, rolling, shaking, getting intoxicated in the new wine of the Spirit, are understandably the focus of the media and the critics but are regarded by those facilitating this outpouring as simply outward physical signs that our powerful heavenly Father is coming near to do a deep inner work; to heal and restore, love up on and play with His children. The prayer ministry teams do not pray things like, "Lord make them laugh, or shake, or fall, or roar." They pray simple, biblical prayers as led by the Spirit, such as, "Father fill them, bless them, breathe fresh life into them, let the river flow, let Your fire fall, let Your power come, and place Your loving arms around them."

John Arnott has encouraged us not to focus on the manifestations but to interview people afterward to find out what God was doing on the inside. It is the gift inside, what is going on in the heart that matters. John likens the manifestations to "packaging on a gift," and insists that they are not the ultimate goal. The Toronto Airport Vineyard leadership considered itself to be immensely privileged and blessed by this sovereign visitation of God and has remained committed to "giving it away" to all who are desperate and thirsty.

John Arnott says,

I've purposed to never be ashamed of what the Holy Spirit does. We desire a profound transformation and deep work of grace that happens in the heart... God is doing something drastic because what we were doing wasn't winning the world.[238]

---

238 Quoted in Christian Week newspaper on October 31, 1995, Doug Koop, article, pp. 1, 4.

John likes to retell the story of Mary and Martha and encourages us to never feel guilty for taking the time to sit at the feet of Jesus; to soak in His presence and enjoy Him.

"You'll end up accomplishing ten times more for the Kingdom than if you just got busy serving. Lovers are more fruitful than workers". He insists, "this is not the world's largest bless-me-club." Time spent soaking in His presence "will propel you to mission."[239]

In a recent interview with John Arnott, when asked about the manifestations, his response was, "Forget the manifestations. We don't care; we want to know what has happened in your heart. Roaring is not so bad. It was the barking that got even greater criticism, and yet it was so rare. I have only seen about three to five people bark out of three million over the twenty years."[240]

Roaring

Aside from all the responses such as laughter, crying, shouting, shaking, falling, being drunk in the Spirit, in the spring of 1994, "roaring" spontaneously broke out. The first person to act out as a lion roaring, that we are aware of, was Gideon Chui, a Cantonese Chinese pastor from Vancouver, British Columbia. Gideon was an educated, intelligent man of God who graduated with a master's degree from Regent College in 1983.[241]

Pastor Gideon Chui came to the renewal meetings fasting. While there, the Lord told him to stop fasting and to enjoy the banquet the Lord had prepared. Gideon attended a small gathering of Vancouver pastors at the home of Marc Dupont during the day. Marc prayed for Gideon for the Lord to fill and bless him. The Lord came upon Gideon powerfully and he began to roar. At first, Marc wondered if it was a

---

239 Quoted in Christian Week newspaper on October 31, 1995, Doug Koop, article, pp. 1, 4.
240 John Arnott, recorded interview, June 14, 2013.
241 Years later, Gideon would go on to complete a doctorate at Fuller Seminary.

demonic manifestation, but then felt the Lord convey that is was not. It appeared to have a prophetic, intercessory, spiritual warfare aspect to it.[242]

This lion-roaring episode first happened while John Arnott was in St. Louis with Randy Clark. When John came home, a few days later, he interviewed Gideon Chui on the platform and he roared again. John whispered to the Lord, "Please, Lord. It has been so wonderful up to now. Don't let it get weird."[243]

After roaring like a lion on the stage, Gideon testified that he thought the roaring represented God's heart over the heritage and domination of the dragon over the Chinese people. He felt that Jesus, the Lion of the tribe of Judah, was going to free the Chinese people from centuries of bondage. When he shared his experience, the audience broke out into spontaneous cheering and worship. People sensed this was a prophetic statement to Christians about God's intense desire for China.[244]

Years later, at the Partners in Harvest Conference in Toronto, on September 23, 2013, Gideon Chui came and shared with the Arnotts and other pastors. He wanted to thank the Toronto leadership for not shutting him down when he experienced the prophetic act of roaring. Gideon gave an update of how God has been using him. Gideon Chui and David Damien, both leaders from Vancouver, met with five leaders of house church movements in China at a conference they organized in Hong Kong in 2012. These leaders represent over fifty million believers in China. They no longer want to be considered generals but fathers in a unified movement and desire to incorporate the Father's love and healing of the heart.[245]

The roaring was not one isolated case, however. On occasion we would see others manifest in this dramatic way. The British bishop, David Pytches, found himself roaring while he was in Toronto for a few days in early June of 1994.[246] David Pytches' worship leader, Matt

242 Telephone interview with Marc Dupont, September 12, 2013.
243 John Arnott, The Father's Blessing, Creation House, 1995, pp. 168-169.
244 Spread the Fire magazine, October 1995, pp. 17, 30.
245 John and Carol Arnott, citing Gideon Chui speaking at PIH conference at Catch The Fire Toronto, September 23, 2013.
246 By Their Fruits, The Lasting Impact of Toronto in the UK, Chapter written by David Campbell, p. 31; also interview with Steve Long, June 3, 2013.

Redman, later composed the song *It's Rising Up*, which includes the words "*And we have heard the lion's roar that speaks of heaven's love and power.*"[247]

The roaring manifestation was not limited to Toronto. At the Anaheim, California Vineyard Let the Fire Fall conference, in July of 1994, the power of God's fire indeed fell, with wild manifestations, including roaring breaking out, leaving those not affected, "bug-eyed" and extremely uncomfortable. John Arnott, one of the conference speakers, recalls:

> It was the party of all parties! At one point, John Wimber was laughing while he bounced down the stairs. More than a few were roaring, including John Wimber's daughter-in-law. The wife of the late David Watson, Anne Watson, was lying on the platform. A microphone had fallen over next to her and, while she was rejoicing in all that God was doing, she also blurted out with, "This is more like a barnyard, than a Vineyard!"[248]

The week of August 8, 1994, the Canadian Vineyard pastors met together.[249] We were honoured to have John Wimber join us for a couple of those days. In one of the prayer times, John Wimber prayed for a Calgary Vineyard pastor, who began to roar like a warrior or a lion. It was a fearsome but holy experience. After this and other dramatic physical and emotional reactions while praying for each other behind closed doors, Bob Fulton commented that the Holy Spirit could be, at times, like a wild man.

In his 1995 book, *The Elijah Years*, Marc Dupont wrote,

> At the close of each year, I typically spend the last few weeks seeking the Lord's overriding theme for my messages in the coming year. In December of 1993, without receiving full insight, the Lord drew my

---

247 Matt Redman and Martin Smith, song: It's Rising Up, Thankyou Music, Copyright, 1995; also interview with Steve Long, June 3, 2013.
248 John Arnott, recorded interview, June 14, 2013.
249 The meeting was held north of Kenora, Ontario at Minaki Lodge.

focus to Amos 3:8, which says, *'the lion has roared—who will not fear? The Sovereign LORD has spoken—who can but prophesy?'*...

In numerous meetings since mid-1994, some people have been literally roaring as lions as the Spirit of God comes on them. Such unusual behavior is particularly difficult for the natural and/or the religious mind to put into perspective, since the manifestation is somewhat similar to that seen in demonized people. The difference, however, is that these people exhibit no demonic anger or agony. Instead, a boldness and jealousy for God is in evidence. I believe this boldness is a prophetic manifestation of the fierceness in which the Lord is pursuing the lost and hurting.

Like everything else God does, people's flesh often tries to imitate it, and Satan tries to counterfeit it. This is where spiritual discernment is specifically needed. It seems the roaring mainly comes on those who have multi-church ministries, church leaders, evangelists, or intercessors. No doubt this manifestation causes a wide array of reaction and criticism, but, as I see it, these are the Father's children imitating by the Holy Spirit what the Lord is doing in the heavenlies.[250]

---

250 Marc A. Dupont, The Elijah Years, Mantle of Praise Ministries, 1995, pp. 91-99.

CHAPTER 11

Fruit of the Toronto Blessing

"Every good tree bears good fruit, but a bad tree bears bad fruit. A good tree cannot bear bad fruit, and a bad tree cannot bear good fruit...Thus, by their fruit you will recognize them." —Matthew 7:17-20

"God cannot do a great work through you without doing a great work in you first" —Evan Roberts, Welsh Revival [251]

"I was busy being a fruit inspector. But I should tell you that I found the fruit to be very good."—David Mainse, Canadian broadcaster, March 1995 [252]

Jonathan Edwards wrote a treatise in 1741 called *The Distinguishing Marks of a Work of the Spirit of God*. Edwards encouraged his readers to discern the Great Awakening by looking past the manifestations to see the ultimate spiritual fruit in people's lives. He affirmed that five "sure, distinguishing, scriptural evidences" demonstrated the authenticity of

---

251 Brynmor Pierce Jones, An Instrument of Revival: the Complete Life of Evan Roberts, 1878 – 1951. Bridge Pub., South Plainfield, NJ, 1995, p. 65. Cited in Guy Chevreau, Share the Fire, self-published, 1996, p. 14.
252 David Mainse speaking at the Toronto Airport Vineyard in March 1995, explaining his delay in embracing the renewal; Charisma Magazine, June 1995, "Mainse Endorses 'Toronto Blessing'", by Daina Doucet.

God's hand in a revival:

    It raises the esteem of Jesus in the community

    It works against the kingdom of Satan

    It stimulates a greater regard for the Holy Scriptures

    It is marked by a spirit of truth

    And it manifests a renewed love of God and of man.[253]

So let us look at some of the fruit that we have seen so far in this move of God.

Fruit of Conversions

Many Christian leaders would argue that the Toronto Blessing couldn't be justifiably called a true revival because we have not seen mass repentance and salvations of the lost in the meetings in Toronto.

We believe, however, that it is vital to realize that when God begins to move in revival power, it usually begins by resuscitating Christians who are practically dead, especially church leaders. DM Panton defines revival as, "The inrush of the Spirit into a body that threatens to become a corpse!"[254]

We have seen wonderful conversions in the Toronto meetings. In just the first two and half years of this outpouring, at least eight thousand prodigals came forward to re-dedicate their lives to Jesus and over six thousand people made first time commitments to the Lord.[255]

Let's compare this with the Cane Ridge Kentucky revival camp meetings in August of 1801. Of the estimated ten thousand people in the meetings, one hundred and forty-four salvations were recorded, which is a fairly small harvest of souls. However, over the next couple of years, Baptist churches in the area baptized hundreds and their memberships more than tripled. With the awakening of God's leaders and God's people to passion for Christ and compassion for the lost,

---

253 Jonathan Edwards, The Distinguishing Marks of a Work of the Spirit of God, Banner of Truth Trust, 1st pub. 1741, reprinted 1984 pp. 109-115.
254 Arthur Wallis, In the Day of Thy Power, Cityhill Pub., Columbia, MO, 1956, p. 46.
255 Guy Chevreau, Share the Fire, p. 8.

we soon begin to see exponential growth in the number of sinners repenting and coming to Christ.[256]

During the three short years of continual meetings in the Azusa Street revival, approximately thirteen thousand Christian leaders attended from around the world.[257] God did a deep work of overhauling their hearts and lives and ministries. The Lord dealt with issues of pride, control, fear, competition and apathy, transforming men and women by the grace of God.

Frank Bartleman, the Christian journalist who chronicled the Pentecostal revival, tells of the founding leader of a holiness denomination, Phineas F. Bresee, who lived in Los Angeles. Eight months into the revival, Bresee predicted that the meetings would have as much impact as tossing a pebble into the ocean.[258] He could not have been more wrong.

The fruit of revived lives and ministries launched through the Azusa Street revival was seen by several million conversions in the next few years around the world. By the end of the twentieth century, it is estimated that there were sixty-five million Pentecostals worldwide, with projections of almost one hundred million by the year 2025.[259]

With three waves or surges of the Holy Spirit in the twentieth century, David Barrett has documented well over half a billion Pentecostal, Charismatic and Neo-Charismatic (third wave) Christians on the planet (523 million to be precise) by AD 2000. This does not include the 175 million who are no longer alive on the earth.[260]

We are thankful for every salvation, but we must not limit God's reviving work to conversions in the revival meetings. We need to see the bigger picture of what God is doing. He is refreshing, healing bodies and hearts, restoring Christians to their first love, and raising up an army of radically Spirit-filled and passionate lovers into the marketplace

---

256 Ibid., pp. 26-27.
257 Ibid., p. 178.
258 The Nazarene Messenger, December 13, 1906, p. 6; cited in Azusa Street, Frank Bartleman, Logos International, 1980, pp. 182-183.
259 David Barrett, The Worldwide Holy Spirit Renewal, Chapter 15, p. 382, in the book The Century of the Holy Spirit: 100 Years of Pentecostal and Charismatic Renewal, Vinson Synan, editor, Thomas Nelson Pub., 2001.
260 Ibid., p. 383.

to take the good news of the Kingdom and the presence of the King to a lost and dying world.

Rather than being focused on an addition model of evangelism (how many salvations in the meeting by the evangelist), we need to step into a multiplication model of evangelism, which seeks a mobilized army of on fire saints that can ultimately lead to community transformation. The river of life that flows from the thronge of God, as described in Ezekiel 47, brings life to everything it touches and its ultimate destination is the Dead Sea where it brings transformation to cities and nations.

A Sociological Assessment of the Fruit

Dr. Margaret M. Poloma,[261] professor emeritus of sociology at the University of Akron in Ohio, first visited the Toronto Airport Vineyard in November of 1994.[262]

She admits:

> When one of my friends first told me about her visit to the Toronto Airport Vineyard in the summer of 1994, I was rather skeptical and indifferent. I had seen too many charismatic comets dash across the sky leaving little change in the larger world. It took a direct call of God to get me to check out the renewal a few months later.[263]

In early 1995, Margaret Poloma approached John Arnott and asked about doing a survey of people who have attended meetings in Toronto to assess the effects of "fruit" of the Toronto outpouring. She developed a questionnaire, which was distributed through the August 1995 issue of *Spread the Fire*, the October 1995 "Catch The Fire Again Conference"

---

261 Since 1980, much of Margaret Poloma's work has been on the sociology of religion. She has written, The Charismatic Movement: Is there a New Pentecost? She has also co-authored a book with the pollster George Gallup, entitled Varieties of Prayer. As well, Poloma has written The Assemblies of God at the Crossroads: Charisma and Institutionalization in 1989 and Main Street Mystics: The Toronto Blessing & Reviving Pentecostalism in 2003. Margaret Poloma has been associated with St. Luke's Episcopal Church in Akron, Ohio.
262 Margaret M. Poloma, Main Street Mystics, AltaMira Press, 2003, p. 20.
263 Margaret Poloma, Fruits of the Father's Blessing: A Sociological Report (of the 1995 and 1997 surveys), 2002, on-line, p. 2. http://www3.uakron.edu/sociology/FRUITS.pdf

and the November 1995 "Healing School".[264]

Nine hundred and eighteen people completed the survey and about twenty-five percent of the respondents included supplemental information through letters, diary entries, email messages and tape cassettes.[265]

In May of 1997, a follow-up questionnaire was sent to six hundred and ninety (75%) of the original respondents who had provided a return address and a willingness to cooperate with further research. Of those sent out, three hundred and sixty-four follow-up questionnaires (53%) were returned.[266]

Poloma writes:

> Shortly after my first 'in-process' report on the Toronto Blessing was released through the Toronto Airport Christian Fellowship, Pastor John Arnott referred to me as a fruit inspector. That is probably a good description for a sociologist who has been researching the move of the Holy Spirit for nearly twenty years.
>
> The limited scope of sociology... should be apparent. Although sociology can provide an objective analysis of certain facets of the revival, it clearly lacks the sensitivity to deal with the deeper mysteries of the Holy Spirit. What sociology can do is to describe the effects or 'fruit' of a social phenomenon, including what has been happening to people through the renewal. It can provide a tool to determine whether individuals perceive their lives as better as a result of the renewal, whether their relationships with family and friends have changed, and whether their experiences have empowered them to reach out to others in the larger community.

As Jesus (Matthew 7:16-18) wisely instructs us: *'By their fruit you*

---

264 Margaret M. Poloma, By Their Fruits, A Sociological Assessment of the 'Toronto Blessing', un-published, 1995.

265 Margaret M. Poloma, Fruits of the Father's Blessing: A Sociological Report, revised 2002, p. 8.

266 The people who responded to the survey were from twenty different countries, although most were from the U. S. (54%) Canada (26%) and England (11%). The average person was a North American charismatic who belonged to a non-denominational church that tended to be well educated, mature and in some form of church leadership. Fifty percent claimed that they came to Toronto "experiencing spiritual dryness and great discouragement."

will recognize them... A good tree cannot bear bad fruit, and a bad tree cannot bear good fruit.' Sociology, as briefly described above, does offer a method to study the tree and its fruit, leaving the reader to make the judgment about whether the 'fruit' that is produced by the Toronto Blessing is in fact 'good' or 'bad.' It offers a way to break the deadlock between defenders and critics by presenting evidence about the impact the renewal is having in the lives of people who have tasted of its fruit and judged it to be good."[267]

In 2002, Margaret Poloma revised the 1997 text, prologue and epilogue but no new statistics or tables were added. A new title was also given, *Fruits of the Father's Blessing: A Sociological Report.* In her highly detailed report she explains that the study lends considerable empirical support to the claim that the revival has changed many lives. She also highlights that one of the main things God had been saying in the prior eight and a half years was that the Father loves us.[268] We will look at that more in the next chapter.

Margaret Poloma's research examines the following:

• Manifestations (including shaking, jerking, weeping, speaking in tongues, laughter, reports of animal noises, drunkenness, "birthing", and more)

• Spiritual healing (including forgiveness, grace, an awareness of sin, holiness, intimacy with God, prizing Jesus, and more)

• Inner healing (including emotional wholeness, changes to marriages and mental health issues, and more)

• Empowerment and service (including people's response to what they have received, such as acts of service, almsgiving, charitable giving, missions and outreaches, offering brotherly assistance to others, and more)

---

267 Ibid., p. 5.
268 Margaret Poloma, Fruits of the Father's Blessing, Prologue to the 2002 version, on-line, http://www3.uakron.edu/sociology/FRUITS.pdf

I highly recommend you read the full version on-line, as it remains one of the only pieces of thorough research conducted regarding the effects of this revival. She provides us with the following insights:

> In the broadest sense, the primary fruit of the Father's blessing can be described as being that of healing and of empowerment... God is healing men and women at TACF—making them whole in mind, body, spirit, strengthening and repairing significant human relationships, and then sending them forth, empowered by the Holy Spirit to share with others what they have been freely given.[269]
>
> What has become even more clear to me as I revised the old manuscript and pondered the survey data is that the Toronto Airport Christian Fellowship has a ministry and a message that has changed lives and ministries. The simple message of the Father's love is revolutionary once it takes root in the human heart. Focusing on the Father's love, revealed through His only begotten Son through the power of the Holy Spirit, is the only way we can be empowered to live out the Great Commandment. Without the Great Commandment of love, there can be no effective carrying out of the Great Commission of evangelism. Both the survey data on individuals and observations of institutional fruit that has come about through empowered individuals suggest that both the Great Commandment and the Great Commission are being better lived out by those enriched by the Father's Blessing.[270]

We have learned much from Dr. Poloma's research and we owe her a debt of gratitude.

Dr. Grant Mullen, a physician with a mental health clinic in Grimsby, Ontario, since 1985 and an occasional speaker at TACF, testifies to the fruit he has seen in the renewal. He likens the process of sanctification, of ridding yourself of your old nature, to being in an ox-cart with all our problems and old nature heaped inside. We plod along and, as time passes, a few chains fall off the cart. But in

---

269 Ibid., p. 19.
270 Ibid., pp. 40-41.

this renewal, it's like the Lord has pulled up alongside our ox-cart in a rocket and called over to us in the cart saying,

> Time is too short. We have a big harvest to bring in before I come back. You can't stay in your chains and be part of my harvest. Why don't we just get rid of them right now? I'll break them all and set you completely free. Get in the rocket and we'll see the world changed… Renewal appears to be accelerated inner healing.

Dr. Mullen develops this analogy a bit further by saying:

> But then, how do many of us respond when Jesus calls to us from the rocket and says, 'Get in.' 'Well,' we hesitate, 'I've never seen God in a rocket before. I don't think he even owns one. I know what God is like, and he doesn't do that. Ox-carts have been the tradition in our fellowship and it's worked fine for my ancestors. It'll work just fine for me. I don't think we should change anything. And you rocket guys, you're nuts. I don't even see in the Scriptures the word 'rocket'. Some of the ox-cart crowd add, 'We're going fast enough. We couldn't handle anything faster.'
>
> Others hear Jesus' offer and answer, 'Alright. How do I get in the rocket?' Their lives are transformed, their chains fall off, they're empowered for service and they have fruits and gifts. But you know what happens in rockets. They're loud. They shake… The physical manifestations are merely the result of the refiner's fire coming with such intensity that it makes flesh react. But the manifestations aren't the goal. They're just a little yellow indicator light saying 'God at work; God at work; God at work.' Everyone has a different response. The point of the renewal is not what people look like during ministry time. The point of renewal is that people think differently afterward. This is why the renewal appealed to me as a mental health physician. People are letting go of bitterness, they're letting go of their old nature, and they are becoming changed so quickly…[271]

---

271 Grant Mullen, Breaking The Chains, Spread the Fire, August 1995, pp. 4-6.

What attracted me to the renewal was the inner psychological transformation that I was seeing in people who had experienced the Toronto Blessing. People who I knew well were losing their bitterness, anger and fear. These 'inner healings' were taking place at a speed that I had never thought possible, often instantaneously. I knew that a lifetime of counseling and medications could never have achieved the same results.[272]

Finally, I'll end with just one story that demonstrates the kind of fruit the revival has grown. This is Terry and Melissa Bone's story:

In 1994, I had been a senior pastor for two years at a church that was in extremely poor shape. I had inherited a small congregation with a new building, and a very large debt at high interest rates. The severe financial troubles exacerbated the other struggles, which included a divided leadership team and other significant dysfunctions.

My personal life and marriage were suffering and, after a few months of traditional counselling, I finally agreed to attend the meetings at the Toronto Airport Vineyard. After only one visit, I returned to a mid-week meeting at our church and, when I tried to lead out in prayer, the Holy Spirit began to manifest His power and presence in almost unimaginable ways. The following two weeks saw a similar pattern—I would visit the pastors' meetings at the Airport church and, immediately following, we would have literal waves of the power of God sweep through our services.

Things had been so bad previously that virtually all of our leadership team was excited at the 'new thing' happening and we decided to begin regular 'renewal meetings'. Within a year, the church attendance had doubled and we were seeing miraculous demonstrations of healing and deliverance. The marvelous thing in our eyes is that this 'new thing' did not dissipate. Though the intensity of manifestations reduced, the strength of anointing continued and we developed workshops

---

272 Grant Mullen, Changing the Way We think through Inner Healing, Spread the Fire, August 1995, p. 5.

and teachings that helped process people through the inner work of the Spirit to prepare them for anointed ministry. Our ministry slogan became 'Loving-Mending-Equipping-Sending'. The result is that today, twenty years later, the church is still moving in the power of the Spirit, many ministries have been birthed, missionaries raised up and sent out, books written by members, and attendance runs regularly between seven hundred and nine hundred.

Now my wife and I are itinerant ministers and the Lord has led us to repeat what we did at our home church in Bangladesh. For the past five years, I have been coaching four hundred pastors in that country, and have conducted many Holy Spirit conferences. The result has been a dramatic increase in the church-planting rate with signs and wonders following. The group I work with has planted approximately 500 churches this year, which is unprecedented in the history of this Muslim dominated nation. The fruit not only remains, but also is increasing both here and overseas![273]

---

273 Terry and Melissa Bone, The Power of Blessing, self-published 2004. Terry R. Bone, The Blessing Handbook, self-published, 2007. Terry and Melissa Bone, The Family Blessing Guidebook, 2012, www.powerofblessing.com

CHAPTER 12

The Father's Blessing

Fresh Revelational Truth Associated with the Outpouring

"With virtually every major wave of revival in church history, there has been a fresh revelational truth highlighted by God and recovered by the church."[274]
—Fred Wright, Founding Coordinator of Partners in Harvest

To more fully understand all that God has been doing in this outpouring, we believe it's helpful to view it as a Father movement, primarily. The Father has been throwing a party, celebrating us coming home and back into His loving embrace. We have found deeper levels of healing and restoration in our hearts, and have come into greater intimacy with our Father God. Out of the Father's affirmation, we have been freshly awakened to who we are in Christ Jesus, to our true identity as royal sons and daughters and to our true calling and destiny.

In his 2007 book, *The World's Greatest Revivals*, Fred Wright points out that with every major wave of revival in church history, there has been a fresh revelational truth highlighted by God and recovered by the church. With Martin Luther and the Protestant Reformation of the 16th century, the church recovered the "justification by faith in Christ alone" truth. John Wesley and others in the Great Awakening of the 18th century took this foundational truth further by proclaiming Christ and the need for a personal heart transformation. Beginning with the

---

274 Fred Wright, The World's Greatest Revivals, Destiny Image, 2007.

Azusa Street Pentecostal revival, and throughout the 20th century, God has brought fresh revelation and experience regarding the person and work of the Holy Spirit.[275]

Restoration of the Truth of the Father's Love

In this heavenly visitation, we have seen hundreds of thousands of desperate, discouraged and exhausted Christians, many of them pastors, come from around the world, willing to sacrifice time, money and even reputation, to be refreshed, loved up on, empowered, and re-commissioned by the Lord. An important ingredient to this restorative process is the powerful release of the revelation of the Father's love.

By the end of the 20th century, after two world wars and other wars and oppression, almost two hundred million people were killed, many of them men. This has made the 20th century the most fatherless century in the history of mankind. The orphan spirit is rampant in our day. Fatherlessness has contributed greatly to our modern social problems. In his book, *The World's Greatest Revivals*, Fred Wright writes:

> To a perishing, devastated world torn apart by the effects of fatherlessness and sin, this powerful Father's love revelation is clearly becoming the answer for man's plight. It appears that Father God is now standing up clearly saying, 'I am here. I am here, and My arms are open wide to all my kids to come to Me to be forgiven, saved, blessed, and healed'... That is what the Toronto Blessing has been and still is all about: the experiential truth that Father God really, really loves us unconditionally.[276]

The Three Cream Bottles

The Lord was preparing the Arnotts years prior to this outpouring in various ways. One significant way was through a prophetic dream that

---

275 Fred Wright, The World's Greatest Revivals, Destiny Image, 2007.
276 Ibid., pp. 202-205.

John Arnott received in 1987. He saw three cream bottles and heard the Lord tell him to go to Buffalo, New York, to a dairy and get the three bottles.[277]

John realized the three cream bottles represented three distinct teachings and anointings that God wanted John, Carol and their leadership team to drink from and help others do the same.

John went to Buffalo, NY and met Tommy Reid, pastor of the Full Gospel Tabernacle. Tommy introduced John to a member of his church, Mark Virkler, who teaches a course on how to hear the voice of God, called *Communion with God*. Mark Virkler had been a dairy farmer before entering full-time ministry. Mark was invited to come teach the Communion with God course at John and Carol's church in Stratford. They developed a good friendship and Mark has contributed to the development of John's churches and schools ever since. The Communion with God theme was one of the cream bottles. Mark has summarized this life-changing teaching in one sentence, "Hearing God's voice is as simple as quieting yourself down, fixing your eyes on Jesus, tuning to spontaneity and then writing it down."[278]

John and Carol Arnott had already been exposed to, and had started to drink of, the other two cream bottles, which were the Father heart of God and the healing of the heart. They were introduced to the revelation of the Father's love through the ministry of Jack Winter around 1982. The healing of the heart, or inner healing, came to the Arnotts and their leaders through the ministry of John and Paula Sandford, directors of Elijah House, around 1986.

The Arnotts believe that drinking in these three revelational truths had prepared them and their people for a fresh and powerful outpouring of God's Spirit that was to be rooted and grounded in love. These three cream bottles became the very DNA of John and Carol's ministry. And these three truths have become key themes taught and imparted at many of the Toronto conferences and renewal meetings of the last two decades.

---

277 John Arnott, interview with author, June 14, 2013; also cited by Fred Wright, Dan Slade, in the unpublished booklet, Prophetic History of Partners in Harvest, 2007.
278 Mark Virkler, email to author, August 28, 2013.

The Father Heart Revelation

Jack Winter was a forerunner and pioneer of this Father's heart revelation. He taught and ministered on occasion in the early days of the renewal. His counselling ministry, called Daystar Ministries, was based in Minnesota but eventually had over seven hundred staff members throughout the US Jack Winter passed away August 17, 2002, at the age of 71.

Other pioneers of the revelation of the Father's heart prior to the 1994 outpouring were Henri Nouwen, Brennan Manning and Ed Piorek. Ed Piorek would become a frequent speaker in Toronto, particularly at The Father Loves You conferences. Since 1994, we have seen an explosion in the number of leaders raised up to take this vital and timely revelation of the Father's love around the world, including John and Carol Arnott, Peter and Heather Jackson, Ian Ross, the late Jack Frost and his wife Trisha, James and Denise Jordan, David and Faith Dalley, Alyn and AJ Jones, and Barry Adams.

Jack and Trisha Frost founded Shiloh Place Ministries in 1991 to provide a place of healing and restoration for those in ministry, particularly pastors and missionaries. Jack, who in his twenties, had been a commercial fisherman and a captain, and who later became a pastor, was a driven, performance-oriented man with a vicious temper and a fear of failure. Since Jack had never received the tender love and affection from his father, he had a deep need to be needed, which resulted in having very little time or emotional energy left to love his wife and children.

The busier Jack became in ministry, the more his marriage went downhill. So Jack decided to take Trisha to TACF in November 1995, to a healing conference in hopes that it would "straighten her out" and help her appreciate what a man of God he was. He had been touched by the renewal in 1994 but it had not yet translated into greater love and intimacy at home. He was seeing the anointing as a means of building his ministry and trying to impress people and gain approval from God.

While on the Fire Hall floor at the Toronto conference in 1995, someone from the platform began to pray. In his book, *Experiencing the Father's Embrace*, Jack Frost wrote:

The words startled me. 'Father God, take all the men in this room who were never held by their fathers. Hold them close right now. Give them the love their fathers did not know how to give.'

The anointing of the Holy Spirit fell on me immediately. I did not understand what was happening, but it felt as if hot, liquid love was pouring into my soul. I began crying like a baby as I lay at the altar. Such displays of emotion were not normal for me... But my mask was off now. I was completely undone... I had a direct encounter with the phileo of God. As I lay on the floor weeping, Father God entered into that dark closet of my childhood and held me in His arms. For forty-five minutes, the Holy Spirit poured the love of God that the apostle Paul spoke of in Romans 5:5 through my body and washed away much of my guilt, shame, fear of failure and rejection, fear of intimacy, and the fear of receiving and giving love.

My breakthrough finally came. My pride had been shattered. Until that moment, I had never realized how deeply in bondage I was to striving and fear... I didn't stop weeping for five months. Every time I looked into my wife's eyes or saw the pain that I had caused my children because of my lack of tenderness, the tears would begin to flow. Then I would kneel at their feet, weeping and pleading for forgiveness for the times I had harshly misrepresented the Father's love to them... The Father's affectionate phileo love began to restore the heart of this father to his children and the hearts of my children to their father, and it was breaking a curse off of our lives. (see Malachi 4:6.)[279]

In a 2004 issue of *Spread the Fire*, Jack Frost wrote:

Healthy leaders do not guarantee a healthy church, but unhealthy leaders guarantee an unhealthy church. Our chaotic world is ripe

---

279 Jack Frost, Experiencing the Father's Embrace, Charisma House, 2002, pp. 2-10.

for revival. But first, this renewal is preparing our hearts so that our character is able to sustain an increase of His power and signs and wonders. If our hearts are not first rooted and grounded in love and intimacy, we are easily tempted to consume the blessings and power of God upon our own lusts, and we leave a trail of broken relationships behind.[280]

The Lord has used Jack and Trisha Frost and Shiloh Place to impact countless thousands throughout the nations. They have built a retreat centre on fifty-eight acres of forest land near Conway, South Carolina. Jack ministered often at TACF's The Father Loves You conferences, as well as other teaching venues around North America and beyond.

On March 5, 2007, Jack Frost lost his battle with cancer and went to be with the Lord. Even though Jack is no longer with us, Shiloh Place, with its many ministry team members, including Trisha, continues to minister to leaders who come from around the world. Shiloh Place teams also travel to the nations to conduct leaders' retreats. Their videos, books, tapes and training materials are being used in many countries and languages to help scores of leaders to experience the Father's affectionate love as well as increased intimacy with their spouse and children.[281]

Barry Adams received a powerful experience with the Father's love after a hug from Jack Winter. This encounter inspired him to write *The Father's Love Letter*[282] ; a collection of Bible verses that expressed God's father's heart of love to us as his children. What started as a simple sermon illustration ended up becoming an international phenomenon.

Here is Barry telling the story in his own words:

As a driven, type A personality, ex newspaper advertising executive turned pastor with more than a few performance issues, I went to Catch The Fire Conference 1997 desperately hoping for a touch from God. During a special prayer time for pastors, a young man on the

---

280 Jack and Trisha Frost, Spread the Fire magazine, Issue 1, 2004, pp. 12-13.
281 Ibid., p. 13; also website: shilohplace.org.
282 http://www.fathersloveletter.com

ministry team prayed for me and he had a picture. He saw me as a little baby in my mother's womb. God was my Father in the picture, and He was re-attaching my umbilical cord to Himself.

At the time, I didn't understand what that all meant but that prayer was the spark that made me realize what I had been searching for all my life... And that was the love of a father. The next month I returned to TACF to only have my 'Father hunger' increase as I heard Jack Winter describe God's Father-heart in more detail at the 1997 Father Loves You conference. Eight months later I found myself at a men's retreat in an embrace from Jack Winter that literally changed my life.

It was in the moment Jack hugged me that I discovered that Almighty God was truly my Dad and He loved me with an everlasting love. In response to this new revelation of Father's love for me, I created a simple sermon illustration for my home church called Father's Love Letter in January 1999. Steve Long then debuted the new and improved Father's Love Letter video at a TACF November 1999 conference and it went viral on the Internet after that.

Never in my wildest dreams would I have imagined that this simple series of paraphrased Bible verses would find their way to almost every nation in the world via the Internet in 100 plus language translations. It has been viewed millions of times online and it has been delivered door to door to homes in entire countries.

People have taken out full page newspaper ads with this message, personally printed thousands of copies to share with their friends and neighbors and it has been broadcast on numerous radio and television stations worldwide. It has been shared in prisons, pregnancy crisis centers and even in some of the darkest places you could imagine. I have heard many stories of suicides being averted, abortions prevented, and many people coming to Christ in response to this simple call to come home.

I am truly thankful to God for TACF's role in my own journey home and the amazing story that has become the delivery of this one love letter from God to the world. I truly believe that the global response that has happened is a powerful testimony to the foundational cry of the human heart that Philip expressed to Jesus in John 14:8 when he said, 'Show us the Father and it will be enough'.[283]

Restoration or Healing of the Heart

John and Paula Sandford, founders and former directors of Elijah House, testify to the fruit of this outpouring in their own lives and also in their ministry of inner healing to others. In 2000 they said this:

The Father's blessing currently being poured out at TACF has been a lifesaver to Paula and me, and to our ministry... there's still nothing more tiring than counseling. Though Paula and I knew that we were to release the burdens to God, it was always easier to say than to do. We had become soggy with people's grief and emotional pain, defiled by the weight of their sins, and fond of saying, 'The gunk keeps coming in faster than we can shovel it up!' Though we didn't know it then, what was missing was the dimension that fell at Pentecost, the power of the Holy Spirit and, within it, the manifest love of the Father. When we arrived in Toronto, we began to receive prayer. Flat on our backs lying on the carpet, we began to rejoice as His refreshing River washed away years of accumulated burdens... Now, even though we sometimes get physically weary, we don't accumulate a backlog of burdens; instead, we bounce back refreshed... We can tell you that, without experiencing the Father's River of love that began flowing over us in Toronto, we couldn't even have survived, much less have felt this great.

These aren't the only benefits of this River of blessing; there have been many others. We have found that experiencing His love and emotional healing go hand in glove. Before, we often saw fear block people from seeing and renouncing their sins and sinful practices. Now we are seeing the perfect love of the Father's blessing cast out fear and transform people's lives so much more quickly than we did

---

283 Source: email from Barry Adams to Adele Richards dated 5 December 2013

before... Now that the Holy Spirit is falling with great love, casting out fear, denial doesn't block as many people as it used to, especially men... Consequently many people who now come for emotional healing are more aware of the need to take responsibility for their own sins, and to repent and make choices to forgive, and then to express love and healing to others.[284]

John and Paula Sandford's inner healing ministry, Elijah House Ministries, is based in Coeur d'Alene, Idaho, and there are now eleven Elijah Houses internationally. This pioneering couple wrote seventeen influential books together as well as teaching and offering prayer ministry together for decades. John and Paula taught and ministered on more than one occasion at the Toronto Airport Fellowship during the renewal. Their son and daughter-in-law, Loren and Beth Sandford, of Denver Colorado, have been a vital part of this outpouring and the Partners in Harvest network throughout the years. Paula Sandford was promoted to glory on May 4, 2012, at the age of eighty.[285]

An American couple, Chester and Betsy Kylstra,[286] have developed an integrated approach and structure to bringing healing to the heart, called Restoring The Foundations (RTF). This effective ministry focuses on four areas: generational sins and curses, ungodly beliefs, soul/spirit hurts and demonic oppression. Chester and Betsy have taught at various Toronto conferences over the last fifteen years and have had a significant impact on the Arnotts, the Toronto leadership team and the Partners in Harvest network of renewal churches. Along with their core leaders, they have trained up an army of RTF ministers, both within Toronto renewal circles and other streams in the body of Christ, to minister healing and freedom to individuals and couples.[287]

---

284 John and Paula Sandford, How Soaking in the River Changed our Lives and Ministries, Spread the Fire, Issue 5 – 2000, pp. 23-25.
285 John and Paula Sandford, http://www.elijahhouse.org
286 The Kylstras are ordained through Christian International Apostolic Network, with Bill Hamon. They were based in Santa Rosa Beach, Florida, in association with Christian International Ministries from 1993 until 2004. In 2004, they established the Restoring the Foundations International Training Center in Hendersonville, North Carolina.
287 Chester and Betsy Kylstra, Restoring The Foundations, Proclaiming His Word Publications, 2nd edition, 2001, http://rtfi.org/

In time, additional values came to be added on to the three pots of cream, as the Holy Spirit gave guidance.

Prophetic Ministry

The Arnotts have also drawn substantially over the years from many credible prophetic voices in the body of Christ, for teaching, training, imparting, and prophetic encouragement. To list all the names would simply be too lengthy but let me acknowledge a few prophetic people who have worked closely with the Toronto church from within, such as Marc Dupont, Jim Paul, Steve Witt, Ivan and Isabel Allum and Patricia Bootsma.

These revelational truths would not only become a major part of the DNA, the core values of the Arnotts and the Toronto church, but also of Partners in Harvest, the network of churches birthed out of this outpouring. The Fire word was used to create an acronym:

F Father Heart of God
I Intimacy with God through hearing His voice
R Restoration of the heart
E Extending the Kingdom through the equipping, anointing and
    empowering of the Holy Spirit[288]

The School of Ministry in Toronto starts every Heart Module ministry course with a core value month.[289] The first four weeks focus on our essential values: Hearing God's Voice, Healing Life's Hurts, The Father Heart of God and Prophetic Activation.

As we experience the Father's loving embrace as His sons and daughters, as we grow in intimacy with Jesus and learn to hear His voice as His bride, and as the Lord heals our hurt and wounded hearts through repentance and forgiveness, we have a foundation in which the Lord can further equip, train and trust us with greater power from on

---

288 The fourth core value to complete the acrostic of "FIRE" came from the years the Arnotts and their team were part of the Vineyard movement.
289 The Heart module is a 5 month long ministry training course

high in order to partner with Him to see great exploits for His Kingdom accomplished on the earth.[290]

The Toronto church's motto, which is written on a banner on the back wall of their auditorium says it all, "Walking in the Father's love and giving it away to Toronto and the world."

Anyone who knows John and Carol personally, will testify to the way they so wonderfully demonstrate the Father's love. British pastor, David Campbell, had this to say about the Arnotts and the manifest presence of God that continues to flow out of the Toronto church:

> John is a naturally loving sort of man, who immediately sets you at ease. His gentle firmness, genuine humility and clear thinking have influenced all that happens in TACF and kept it safe from being carried away with its own success. I don't think I have ever met anyone more alive in the Spirit than Carol Arnott. Seven years on, her eyes still sparkle with the joy and excitement of seeing the river overflow. I believe that Carol's role in keeping the river fresh and full of godly fun is one of the great-unsung triumphs of the Father's blessing at Toronto... The lasting impact of Toronto on me has been to release me into a new intimacy with the Father, a fresh experience of His power, and give me a foretaste of revival sufficient to encourage me to spend the rest of my life seeking God for it to happen.[291]

Let me add one further point in regards to Carol Arnott. This woman of God has not only kept "the river fresh and full of godly fun", but has so patiently and persistently laid hands on tens of thousands of people, many of them leaders, for extended periods of time, prayerfully soaking them in the intimate presence of the Lord. With a delightful grin on his face, John recently told me that Carol's record is four hours with the same person![292]

---

290 Fred Wright and Dan Slade, Prophetic History of Partners in Harvest, 2007, pp. 3-4. Fred Wright and Dan Slade, Prophetic History of Partners in Harvest, 2007, pp. 3-4.
291 David Campbell, By Their Fruits: The Lasting Impact of Toronto in the UK, Word Pub. 2001, p. 46.)
292 John Arnott, interview at Catch The Fire, June 14, 2013.

CHAPTER 13

1996: A Significant Year

"All I know is that God wanted Hebrews 13:13 to be the first sermon preached at Airport Christian Fellowship because He had given them a mandate to go outside the camp."[293] —RT Kendall

With the separation of the Toronto church from the Vineyard movement in December of 1995, the church was officially called the Toronto Airport Christian Fellowship, as of the second anniversary of the outpouring, January 20, 1996.

Just before the anniversary, something unusual happened on the first night of the pastors' conference, January 17, 1996. Dr. R. T. Kendall from Westminster Chapel in London, England, got up to preach. He made a few introductory comments to the four thousand people in attendance. He then attempted to launch into his sermon, based on Hebrews 4:14-16, which he claimed he had preached over a hundred and fifty times before.

But as he stood there, R. T. was not able to get into his message. He would utter a sentence, pause, and then find either himself or the crowd breaking out in laughter. Believing that God was touching the speaker, the people began to pray out loud, "More Lord!"

---

293 R. T. Kendall, editor, John Arnott, Experience the Blessing, Renew, 2000, p. 46; also the video of January 17, 1996.

R. T. Kendall was obviously embarrassed and extremely frustrated. He asked John Arnott to pray for him. Then he asked Paul Cain, a member of his church, who was also sitting in the front row, to pray for him. He said, "I sincerely hope that I'm in bed dreaming! And if I'm dreaming, it's a nightmare. And if I'm not dreaming, it's worse!" Everyone roared with laughter. He tried desperately to muster enough mental and physical strength to launch into his pre-determined sermon, without success. At one point, Carol Arnott went up on the platform to pray for R. T. and give him a supportive hug. The speaker's inability to make headway into his message went on for what seemed like fifteen or twenty minutes.

Finally, R. T. Kendall got an impression that maybe he needed to turn to a different Bible passage. When he turned to Hebrews 13:13, it dawned on him that it was probably God who was keeping him from preaching the previous biblical text. Once he had us turn to the new passage and he had read it, his mouth was liberated and the unction of the Spirit came upon him with great clarity, authority and conviction. The crowd immediately recognized the shift and settled down to reverently listen and respond to the word of the Lord. Hebrews 13:13 states, *"Let us, then, go to him outside the camp, bearing the disgrace he bore."*

After this very anointed message was delivered, R. T. Kendall gave an invitation to those who were willing to pay whatever price, including their reputation, to obediently follow the Lord, wherever He may lead. Hundreds came running forward, many of them pastors. Wesley Campbell, of Kelowna, BC, was the first to respond.

R. T. Kendall, in his testimony in the book, Experiencing the Blessing, states, "All I know is that God wanted Hebrews 13:13 to be the first sermon preached at Airport Christian Fellowship because He had given them a mandate to go outside the camp."

Rolland and Heidi Baker's first visit to Toronto in 1996

When missionary Rolland Baker first heard of the manifestations at the Toronto church in 1994, he hardly took notice of it. He considered such things as normal when God was on the move. As a young boy, he remembers hearing his grandfather tell him stories of a revival in China, among the mountain villages of southern Yunnan Province, as well as in his orphanage. Rolland writes:

> Each time we were together, I would hear more about angels, demons, power encounters, the grace of God, the beauty of Jesus and how people would shake, tremble, fall and cry out when under the power of the Spirit... His orphans were caught up in heavenly visions for days, weeks and even months. While being shown the glories of the New Jerusalem, they would roll on the floor, laugh and shout with joy. They would also weep for the lost and groan over their own sin.[294]

Rolland's grandfather, H. A. Baker, chronicled this revival in the book, *Beyond the Veil*.[295]

Rolland and his wife, Heidi, were missionaries first in Asia, then ministering to the homeless and planting a church in London, England, while working on their PhDs in theology. They had moved to Mozambique at the beginning of 1995 and were now completely worn out and exhausted. Rolland came from Mozambique to Toronto and during his first visit, he stayed for about two weeks, then came again later for another two weeks.[296] After a powerful time of refreshment and recharging, Rolland returned to Mozambique.

Heidi, seeing her husband's fresh faith, compassion and tender thoughtfulness, intensified her resolve to get to Toronto. She had been beaten up, shot at, and had been crying out, "God, I got to get to

---

294 Rolland and Heidi Baker, editor, John Arnott, Experience the Blessing, Renew Book, 2000, pp. 47-48.
295 H. A. Baker, Beyond the Veil, Sovereign World, 2000; Iris Ministries website, http://www.irisglobal.org/pemba-center-village-of-joy/team, (accessed July 6, 2013)
296 Rolland Baker, email from their assistant, Marta Soderberg, to author Jerry Steingard, October 23, 2013.

Toronto." With little finances, somehow Heidi got a ticket and checked herself out of hospital, against the advice of her doctor. She had double pneumonia, her lungs were filled with fluid, and she could hardly breathe. She stopped in California to see her parents and ended up in the hospital again. But she was so desperate for more of God and very determined to get to Toronto.[297]

During the very first meeting that she attended in Toronto, in the summer of 1996,[298] someone called out "There's a missionary in the room with double pneumonia and God is healing you right now. Take a deep breath." The Lord healed Heidi completely. She could breathe freely for the first time in weeks. Then the person at the microphone called for the missionary who had just been healed of pneumonia to come to the front. There she was prayed for by Carol Arnott and others. She was out on the carpet laughing, screaming, crying and swimming like a fish, and no one stopped her.

Heidi admits she was a type A, driven person. After years of constantly preaching and giving out in ministry, she was now on the receiving end. During her time in Toronto, Heidi soaked in hours of prayer from the ministry team, especially from Carol Arnott and Sharon Wright. She had never experienced such loving and unhurried prayer ministry before.[299]

One night, while out on the floor in a meeting, Heidi was praying for the children of Mozambique. She saw thousands of children coming towards her and she was crying out, "No, Lord, there are too many!" She then had a powerful and vivid vision of Jesus. She saw His shining face and His fiery, loving eyes, with thousands of children surrounding them both. She also saw Christ's body, bruised and beaten. Jesus said to her, "Look into My eyes. You give them something to eat." Then the Lord took a piece of His broken body and gave it to Heidi. It turned into bread in her hands, and she began to distribute it to the children, as it multiplied.

---

297 While in Toronto, Heidi stayed at a TACF Rest and Renewal home for tired pastors and missionaries established by new associate staff members, Fred and Sharon Wright as a sabbatical ministry to tired pastors and missionaries.
298 Margaret Poloma, Main Street Mystics, Altamira Press, 2003, p. 226.
299 Rolland and Heidi Baker, There is Always Enough, Sovereign World, 2003, pp. 48-49.

Jesus said again to Heidi,

"Look into My eyes. You give them something to drink." He then took
a simple poor man's cup and filled it with blood and water from His
pierced side. She took the cup of suffering and joy and drank from it,
then shared it with the children. The cup did not run out. Heidi was
completely undone, as she realized what it had cost Him to provide
spiritual and physical food for us all. Jesus again spoke to Heidi and
said two times, "Because I died, there will always be enough."[300]

Heidi Baker at TACF
January 1997

At the January 1997 pastors' conference, Randy Clark was preaching
one night about the fire of God, laying down our lives and the apostolic
anointing. Heidi Baker came forward during the message and knelt at
the front. Randy pointed to Heidi and said, "God is asking, 'Do you
want Mozambique?'"

She replied, "Yes." Heidi experienced the fire of God fall upon her.
She thought she was going to burn up and die. She cried out, "Lord,
I'm dying!" The Lord clearly spoke to her, "Good, I want you dead!"[301]

Heidi Baker was bothered with Randy's use of the word "apostolic"
because of its association with arrogance. And with the fire of God
upon her, God flipped her on her head and told her that the apostolic
is upside down, it's the lowest place. She was bruised from head to toe.

While upside down, Ian Ross asked her, "Can I pour water on your
feet?" As he did, God hit her even more.[302]

Heidi spent seven days in the Toronto meetings, on the floor and
unable to move, because of the weightiness of the glory upon her. To
her, it was a week of being like a quadriplegic. The Lord taught her
much that week. She could do nothing without the Lord's strength and
the body of Christ. Betty Richards, the security guard, was a real gift

---

300 Ibid., pp. 49-50; also Heidi's testimony on YouTube, Catch The Fire, uploaded May 16, 2011.
301 Rolland and Heidi Baker, There is Always Enough, Sovereign World, 2003, pp. 67-68.
302 Heidi Baker's testimony, Catch The Fire TV on YouTube, uploaded May 16, 2011.

of love and care while she was in this humbled state of paralysis. She needed assistance to drink, go to the bathroom and get back and forth to the meetings. Heidi claims:

> "I learned more about the Lord, His nature and His priorities in those seven days than in ten years of academic theology. Ephesians 6 came alive to me. I did not have any desire to eat that week. I needed help to even get a drink of water or go to the hotel. I used to try to control things. Now I realized it was all about dying to self and being filled with the Holy Spirit. This could only happen as I soaked in His presence, and that takes time."[303]

She admits:

> "I am a type A, driven person, and God had to break and humble me. He showed me my total inadequacy to do anything in my own strength. Being unable to move for seven days drove the point home as nothing else could have ever done. I remember several times hearing people whisper with pity that I was crippled, a quadriplegic. I never liked being dependent on others. I have been a leader as long as I can remember... After that transforming experience, everything in my ministry changed. He brought me to a place of utter dependence on Him. When I returned to Mozambique, I began releasing people in ministry. I began to recognize potential ministers even in children as young as eight. I began relinquishing control and delegating responsibilities... As I became less and He became more, the ministry grew at a phenomenal rate."[304]

Heidi Baker wrote of another experience with the Lord while on the floor in Toronto.

---

303 Heidi Baker, Spread the Fire magazine, Issue 3 – 2001, p 18.
304 Rolland and Heidi Baker, There is Always Enough, pp. 69-70.

In 1999, during one of my always-memorable visits to TACF, I received a further vision of Jesus the Bridegroom... His weighty glory again fell on me, and I found myself prostrate before Jesus. He showed me a delightful feast, elegantly laid out on long tables, which had no end. Jesus spoke to me and said, 'My feast is about to begin! The church is not ready. Wake up, Church! Wake up!'

Then He showed me the garbage dump in Maputo, Mozambique. I was walking with Jesus on mountains of garbage. Jesus and I were calling the people to come. And they came in their rags, with their bloated bellies, open sores and bare feet. As we placed our hands on them, they were healed. Jesus, my Bridegroom, allowed me to participate with Him as we placed stunning robes of blue, red, purple, silver and gold on the people. We began to dance and sing until we danced right out of the garbage dump into the wedding feast. Jesus pointed to our friends and told them to sit in front. The Lord said, 'I want my house full!'[305]

Since 1999, Heidi and friends have been going regularly to the garbage dump in Maputo, calling the poor to the wedding feast. Although the filth and smells can be overwhelming, to Heidi, it is one of the most beautiful places on earth because people are hungry for Jesus. In her book, *There is Always Enough*, Heidi claims:

Not one person in the garbage dump has said no to an invitation to meet Jesus. They are all hungry for the Bread of Life. We started our dump church in a tiny, blackened shell of a building, and it's one of my favorite churches in the whole world. We sing, preach and worship in eye-stinging smoke. Our arms are black with swarms of flies... Many are diseased and hungry, and some know they will die within weeks, but they are thrilled to find their Savior.[306]

---

305 Heidi Baker, The Revelation of Jesus and His Call on my Life, Spread the Fire, Issue 3, 2003, pp. 11-12.
306 Rolland and Heidi Baker, There is Always Enough, pp. 55-56.

In 2001, Heidi reported,

> Since the Lord touched us in Toronto and we learned to soak in His presence, Iris Ministries went from four churches in 1997 to six hundred and twenty churches in Mozambique, over one hundred churches in Malawi, and sixty-three churches in South Africa by January of 2001... We now run medical clinics, schools, a Bible College, eight farms, countrywide food distribution, and host two thousand plus visitors per year. This renewal has helped us learn that abiding in Jesus is the secret of real fruitfulness.[307]

Rolland says,

> We value immediate intimacy with Jesus, a life of utterly-needed miracles, concentration on the humble and lowly, willingness to suffer for love's sake, and the unquenchable joy of the Lord, which is our energy, motivation, weapon and reward—not optional.[308]

Rolland tells of how, in 1998, he began to travel north with his Mozambican friend and pastor, Surpresa Sithole, who had started a handful of churches.

> Surpresa speaks fourteen languages, ten given to him supernaturally. Fasting and prayer are a way of life for him, and he sees visions regularly. But Supresa's most impressive quality is that he is filled with love and joy. He is virtually incapable of a negative thought, laughing easily and often in all circumstances. He still travels with me preaching all over Mozambique and surrounding countries to our churches, which now number in the thousands... As far as we know, at least eight people have been raised from the dead in this revival between 2000 and 2002, and maybe fourteen since 1998. Several of these resurrections took place

---

307 Heidi Baker, Spread the Fire magazine, Issue 3, 2001, p. 19.
308 Iris Ministries website, http://www.irisglobal.org/pemba-center-village-of-joy/team (accessed July 6, 2013)

in heavily Moslem areas, and many Moslems have come to Jesus as a result."[309]

In his article, 'Remember the Poor,' in *Spread The Fire*, Georgian Banov, the Bulgarian born musician, told of how the 1994 river of renewal dramatically changed him and his wife, Winnie, and their ministries. He claimed,

> It was as though huge, invisible jets were attached to us propelling our lives with new power of the Holy Ghost… We were not only renewed, but we found ourselves ministering under a whole new anointing. We began to immerse ourselves in the depths of the Father's love and began experiencing His pleasures in almost unbearable degrees. The joy of Jesus, the joy unspeakable and full of glory we've read about in the Bible, became our daily portion, altering the way we used to preach and lead praise and worship. We became more radical and free as the glory of God intensified.[310]

Georgian and his wife take teams to Bulgaria twice a year to do evangelistic outreaches. They love to throw Jesus parties and celebrate the extravagant love of God with joyful song, dance and feasts on the streets, among the gypsies and the poor. Many of them give their lives to Jesus.

In early 2002, the Banovs were invited by Heidi and Rolland Baker to come to Mozambique for a Jesus Celebration Conference. At the time, the Bakers were caring for over eight hundred orphans on their main base in Maputo. Georgian asked about the children's favourite meal. "Fried chicken," Heidi said, "but they get to eat it only twice a year, on Christmas and Easter."

"Well," he told her, "let's have a chicken dinner at the end of the conference for everybody. You organize it and we'll cover the expenses."

---

309 Rolland Baker, Spread The Fire magazine, Oct 31, 2002 http://revivalmag.com/article/remember-poor
310 Georgian Banov, Remember the Poor, Spread the Fire magazine, Issue 5 – 2002, p. 12.

So the cooks spent all night cooking twelve hundred pieces of chicken. However, the next day, twenty-four hundred people showed up for the Sunday service. All they could do was pray,

"Lord, help us!" Georgian reports that they kept serving the chicken and the pile of chicken finally ran out after the last unexpected visitor ate their portion. The Lord doubled the chicken![311]

Other Moves of God Around the World in 1996 (and beyond)

Over the years, it has been a sheer joy to continue to hear reports of the Holy Spirit breaking out in various churches, places and lives, sometimes connected with what God has been doing in Toronto and sometimes completely unconnected. During this sovereign season of visitation in the mid-1990s and beyond, it became apparent that the God of suddenlies was accelerating His Kingdom plans and purposes for this generation. Here a few of the stories of what God was doing in 1996.

Canadian Arctic Outpouring
1996 and 1999

Revival broke out in various communities in the Canadian territory of Nunavut, in the eastern Canadian Arctic. In Pond Inlet, on Baffin Island, in late January and early February 1996, God began to move and bring conviction of sin and repentance to many. Converts wanted to get rid of their heavy metal music materials, pornography, drugs, and other materials from hell. So, with the logistical assistance of the Royal Canadian Mounted Police, they had a large bonfire out on the ice. Practically the whole community came out to watch as eighty to one hundred thousand dollars worth of junk went up in smoke.

In February 1999, a week of revival meetings took place at the Anglican Church in Pond Inlet. Because of the level of hunger for God, they added a Sunday afternoon youth service. Various Christian

---

311 Ibid., p. 13.

leaders such as Billy Arnaquq, Moses Kyak, James, Joshua and Looee Arreak were there to witness the extraordinary visitation of God that afternoon. Looee Arreak, the worship leader in that meeting, got the word, *"Blessed are the pure in heart, for they shall see God."*

According to Pastor Billy Arnaquq, while praying over the youth at the altar, "Something started to happen that was out of our control." A quiet sound started, then got louder and louder. The dual-cassette tape deck that was used to record the service was still running off the soundboard. The soundman, however, shut the sound system off completely, thinking the sound was feedback of some kind. The sound got louder and louder as if a freight train was coming through the building. As it got louder, the place began to shake and people began to shake and weep.

On the Transformations II video, you can hear the tape recording of that extraordinary rumbling sound growing louder and louder, and of people started to shout the word, "Fire, fire!" A year and a half after this mighty visitation of the Holy Spirit, the people were still moved to tears as they recalled that day.

A string of small communities in the eastern Canadian Arctic, particularly northern Quebec and Baffin Island, have been impacted by this visitation from God. Suicide and drug abuse among youth have declined, as has domestic abuse and crime in general. A number of Christians and pastors have also been involved in the political realm, as mayors and community elders. Upwards of sixty percent of many northern community populations claim to be born-again or Spirit-filled. And signs of restoration have not only been seen in hearts and relationships in the home and community, but also in the land and water. Caribou and fish seem to be returning and the land is more productive.[312] Ontario leaders such as Bill Prankard and Andy Koornstra, as well as Roger Armbruster of Manitoba, have travelled to the Canadian Arctic over the years to be a support and to bring Kingdom healing and restoration.

---

312 Transformations II video, The Sentinel Group, George Otis Jr., host, 2001; Roger Armbruster, Harvest Field Ministries newsletter 1996; Spread the Fire magazine, August 1996, p. 32; Christian Week, Northern Church Grows and Matures, May 16, 2000 by Debra Fieguth, http://www.christianweek.org/stories.php?id=1367)

Randy Clark and the "Moscow Blessing"
March 1996

Randy Clark took a team of twenty-one people to lead a renewal conference in Moscow in March of 1996.[313] Pastors and leaders from many denominations attended—some traveling by train for up to thirty hours.[314]

In 1995, Randy Clark spoke to his worship team and told them that they would be going with him to Russia in the near future and that they needed to learn to sing some worship songs phonetically in Russian. Randy and some of his team did some preliminary meetings in Moscow in the fall of 1995 to establish a foundation of relationships and unity among the church leaders before the conference in March of 1996.[315]

This conference was considered by many to be "historic". A member of the team, Teresa Seputis, wrote:

> I was privileged to be a part of the ministry team for this conference. It was like living the book of Acts... God showed up with incredible power and with more love and anointing than I think I've ever seen in one place before. He accomplished such a major thing with this conference that I think one day church historians may look back on this as a significant event in Church history.[316]

After being asked by Moscow pastors to come back the next year, Randy Clark and a renewal team returned to conduct another Catch The Fire Conference in May of 1997, which saw many salvations, many children powerfully touched, and significant healings and impartations.

---

313 In his book, Lighting Fires, Randy Clark told of some amazing things about this venture to Moscow. Back in April 1990, Mike Bickle had taken up an offering for Bibles for Russia at his Kansas City conference. During that offering, which brought in 1.2 million dollars for Bibles, the Lord spoke to Randy that someday he would be going to Russia and that he would be taking his worship team.
314 Roger Helland, Let the River Flow, Bridge-Logos, 1996, pp. xxiii-xxiv.
315 Clark also promised to pay for the costs for the pastors to come to the conference, as a service of love to the Moscow church leadership. But shortly before the event, they realized that, due to inflation, they were thirty thousand dollars short. Thanks to the generosity of Rodney Howard-Browne and John Arnott, they eventually had sufficient funds to pay for nine hundred and eighty pastors to attend.
316 Teresa Seputis, http://www.godspeak.net/moscow/moscow_index.html (accessed July 12, 2013)

Smithton Outpouring
March 24, 1996

Steve Gray, pastor of Smithton Community Church in Missouri, practically crawled to the Pensacola revival to find more of God, leaving the pastoral responsibility of the church to his wife, Kathy, for two weeks. He was a broken, burned-out man who had pastored this little country church for twelve years and had nothing left to give.

After basking in the presence of God at the Brownsville revival, he drove home and walked into the Sunday evening church service, on March 24, 1996, to the sound of the worship music. He saw his wife, Kathy, and as he proceeded to go give her a hug, the power of God hit him and he started glowing, jumping and twirling for joy. The worship leader switched the song to a high-energy praise song of joy and immediately the people, who had never seen their pastor display such rejoicing, came forward, many kicking off shoes, and began to jump and dance for joy in the river of God's joyful presence. As the pastor later prayed for them, many were collapsing to the floor laughing or weeping.

This was the start of an outpouring in the most unlikely of places. The small town of Smithton with only five hundred and thirty-two residents, had no gas station nor even a Coke machine. Yet, in the first three and a half years of the outpouring, over two hundred and fifty thousand people attended the small church from every state in the USA and over sixty foreign countries.[317]

Towards the end of 1999, they began a transition from the little town of Smithton into the city of Kansas City to continue the worldwide impact of the revival. The last outpouring meetings in Smithton were conducted the weekend of February 11–13, 2000.[318]

---

[317] Source: Ron McGatlin, I Saw the Smithton Outpouring, Basileia Pub., 2002, back cover.
[318] The World Revival Church began on Friday, June 30, 2000, in the "tent of meeting" erected on the beautiful sixty-two acres of land off I-470 in Kansas City, Missouri. September 11, 2000 marked the first day of classes for their World Revival School of Ministry. On March 24, 2001, the fifth anniversary of the Smithton outpouring, pastor John Kilpatrick of the Brownsville revival in Pensacola, Florida, was the guest speaker in their celebration of the anniversary as well as the dedication of World Revival Church's new facility. Source: ibid., p. 90.

Pulpit split in half – Tommy Tenney in Houston, Texas
October 20, 1996

Christian Tabernacle pastor, Richard Heard, brought Pentecostal evangelist Tommy Tenney to his church to conduct revival meetings. At the 8:30 AM Sunday service, October 20, 1996, God showed up in a startling way. At the end of the worship time, with the worship atmosphere thick with the presence of God, Richard Heard and Tommy Tenney were hesitant to move into a time of preaching. When asked by Pastor Heard if he was ready to lead the service, Tenney stated that he feared going to the pulpit because he sensed that "something big" was about to take place.

Richard Heard eventually went to the pulpit and read 2 Chronicles 7:14. After reading the text and making a few comments about seeking God's face rather than His hand, suddenly "a loud clap of noise hit the sanctuary." It was as if a bolt of lightning had come in and struck the pulpit. The pastor was thrown backwards eight or nine feet and landed flat on his back. The pulpit, made of half-inch thick Plexiglas was split into two pieces, landing six or seven feet apart. The congregation was awestruck.

Tommy Tenney gave several altar calls and people responded, leading to many salvations that day and over subsequent days. The meeting ended around midnight that night. Tenney interpreted the pulpit splitting in two "as a symbolic slap in the face for the tight human control of the church across America." The manufacturer of the podium claimed that the material would never split by natural means the way it did—along a diagonal jagged line.[319]

The carpet in the auditorium became wet from the tears of repentance and was covered in white tissue paper. For about one month, many claimed seeing angels and having visions. Some smelled a fragrance like perfume. Still others saw the glory cloud. For about three months, the Lord moved them into deep repentance and intercession. Preaching and

---

319 James H. Rutz, Houston Pastor Says God's Power Split His Pulpit in Half, Charisma magazine, June 1997, pp. 27-28.

choir performances could not take place during this time, unless God allowed them to. Whenever anyone attempted to either preach or sing, they would end up on the floor, be stuck in their seats, or find themselves laughing or crying as the Spirit moved. People and leaders alike found themselves changed in terms of having a deeper love, humility, fear of the Lord and hunger for God.[320]

Tommy Tenney, Baltimore, Maryland, Rock City Church, *January 19, 1997*

Pastor Bart Pierce and his wife had just come back from a pastors' retreat in Florida where Tommy Tenney had shared what God had been doing over the last couple of months in Houston, Texas. Bart Pierce invited Tommy Tenney to come to their church to minister on Sunday, January 19, 1997. Neither of them got to preach due to the fact that the manifest presence of the Lord came down and people were on the floor weeping for hours.[321]

Over the next two years or so, Monday and Tuesday nights were dedicated to meeting with the Lord. Tommy Tenney[322] came most weeks to help facilitate these times of ministering to the Lord in the glory. They determined not to set an agenda for the meetings and each meeting was unique. Sometimes the Lord would direct them to continue worship, be silent, pray, repent, give a short message from the Word, or give a prophetic word. At times, they were on their faces before the Lord. Other times, they felt God was calling them to praise Him with song and abandoned dance and celebration.

This Baltimore church was not only enjoying the awesome and holy presence of the Lord in their revival meetings, but also had been taking His love and presence to the poor and downtrodden of their city.

320 Email to Richard Riss, Awakening List, from leadership of Christian Tabernacle, March 18, 1997.
321 Baltimore Revival, Elizabeth Moll Stalcup, http://renewaljournal.wordpress.com/2011/08/13/baltimore-revival-byelizabeth-moll-stalcup/ (accessed September 5, 2013)
322 Marc Dupont first met Tommy Tenney in Houson, Texas. Later, when Marc had Tommy Tenney in Toronto to speak and minister, Bart Pierce came to Toronto as well. After they met, Bart invited Marc to come down to help facilitate the precious and glorious visitation of God taking place in Baltimore. Marc recalls going to assist in Baltimore maybe ten to twelve times; sometimes all three of them (Bart, Tommy and Marc) were together seeking to facilitate what the Lord was doing in that place. Source: Bart Pierce, Seeking Our Brothers, Destiny Image, 2000, p. 118.

In Pierce's book, *Seeking Our Brothers*, he states,

"In the past we have had program evangelism. John Wimber taught us about power evangelism. Now we are entering the day of what Tommy Tenney calls 'presence evangelism.' This means going into the street, or into a bar, or into a jail, or into a drug-infested area with the glory of God on you... Since January 1997, we have seen the same presence and power of God that happens in church happen right out on the street during our block parties. People are being saved by the hundreds and experiencing the fullness of the Spirit... If we create a true house of worship, He will show up. That's what He is looking for. At the same time, He loves being out there with Bartimaeus and Zacchaeus, and with lepers and demoniacs—anywhere there are people in need. The Church must love what He loves. We must cultivate a passion for both. It is already beginning to happen in many places."[323]

God Moves in Prisons

Full-time prison chaplain, Bill DeHart first visited TACF late in 1995. At a TACF conference in late 1996, Bill DeHart testified of God's power breaking out at his Michigan prison. "The fire has fallen on Genesee County Jail, and it's ablaze with the Holy Spirit," said DeHart, one of two full-time chaplains to the jail's six hundred and fifty prisoners.

He prayed for hundreds at the prison; with some around him actually seeing rays of light beaming from his hands. DeHart said,

I was leaving one night, and a deputy asked me, 'How do you get that light to come out? Three of us saw it tonight when you put your hands on their heads.'... 'The deputy said the men sometimes hear it crackle!' The prisoners were praying in tongues and prophesying. Many of them stayed in touch with DeHart after their release. "Everything's changed," he said, "they want to live holy lives."[324]

---

323 Bart Pierce, Seeking Our Brothers, Destiny Image, 2000, p. 118.
324 Spread the Fire, April 1997, Anointing Transforms Michigan Prison, pp. 29, 31.

Prison chaplain, David Powe reported that upwards of nine hundred inmates had come to Christ in two years at Lewes Prison, near Brighton, England.[325] And Rev. Bill Birdwood saw close to 200 inmates come to Christ within a year at Exeter Prison. "They were hit by the so-called 'Toronto Blessing'—with reports of repentant prisoners shaking violently or crashing to the floor."[326] In 2001 Gerald Coates reported that over six thousand prison inmates in the UK have come to faith in Christ since the summer of 1994, as a direct result of the Toronto Blessing.[327]

New to TACF in 1996

In early 1996, at John Arnott's request, Fred and Sharon would also work with John in forming a new family of churches. The Wrights would become the founding international directors of the new Partners in Harvest network of churches.

In March 1996, TACF launched a thirty-minute television program, *Catch The Fire*, which aired for the first time nationally on Vision TV.[328]

By August 20, 1996, TACF had held thirty months of nightly meetings. Steve Long reported that:

The evening renewal meetings at the Toronto Airport Christian Fellowship began on January 20, 1994. By August 1996, they had passed one million in total attendance or about two hundred thousand different people. The average stay is five days according to the hotels. They have had over ten thousand people come to the front to receive prayer as first-time commitments or backsliders. Of the people who attend, twenty-five percent are leaders in their churches as pastors, elders, church staff, etc. The Toronto Airport Christian Fellowship staff estimate that there are over one hundred thousand renewal churches in the world today and growing.[329]

---

325 Spread the Fire magazine, April 1997, "UK Prison Awakening Continues", p. 28.
326 Spread the Fire magazine, April 1997, "UK Prison Awakening Continues", p. 28.
327 Gerald Coates, By Their Fruits: The Lasting Impact of Toronto in the UK, Word Pub. 2001, p. 25.
328 Spread the Fire magazine, January 1998, p. 26.
329 Steve Long, pastor of Administration at TACF, in an e-mail message to Roger Helland, August 25, 1996; Let the River Flow, Roger Helland, Bridge-Logos, 1996, p. xxi.

CHAPTER 14

The Rest of the First Decade (1997-2004)

Healing, gold teeth and the golden sword prophecy

Carol Arnott – The Golden Sword Prophecy
January 20, 1997

When Randy Clark announced his sermon title, "The Making of a Warrior," at the third anniversary, January 20, 1997, in Toronto, the Spirit fell powerfully on many people and especially on Carol Arnott. For about twenty minutes, while on the floor, she was slashing violently with a two-handed sword in her hands (her hands were together as if holding a sword). After Randy finished his message, Carol got up and powerfully delivered the following prophecy:

> This is My sword, this is not man's sword, this is My golden sword.
> The ways you have been using My weapons, the methods that you
> have been using in the past, you are to throw them away because I am
> giving you My sword now and the old ways of doing things will not
> do. The old methods will not be acceptable to Me anymore because I
> am doing a new thing. Do not look to the yesterdays but look to the
> future because I am doing a new thing and this new way is not the old.
> This new way is new and you must throw away the old ways of doing
> things and take up My sword because My sword is made of pure gold
> and is purer and is mighty. If you wield it the captives will be set free,
> the chains will be broken and the healings will be manifest because it

will not be by might, nor by power, but by My wonderful Holy Spirit. It is by Him, it is by Him that this new wave will be brought forth, it is by Him that the King of Kings and Lord of Lords will ride again. In this next wave I am requiring those who take up this golden sword to be refined, to be pure, to have all the dross refined in the fire because if you take this sword and there is secret sin in your life this sword will kill you. This next wave is no joke. It is not a laughing matter. All those who do not want to give up their sin and are fearful, like Gideon's men, stand back, because I am calling men and women in these next days that will allow me to refine them, that will allow me to chasten, but not with anger because I am a loving God. I am a God full of mercy but I am serious as the time is short. The bridegroom is most anxious for His bride, so those of you that will, let Me refine you and come and take up that golden sword for I will use you in ways, I will use you in ways that you can't imagine, but I must purify you first."[330]

Healing Miracles

In 1998, John Arnott believed a stronger healing component was beginning to emerge in the river of revival and so he invited healing evangelist Bill Prankard to join TACF's renewal team for a season. Bill loves to see miracles, especially miracles that transform lives. Bill recalls that, during one renewal meeting,

A fourteen-year-old boy who was born with a severely deformed hip, wore special shoes and had never been able to run. As God's power hit him, he began running up and down the aisles, perfectly healed. He and his parents committed their lives to Christ and the following evening, they brought two entire rows of relatives, many of whom came to Christ as well.[331]

---

330 Golden Sword Prophecy, http://www.apologeticsindex.org/s01.html
331 Melinda Fish report, "Bill Prankard, Toronto's Healing Messenger", in Spread the Fire magazine, Issue 4, 1999, pp. 21-22.

As of January 1998, TACF began broadcasting audio and video live on the Internet. Many people have testified, from around the world, of the power of God touching them via cyberspace.[332]

Gold Teeth Appearing

Beginning on Wednesday, March 3, 1999, during TACF's Intercession Conference, with guest speakers Dutch Sheets and Cindy Jacobs, a new miraculous manifestation of God's powerful presence fell; that of gold teeth appearing. This sign and wonder has been reported frequently since the 1980s in the Argentina revival.

The first night of the Toronto conference, John had two women from Capetown, South Africa, give the testimony of their father having received a gold filling while watching a video of a meeting that took place in February in Pretoria, South Africa. In this South African meeting, John and Carol had been ministering and several people had reported receiving gold fillings. After their testimonies, John encouraged everyone who needed a healing touch from God in their mouth, teeth, gum or jaw, to stand. Virtually everyone rose to their feet. They prayed and, within minutes, about twenty people marched to the front to report that they had gold teeth miraculously appear in their mouth.

As the meeting continued that night, and over the next couple of days, more and more people reported similar healings and manifestations. By the Friday evening service, well over one hundred people crowded into the café next to the sanctuary to fill out testimony forms. As attendees, including a dental hygienist from Germany, shone flashlights into each other's mouth, many reported witnessing changes in the metallic composition of the fillings taking place before their eyes. Some came into the café because they had one filling turn to gold but, with the child-like faith in the room, came out with three gold teeth! By Saturday night, one hundred and ninety-eight people stood at the front to testify of God's miraculous work in their mouth. They were encouraged to go home

---

332 Spread the Fire magazine, June 1998, p. 28.

and make appointments with their dentists to confirm and validate the changes that have taken place.[333]

TACF sought to follow up with these testimonies. About one third actually went to see their dentist. A number of them did not see their dentist because they had checked their dental records and insurance forms at home and found that, what was in their mouths reflected a definite change, which was enough evidence to satisfy them. About a third of those who saw their dentist found that their gold fillings had been put in previously by the dentist and they'd forgotten about them. Some dentists were unwilling to comment, or stated that the teeth looked polished, or asked if the patient had been elsewhere. Some dentists were skeptical or fearful and simply said that an error must have been made on the records. About five percent of the dentists were willing to say that some kind of miracle appeared to have occurred.[334]

While many were speculating what this outbreak of gold teeth means, maybe John's explanation sums it up best, "I just believe God loves people and wants to bless them."[335]

In 1999, Marc Dupont ministered in Seoul, South Korea. He received a word of knowledge to pray for healing of people with teeth problems. Several people received healing. One man in particular had seven bad teeth. He was not only healed but these seven teeth became completely covered with gold. This man was a custom designer in the fashion industry. When Marc came back to that place about a year and a half later, he talked with this man and got an update report. Not only was the miracle permanent, but this man had also led about twenty of his colleagues in the fashion industry to the Lord, simply by showing them the miracle in his mouth and testifying of God's love and kindness![336]

Cal Pierce, an elder and board member for years at Bethel Church in Redding, California, was forever changed by the power of God in a Bethel service in June 1996. In late 1997, Cal Pierce and his wife, Michelle, moved

---

333 Melinda Fish report, "Gold Teeth Make Their Mark on Toronto", Spread the Fire magazine, Issue 2, 1999, pp. 4-5.
334 Connie Janzen and Melinda Fish reporting, "What About the Gold Teeth?" Spread the Fire magazine, Issue 3, 1999, p. 4.
335 Spread the Fire magazine, Issue 2, 1999, p. 5.
336 Marc Dupont, telephone interview, September 12, 2013.

to Spokane, Washington and sought the Lord as to what He would have them do. Cal had studied revivals and had read of the "Healing Rooms" ministry of John G. Lake, in Spokane, earlier in the century. Cal went monthly to pray at John G. Lake's gravesite and in early 1999, he felt the Lord challenge him to re-dig the wells of healing in Spokane.

After training some intercessors as prayer teams, on July 22, 1999, the Spokane Healing Rooms were re-opened in the same location they had been eighty years earlier with John G. Lake and The International Association of Healing Rooms was officially founded. The Healing Rooms are set up similar to a walk-in clinic; people can come in and receive free prayer, from a trained and compassionate team, for physical healing. Currently there are over two thousand Healing Room locations established in sixty-three nations of the world.[337]

Randy Clark's Ministry in Brazil

Randy's 'land of anointing,' the country where he and his team have the most favor, is Brazil. In five years (1999-2004) approximately one hundred thousand healings have occurred when Randy and Global Awakening teams prayed for the sick. Truly the blind have seen, the deaf have heard, the paralyzed have walked, and those dying from disease have been healed. Thousands have been born again and thousands of pastors and leaders have received a strong impartation. As a result, evangelism in their churches has multiplied and even more people are being led into the Kingdom.[338]

IHOP

On May 7, 1999, Mike Bickle and twenty full-time "intercessory missionaries" founded the ministry of the International House of Prayer of Kansas City (IHOPKC). They began with prayer mingled with worship

---

337 International Association of Healing Rooms, https://healingrooms.com/ also https://www.facebook.com/healingrooms
338 Global Awakening website: http://globalawakening.com/home/about-global-awakening/history-of-global-awakening

for thirteen hours each day. On September 19, 1999, prayer and worship was extended to the full 24/7 schedule.

Spontaneous Healings at TACF
2003

At TACF's ninth anniversary renewal meeting, January 20, 2003, at the end of the worship time, a sense of the weighty presence of God landed in the room. The musicians remained on stage. Nobody said or did anything. There was a holy hush in the room. Eventually Lynley Allan, who was sitting in the front row, began singing prophetically. After she sang, John Arnott sang out about God's glory, followed by Lynley singing another line, then John again. Soon April Stevenson came up the aisle to the front, sharing how she felt water dripping, a fine misty rain. She had looked up but could not see water dripping but she felt it.

Soon more than a dozen people were looking up and were stunned to see what appeared to be glory dust. It looked like snow drifting across the room. Under the weight of the glory, Carol Arnott slid off her seat. Meanwhile, spontaneous healings were taking place towards the back and side of the auditorium, near the Noah's ark children's ministry area. John never did preach that night.[339]

Soaking Prayer Centres
2003

To further promote the cultivation of intimacy with Jesus and taking the time to soak in His presence, in 2003, the Toronto church launched their vision of seeing thousands of "Soaking Prayer Centres" spring up around North America and around the world. They offered a starter kit to get people going as well as a one-week training course in Toronto.[340]

---

339 Connie Sinnott, telephone conversation, August 23, 2013.
340 John Arnott, "Soaking in His Presence", Spread the Fire magazine, Issue 3, 2003, pp. 5-7.

2003 was also the year that the International Leadership Schools were first launched. Duncan Smith started the first school in Ghana. It was a three-week school. The next school, which was trimmed to one week, was in Kyrgyzstan. The course entailed teaching and ministry regarding the Father's love, healing of the heart, intimacy with Jesus, hearing God's voice and impartation of the fresh anointing. They discovered that the churches of the leaders that attended the leadership school grew, on average, by three hundred percent in the next year.[341]

---

341 Steve Long, teaching at Catch The Fire conference, Toronto, September 28, 2013.

CHAPTER 15

Second Decade of the Toronto Blessing (2004–2014)

There are no toxic levels of the Holy Spirit

In 2003, Bill Johnson, of Redding, California, reported, "Since 1995 we have seen several thousand people healed from various afflictions and diseases. In recent months, a shift has taken place where we are now seeing more people healed in public places than in church services. The church is learning to be the Church."[342]

> A lot happens when you do 'carpet time' whether in TACF or anywhere else. Your heart is healed, your dreams are born and you get up ready to take on the world. My two times in Toronto proved that. When I attended the Pastors and Leaders Conference in 2004 and 2006, I saw the church there in the river—still alive and still active and still seeking more of God. Some said it would all fade and prove to have been a temporary excursion into Holy Spirit excess. But a phrase I heard at TACF, 'There are no toxic levels of the Spirit,' shows that you can never max out on the Spirit."—Colin Dye

Colin Dye, senior leader of the Elim Pentecostal mega-church, Kensington Temple, in London, England, was a speaker at the Toronto's Pastors' Conference in 2004 and again in 2006. In the spring of 2006, Colin Dye wrote:

> During my personal 'carpet time' in TACF, I found myself refilled, renewed and re-commissioned to take the gospel to the nations. I

---

342 Bill Johnson, Spread the Fire magazine, Issue 2, 2003, pp. 18-19.

was freshly equipped to lead our great church in London into new levels in the Holy Spirit, and to take our people into the real purpose of the Spirit, to touch lives as we ourselves have been touched with the blessings of the Father's House.[343]

In the year 2000, Colin and his leadership team implemented the G12 cell group model into their church for discipleship and evangelism purposes.

Soaking Prayer and Houses of Prayer

Bob and Cindy Parton of Hurst, Texas, started inviting people to soaking prayer in their home in 1995. It became known as The River Centre, with some people driving for hours to attend the soaking meetings that were often characterised by holy laughter and great refreshing in the Holy Spirit. Bob and Cindy's soaking prayer model became the first of what has become an expanding network of thousands of soaking prayer centres.

Since 2005, inmates in Brunswick Correctional Facility, in North Carolina, have been holding regular weekly "soaking" meetings in Room 113 of their prison. Prisoners testify that in a place "where sin abounds, grace does much more abound." Many men who never had a relationship with a father are discovering their heavenly Father.[344]

June 21, 2005 marked the first meeting of TACF's very own Soaking Prayer Centre. Led by June Bain, the Soaking Centre was held every Tuesday evening in the chapel room [345]

By late 2007, the network of Catch The Fire Soaking Prayer Centres had spread to seventy-seven nations and is still growing. People meet regularly in God's presence, not only in homes but also in offices, in prisons and even on a US naval aircraft carrier.[346]

On September 23, 2005, TACF dedicated the Chapel Room as a House of Prayer. This became a quiet place to meet with the Lord and

343 Colin Dye, The Pathway to Renewal, Spread the Fire magazine, Issue 3, 2006, pp. 19-21.
344 John Arnott, Reflections, Spread the Fire magazine, Issue 3, 2006, p. 4-5, 14.
345 Spread the Fire magazine, Issue 4, August, 2005, p. 16.
346 John Arnott, Reflections, Spread the Fire magazine, Issue 3, 2006, p. 4-5, 14.

pray, and it was available Monday to Friday between 9 AM and 5 PM April Stephenson, head of intercession at TACF wrote:

> They kept the room simple and uncomplicated – very few chairs, plenty of carpet space, colourful banners and a CD player. This leaves lots of room for the Holy Spirit and creates anticipation of entering the glory of His presence... People began to be aware of different fragrances in the room... Incense, sweet fragrances or spices and even smoke were noticed many times. Angelic visitations increased... From the Bride's privileged position of intimacy will come the intercession for the harvest in Toronto.[347]

On Sunday, January 22, 2006, John and Carol Arnott laid hands on Steve and Sandra Long and commissioned them as the new senior pastors of the Toronto Airport Christian Fellowship. John had just turned sixty-five years of age. John and Carol are now considered the Founding Pastors.[348]

This freed the Arnotts up to do more apostolic and international ministry, such as lead Catch The Fire Ministries, the outreach arm of TACF. Started some years before, Catch The Fire Ministries operated as a department out of TACF focused on external work. They operated a television station for a time, coordinated thousands of Soaking Prayer Centres, and ran conferences and training schools around the world. When the first church was planted directly by a Toronto team, the name "Catch The Fire" was chosen for that church, and within a short span of time the entire ministry of TACF was renamed "Catch The Fire", with the Toronto church becoming "Catch The Fire Toronto."

In February 2006, Toronto sponsored the Catch the Wave Cruise Conference at Sea in which twelve hundred Christians sailed on a cruise ship through the Caribbean. The cruise consisted of leaders such as the Arnotts, Bill Johnson, Heidi and Rolland Baker, R. T. Kendall

---

347 April Stephenson, Harvest Family Newsletter (Partners in Harvest), The Birth of a House of Prayer, July 2006, pp. 8-9.
348 Spread the Fire magazine, Issue 2, 2006, p. 25; also Steve Long's on-line article in Revival Magazine, called Spiritual Milestones and Large Stone Stories, accessed August 2, 2013.

and worship leaders, Georgian Banov and Lindell Cooley.

Part of the conference included docking in Montego Bay, Jamaica, for a day and conducting an evangelistic outreach. They, in partnership with twenty local churches, fed a hot chicken meal to over four thousand people at a park while providing a gospel concert. Many of those who came for a free lunch were the poor from the squatter camps that surround Montego Bay. Worship leader, Georgian Banov led a musical procession through the streets, with his fiddle. The Christian cruisers ministered to many on the downtown streets and in the park. Hundreds of people received a healing, including a blind man, two deaf people and a woman with a cancerous tumor that literally fell off her back. Many came to faith in Christ.[349] Catch the Wave cruises became an annual event for a number of years.

Although the protracted nightly renewal meetings at TACF (with the exception of Mondays) came to an end after twelve years (2006), the presence of the Lord had not lifted. Conferences continued to be well attended and God was faithful to keep touching those that came. With other renewal centres operating around the world, and with so many people and churches freshly touched and impacted over the previous decade, more and more, the focus became that of taking teams out to preach the gospel, train and equip believers and leaders, and continue imparting this fresh anointing to all who were hungry and thirsty around the world. As you'll see in the next chapter, this continues today.

In October 2007, Connie and Jeremy Sinnott travelled with TACF members Bill and Sue Dupley to Reykjavik, Iceland, to conduct a "Soaking in His Presence" weekend with about four hundred people. Connie reports:

At the end of the weekend, some unusual things started to happen. When a woman had a vision of oil and gold being poured out on her, she opened her eyes to see that there was literal oil and gold on her hands. Her son immediately gave his life to the Lord. Gold dust and a

---

349 Ibid., p. 6; also Janice Davis, Spread the Fire magazine, Issue 4, 2006, pp. 22-23.

jewel appeared for others. A girl, who was passing by the school where they were meeting, came to see what was happening at her school and heard the message of the power of the cross and asked someone how she could become a Christian too. There were a few new Christians at the meeting who had just been radically saved and set free from drugs, [and] who were being dramatically impacted by the love of Father God for the first time. One of them brought a girlfriend who gave her life to the Lord that day.

The day after the conference ended, one of the ex-drug addicts and six Bible School students who had been at the weekend conference, stopped in at the same school to see if God's presence was still in the place. As they walked into the cafeteria, the ex-drug addict boldly shouted out his testimony of how God had radically saved him, and when he asked if anyone wanted to accept a God like that, thirty young people stood to their feet to accept Jesus. The same group went into schools the following couple of days with the same results. Another group of people went into a women's prison and seventeen gave their lives to the Lord. One woman who was so angry when she heard about the gold, saying she didn't believe that stuff, came back later with tears in her eyes, showing the gold covering her hands, [and] now believing.

A group of people from the conference met at their home the evening after the conference, and the glory of God landed heavily upon them. When they got up afterward, there was gold and jewels on the floor. Another group met in their home three days later and the same thing happened.

Sigga Helga Agustdottir reported that there were at least two hundred people that accepted Jesus in just the first two weeks following the conference, with more following. A new church was started over the next few months in order to nurture the new converts, which included drug addicts, prostitutes and prisoners who came to the Lord in those days.[350]

---

350 Connie Sinnott, email to author Jerry Steingard, October 10, 2013.

In 2008, after eight years as executive directors of Catch The Fire Ministries in Toronto, Duncan and Kate Smith moved to Raleigh, North Carolina to plant the first Catch The Fire church. They have also established the Catch The Fire School of Revival in Raleigh; a leadership and church planting school. Duncan and Kate are now co-vice-presidents of Catch The Fire World (along with Steve and Sandra Long), directors of Catch The Fire USA, pastors of Catch The Fire Raleigh and revivalists who love to carry the love, power and presence of the Father to the nations of the world. [351]

Catch The Fire in India

On the day of the Mumbai bombing, November 26, 2008, when Pakistani terrorists converged on Taj Mahal hotel, about one hundred and thirty Christians from around the world also converged on Mumbai, joining many of the Catch The Fire staff from Toronto who were going to minister the love of God to the people there. The terrorists attacked about ten places within the city. The Catch The Fire team were going out from Mumbai to ten of the largest cities all around India to minister and lead International Leaders Schools (ILSOMs) simultaneously.

Approximately two hundred pastors and leaders and their spouses came to each of these ten schools. The transformation that took place in people's lives that week was truly amazing, as people's hearts were so healed up in the Father's love and people came into new levels of freedom and empowering.

At the end of the school that Connie and Jeremy Sinnott were leading in Nagpur, a city in the middle of India, three of the pastors got on the train to go home. They stopped at the station where one of the pastors lived and a young blind beggar got on the train. One of the pastors, full of the Holy Spirit from the time spent at the ILSOM, boldly asked the young man if he wanted to see. He prayed for the man in the name of Jesus, and that young man was able to see. It started a revival at the train station, as everyone there knew this young man. When they took him

---

351 Catch The Fire website: http://www.catchthefire.com/media/profiles/duncan-kate-smith

to his home it began a revival in his neighbourhood. That young man went on to pray for many others, and everyone he prayed for was getting healed. He became so on fire for God that after a couple of months he said he wanted to be a full time evangelist, and everywhere he went, revival was breaking out.[352]

Other Outpourings of the Spirit

The Lakeland, Florida, healing revival broke out at Ignited Church,[353] pastored by Stephen Strader, on April 2, 2008, with Canadian evangelist Todd Bentley of Fresh Fire Ministries.

Todd Bentley had grown up on the west coast of British Columbia, being raised by his mother. Prior to his radical conversion to Christ at the age of eighteen, Todd had been an alcoholic, drug addict and in trouble with the law. But soon after gobbling up the Word and being discipled, this young man, in his late twenties and early thirties, became "a sign and a wonder" in terms of becoming a Holy Spirit-empowered healing evangelist travelling throughout North America, Africa, India and other nations of the world. One time, while ministering at TACF in 2007, Todd had those in the meeting get out their cell phones and call friends and family members who needed a healing, resulting in a rash of instantaneous healings.

Todd Bentley was originally invited to conduct five days of meetings in Lakeland but it was decided to extend them since God was moving powerfully to heal and save people and the crowd was growing larger. The daily meetings would continue for over six months. With GOD TV soon featuring the nightly healing revival meetings, the outpouring soon became well-known in the Christian community worldwide. After meeting in increasingly larger venues, a large tent was rented to accommodate the large crowds. By June 30, it was estimated that over four hundred thousand people had attended from over one hundred nations of the world.

---

352 Connie Sinnott, email to author Jerry Steingard, October 26, 2013.
353 Ignited Church was an offshoot of Carpenter's Home Church, pastored by Stephen Strader's father, Karl Strader, which was well-known for the "laughing revival" that broke out when Rodney Howard-Browne conducted sixteen weeks of revival meetings there in 1993.

During the last week of June, a number of apostolic fathers and mothers came to pray and show support for Todd Bentley and this move of God. Todd began taking the healing revival on the road to a few other cities. Some of his ministry team was also taking the fire of healing and evangelism to other locations. Partners in Harvest pastor, Trevor Baker, had a Fresh Fire ministry evangelist come to conduct meetings at his Revival Fires Apostolic Resource Centre in Dudley, England. The Toronto church also had several Fresh Fire team members conduct healing meetings in July of 2008.

But by August 11, 2008, Todd Bentley and the Fresh Fire Ministries team were finished leading the meetings. However, back at the Ignited Church, the revival meetings continued until October 12.

Revivals always generate controversy and this outpouring certainly had its share. Todd's tattoos, body piercings, t-shirts and unorthodox ministry style all added to the offence taken by many in the religious community. At times, Todd would yell "Bam" when he prayed for someone and, on rare occasion, would be quite forceful in handling and praying for people (not unlike Smith Wigglesworth). But the real clincher for the critics of this move was when word got out that Todd Bentley's marriage was in grave trouble.

After leaving the revival meetings in August, he separated from his wife, Shonnah, and resigned from the board of Fresh Fire Ministries. The board announced that Todd was having an unhealthy emotional relationship with a woman staff member and needed to refrain from public ministry for a season and receive counsel. Bill Johnson, Jack Deere and Rick Joyner, sought to bring spiritual restoration to Todd's family. On March 9, 2009, Rick Joyner announced that Bentley had re-married.

This further piece of news brought considerable devastation and disillusionment to many in the body of Christ. Many of us had high hopes for this healing revival to ripple out around the world and be long-lasting.

Rick Joyner felt led of the Lord, at the risk of his own reputation, to help bring firm but loving discipline and restoration to Todd Bentley and his new wife Jessa. Sometime in 2010, Rick Joyner partially released Todd back into ministry, but only within his Morningstar church. Eventually Todd was given the green light to minister without restriction. In April 2013, a revival of healing and miracles broke out in the meetings conducted by Todd Bentley in Durban, South Africa, with approximately three thousand coming to faith in Christ the first week.[354]

During this same time period in 2008, another outpouring of the Holy Spirit fell at Rick Joyner's Heritage International Ministries in South Carolina. This sovereign move of God was called "Holy Spirit Breakout". Video highlights can be viewed on YouTube.[355]

Nathan Morris, Bay Revival

On July 23, 2010, the last night of the Open the Heavens Conference, hosted by pastor John Kilpatrick and the Church of His Presence, in Daphne, Alabama, a fresh visitation of God was unleashed. The young British evangelist, Nathan Morris, was preaching and ministering that night. Many miracles and healings took place. They decided to extend the meetings at the Civic Center and the Bay outpouring continued each weekend for the next nine months. In April of 2011, John Kilpatrick and Nathan Morris felt they were to take the revival meetings on tour to various cities around the United States and they continue to do so to this day.[356]

7 Mountain Teaching

In the last half a dozen years, fresh revelation called the "7 Mountain Teaching" has gained momentum in the body of Christ. This revelation first came to Bill Bright and Loren Cunningham in 1975. Lance Wallnau, C. Peter Wagner, and Jonny Enlow have become key communicators of

---

354 John Arnott, article, Revival Magazine, August 1, 2008, http://revivalmag.com/article/lakeland-healing-revival, also: http://en.wikipedia.org/wiki/Todd_Bentley
355 http://www.youtube.com/watch?v=oLQvOyiJm-s&list=PLB5A49282FFD923C2
356 http://en.wikipedia.org/wiki/Bay_Revival, also: http://bayrevival.org/about.php, accessed August 5, 2013

this teaching, which encourages believers to go on the offensive and take the Kingdom of God into various sectors of society to see transformation. The seven spheres or mountains of influence are: government, business, religion, family, education, media, and arts and entertainment.[357]

At the Catch The Fire Pastors & Leaders' conference in January 2011, Lance Wallnau and C. Peter Wagner taught on the seven mountains of influence. Jonny Enlow has also taught on this vital revelation in Toronto. John Arnott has also encouraged pastors and leaders to draw on the resources of the La Red business network and programs that God has used tremendously, particularly in South America.[358]

Three Streams Prophecy

Patricia Bootsma, of Toronto, prophesied that the three streams of Toronto, Redding and Kansas City would converge, strengthening and increasing the move of God; Toronto with its emphasis on the Father's love, Kansas City, with its message of the soon coming Bridegroom, King Jesus, and Redding California, with its priority on the supernatural power of the Holy Spirit in extending the Kingdom of God.[359]

Outpouring at IHOP University

In Kansas City, on November 11, 2009, a fresh and sovereign outpouring of God's Holy Spirit broke out during a 9 AM class at the International House of Prayer University. Facilitated primarily by the school leaders, Wes Hall and Allen Hood, IHOP began evening revival meetings which lasted for months.

A report posted on the CBN website quotes the leaders of IHOP Kansas City as saying:

---

357 http://www.7culturalmountains.org/ (accessed December 13, 2013)
358 http://www.lared.org/principles/ (accessed December 13, 2013)
359 The Lord spoke this to Patricia circa 2008. http://revivalmag.com/article/river-rising (accessed December 11, 2013)

We recognize that the Holy Spirit is awakening our students and many others. In each of these meetings, many people are being set free from addictions, shame, depression, demonic activity, and every sort of emotional pain. We are also witnessing an increase of physical healings, as God is touching and restoring bodies inside the building, as well as healing people watching via the web stream. Moreover, we greatly rejoice as we are seeing lost souls being added to the kingdom of God during these meetings. We are receiving many testimonies and reports that this move of the Spirit is spreading to other churches and prayer rooms that are joining with us each night via the web stream.

The CBN report goes on to state:

It is being reported that college students are gathering across the country to watch the services on-line. Testimonies have poured in from such schools as Georgia Tech, Wheaton College, Asbury College and the University of California-Berkeley, where students reportedly are experiencing great joy, deep peace, and emotional and physical healing...[360]

Bill Johnson, senior pastor of Bethel in Redding, California, and his leadership team have developed a revival resource centre for the body of Christ. Through their training conferences, books and Supernatural School of Ministry, they are helping to equip believers and leaders in partnering with God to bring heaven to earth with signs and wonders.

Their weekly church staff meetings begin by hearing the testimonies of miracles of that week and they have someone who records them. They are not only seeing an increase of healings but also of creative miracles and manifestations of the glory of God, both in their gatherings as well as in the marketplace. They are even contending for their church property to become a "cancer-free zone". Bethel also gives leadership to

---

360 CBN.com website, article by Craig von Buseck, Revival Breaks out at Kansas City IHOP, http://blogs.cbn.com/ChurchWatch/archive/2009/11/25/revival-breaks-out-at-kansas-city-ihop-spreads-via-web.aspx (accessed August 8, 2013)

a network of churches, ministries and revivalists, dedicated to global, multi-generational revival, called Global Legacy.[361]

John and Carol in The Glory Cloud, Bethel

In 2011, John and Carol ministered at Bill Johnson's Bethel Church in Redding one night. As the Bethel team prayed for them, Beni Johnson remarked, "John, you've got gold on your face," Little did she know, gold was already on John's mind. I'll let John tell his story:

> As I preached that night about claiming the city for God, the Holy Spirit wouldn't let me forget about the message of 'gold'. I asked, 'Who needs a dental miracle tonight?' People were miraculously given dental crowns! God wants to deal with the simplest situation as much as he deals with the impossible. God's glimmering presence did not end there. At 11:15 p.m., when we were just about to close the meeting and move into fire tunnels, shouts erupted. 'It's the gold, it's the glory!' a person shouted.
>
> I looked up, and the ceiling became radiant. It was like tiny little fire flies, explosively flickering their shimmering light. The cloud began to thicken in our midst with more golden flecks appearing. It burst and engulfed us with golden mist. People were trying to roll in it, grasping it and bathing in the glory.
>
> 'Lord, what does this mean?' I asked. God reminded me that the Bridegroom is coming. It's time for us to press in to intimacy with God. 'We're gearing everything we're doing [in Bethel] for God's glory,' Bill Johnson said. We continued to worship God with all our hearts in the midst of the glory cloud.[362]

---

361 Global Legacy website: http://www.igloballegacy.org/ Bethel Redding website: bethelredding. com
362 John Arnott, Revival Magazine, Raining Gold, Wandering Bucks, Wedding Bliss, December 2, 2011. http://revivalmag.com/article/raining-gold-wandering-bucks-wedding-bliss

Where are the millions of people that have been saved? And where are the thousands of churches that real revival should produce? They are in Mozambique! They are in parts of the Middle-East—underground. They are in Eastern Europe, in Africa, and Brazil. They are where the church did not rise up and fight God. And God wants to give England a second chance.[363]

—Randy Clark speaking in Birmingham, England, on August 13, 2012.

---

363 Randy Clark, speaking in Birmingham, England, Revival Alliance, August 31, 2012, YouTube http://www.youtube.com/watch?v=W3Ffalvq2BA (accessed September 8, 2013). Just before the part I've quoted, Randy says, ""This has been a much more cordial welcome than the last time I spoke in Birmingham. I was met with placards and protesters outside the door of the church the last time. So this is much nicer. When people ask, 'why don't you defend yourself?' It's very difficult to defend what God is doing in the midst of the moment. History always comes out on the side of favour and honour of those who lead revival … Now, some eighteen years later, time has been on our side. And there has been a great testimony of millions of people. Even as one book that was written in England about this outpouring said, 'it came in like a lion and went out like a lamb.'"

CHAPTER 16

Where is the revival at now, after 20 years?

Many have erroneously assumed that this revival is basically over. But if you ask the Arnotts, Randy Clark, Heidi and Rolland Baker, Che Ahn or Bill Johnson if this move of God is history, they would probably give you a warm smile and begin to tell you fresh and first hand stories of scores of healings, miracles, salvations and other evidence of supernatural Kingdom advancement that would blow your socks off.

When the outpouring first began in 1994, and for several years, the world made the pilgrimage to Toronto to drink deeply of God's presence. We sometimes referred to Toronto as an "international filling station!" In 1994, other centres of revival were popping up around the world, most notably: Holy Trinity Brompton in London and Sunderland England. By 1995, revival centres were breaking out in Melbourne and Pensacola, Florida, Fort Mill, South Carolina, Seattle, Washington and Pasadena, California, and by 1996 and 1997, in Houston, Texas, Baltimore, Maryland, and Smithton, Missouri.

This first stage of revival was primarily the "gathering" stage ("centripetal forces"). Hungry people hear that God is moving in a fresh and powerful way and they flock to that location to receive. But within a few years, with many churches throughout the world touched and flowing in this new level of God's manifest presence and power, the second stage of revival became more prevalent. The gathered crowds dwindled in numbers and the focus became primarily on the "sending" stage; that of sending teams out ("centrifugal forces") to keep giving it away, spreading the fire, preaching the good news of the Kingdom, doing the works of Jesus and healing up and equipping leaders.

While the protracted nightly meetings have been cut to one night a week, the half a dozen major conferences still held in Toronto each year continue to be well attended and, more importantly, well attended by the precious presence of the Holy Spirit. Lives continue to be radically changed by encounters with a loving Father, and people still come who say "You know, I always meant to come back in 1994, but it's taken me this long to get here. And I am so glad I came!" In two decades, Toronto has hosted well over one hundred major conferences and the leaders have ministered in hundreds, if not thousands, of conferences around the world, and they continue to do so every day.

Some mistakenly conclude that when the crowds subside in a revival centre location, the revival must have petered out. Again, I love John Arnott's delightful response to those folks who ask if this revival is over: "It is [over] for you, if you think it is!"[364]

The river of God's renewing presence continues to flow, leaving bodies on the floor, marriages restored, and the hearts of fathers turned back to their children. You need only look at a fresh batch of handsome 18-35 year olds at one of the Catch The Fire College locations to see the ongoing, radical work of God, that is still not as widespread in Christendom as we would love to see it. When the first French-language School of Ministry opened in Montreal in 2013, many students came from France and said that there was simply no teaching like this anywhere back home.

The teaching and revelation continues to grow. In the last twenty years, the three pots of cream have continued to be DNA-level messages. Added to these are an ever greater understanding of the importance of intimacy with God, the life-changing dynamic of oneness with Christ, and the importance of a worshipful lifestyle.

John and Carol Arnott authored a book in 2013 titled *The Invitation*,[365] which is a call to cultivate a life of intimacy, especially in view of the

---

364 John Arnott, interview, June 14, 2013; Jeremy Sinnott, Australia, November 5, 2012.
365 John and Carol Arnott, The Invitation, Catch The Fire Books, 2013.

approaching end-times. Rather than a fear-laden eschatology study (though there is useful study contain within), John and Carol make the effective plea that we not end up like the foolish virgins, who fail to cultivate a sense of longing for their soon-returning Bridegroom.

In *The Invitation*, Carol also introduces us to the "10 Minute Worship Revolution".

Following much serious battle with digestive difficulties that robbed her of the sense of God's closeness, Carol began to find healing after adopting a radical practice of worshiping God literally every 10 minutes, with the help of a simple gym timer. Inspired by the testimony of a German medical doctor, Dr Arne Elsen, this profound expression of surrendering our time undo the Lord has sparked a movement and is drawing people into continued intimacy, physical healing, and more.[366]

For many, the water table of the Spirit is much higher than prior to 1994. Toronto is not the only revival gig in town anymore, and for that we praise God! Many in the body of Christ have simply been ruined for anything less than the precious manifest presence of the Lord in their lives and in their churches.

Millions of Christians and tens of thousands of churches have had fresh and powerful encounters with the Living God at some point during these twenty years of God's visitation. They can't go back to "business as usual". They have tasted of a greater level and dimension of the Kingdom of God and are ruined for anything less.

Sadly, there have been those who did not highly cherish God's presence and jealously guard it. They did not persist in soaking in His sweet presence and cultivating intimacy in the secret place nor did they continue to give away what the Lord had given them. As a result, there are those who would have taken ten massive spiritual steps forward in the revival but, over time, have taken a few steps back—not intentionally, but by default. Life can get busy; with many distractions that can keep you from doing the one thing that Mary did, sitting at the feet of Jesus in intimate communion.

---

366 Ibid, and revivalmag.com/article/battle-intimacy-and-worship-revolution (accessed December 11, 2013)

We must not forget that we are in a spiritual war. The thief comes to kill, steal and destroy. He has distracted, dis-heartened, seduced, wounded and offended many hearts. Some have not learned to overcome in adversity and have become bitter rather than better. So, regarding this precious and sacred outpouring of God's amazing grace and refreshing presence, some have taken it for granted, saying, "Been there, done that and got the t-shirt." They have "gone back to business as usual," although they may have nostalgic feelings, fond and faint memories of God touching and blessing them during the "glory days" of the mid-1990s. Some have even questioned whether their experiences were real and valid.

However, the great news is that, like a sponge that dries out over time, it can easily be reversed and begin to get saturated again. God and His sweet manifest presence have not left the planet. It is only ever we who have gradually distanced ourselves. James 4:8 invites us to "Come near to God and He will come near to you." The question is: How hungry and desperate are we for more of Him? Seek Him in the secret place. Go get prayer again from others who are continuing to flow in the river.

Global Impact of the Toronto Outpouring,
By 2014

Let us now take an overview of the current, ongoing fruit of this revival as it has impacted the church and the world at large.

Significant Fruit: Conversions

Randy claims there has been significant fruit of conversions from the outpouring. [367] Talking in 2013, he gives examples of just three ministries, namely Henry Madava in Kiev, Ukraine, Leif Hetland among Muslims in the Middle East and particularly in Pakistan, and

---

367 In interviewing Randy Clark at the 20th Catch The Fire Conference in Toronto on September 26, 2013,

Iris Ministries with Heidi and Rolland Baker throughout Africa, each of which has seen over one million converts.

Iris ministries, which has established mission bases, orphanages, Bible Schools, feeding programs and churches in various African countries, has also given particular attention, in recent years, to the Makua people group, in the north of Mozambique. This group consists of about four million people and has been considered by musicologists to be an "unreached and unreachable" people group. According to Rolland's article on the Iris website, with significant assistance from missionaries and nationals, approximately two thousand churches have been planted among this people group in the last decade.[368]

Leif Hetland – the Reinhard Bonnke of the Islamic Nations

In his Spread the Fire article, *God is Still Using Little Old Me*, Randy Clark shared how amazed he has been that God has caused this outpouring to impact so many people, including leaders like Rolland and Heidi Baker, who then have gone forth to truly shake nations. Randy also talks about Leif Hetland, whose life and ministry has been radically impacted.

Randy says, "I met him in Norway where he was to be my interpreter. At a meeting in the basement of a small missions church, with about thirty other pastors, I found myself walking over to Leif and prophesying, 'God is going to make you a bulldozer among the unreached people groups, especially the Muslim nations.' The power of God knocked him down where he experienced a mighty impartation of the Holy Spirit. That was around 1995."

"Since then Leif has become a mighty evangelist in the Islamic nations, especially Pakistan. My friend, Jack Taylor, told me he is to the Islamic nations what Reinhard Bonnke has become to Africa. Leif has led hundreds of thousands of Muslims to the Lord since that impartation. He is no longer pastoring a small Baptist church, but is leading a powerful international ministry to the Islamic nations."[369]

---

368 Rolland Baker, Iris website http://www.irisglobal.org/pemba-center-village-of-joy/team, (accessed July 6, 2013)
369 Randy Clark, God is Still Using Little Old Me, Spread the Fire, Issue 1 – 2004, pp. 8-10.

The number of ministries birthed as a result of this move of God are hard to estimate, but we have selected a few to focus on.

Significant Fruit: Restoration of the Apostolic and Prophetic Ministries

Many new and credible prophetic voices and apostolic fathers and mothers have been raised up to mentor, equip and empower new believers, take teams to the nations, and establish new apostolic networks for coming Kingdom advancement and harvest ingathering.

Bill Johnson's Bethel Church and School of Supernatural Ministry in Redding, California, continues to grow, mature and expand in its breadth and depth of influence. They are seeking to promote a "culture of revival" and "culture of honour" as well as develop a "Global Legacy" network for equipping and encouraging revival around the world. Prophetic, apostolic and fatherly wisdom and insight flow out of Bill Johnson and a number of their leaders (such as Kris Vallotton and Danny Silk), both in speech and prolific writing, and the larger Church is much richer for it.

Wesley and Stacey Campbell's New Life Church in Kelowna, BC, has become an apostolic resource centre with over one thousand people in regular attendance. In 1995 "Revival Now!" Ministries was birthed and the Campbells began to minister at about fifty conferences a year. Over the years, they have ministered in over sixty nations. In the late 1990s, Wes and Stacey added prayer and solemn assemblies to the revival focus. They launched Praying the Bible International and also joined Lou Engle and Mike Bickle as International directors of "The Call". In addition, they have developed a global missions component of mercy and social justice ministry to widows, orphans, at risk children and refugees. This ministry is called "Be a Hero". And most recently, they have become overseers of Eaglesnest School of Supernatural Ministry in Kelowna—an affiliate of the Bethel School in Redding.[370]

---

370 Revival Magazine, http://revivalmag.com/author/stacey-campbell

Steve and Christina Stewart, former pastors of the Cambridge Vineyard, were both blasted by the power of God in 1994. Later they would plant a Vineyard church in Vancouver as well as oversee the establishment of thirty Healing Rooms in communities throughout Canada. In 2005, Steve and Christina Stewart founded Impact Nations International Ministries, which networks with organizations to "save lives" spiritually, socially, physically and economically in developing nations. They have taken dozens of teams on "journeys of compassion" to various nations to help bring Kingdom transformation. They seek to address needs with such resources as clean water, micro businesses, medical assistance, food and nutrition as well as bring the gospel of the Kingdom with signs and wonders following.[371]

Patricia King (Pat Cocking) had been President of Christian Services Association in Mission, B. C., and associated with Mary Audrey Raycroft. Patricia was one of the first Canadian Christian leaders to come to the renewal in Toronto and soon the fresh reviving power of God took her ministry to a whole new level.[372] Patricia is presently based out of Phoenix, Arizona. Her ministry, called Extreme Prophetic, is a multi-faceted glory or "presence-based" ministry involving TV and media, a publishing arm, conferences, prophetic evangelism on the streets and mercy/justice ministry to kids trapped in the sex trade in South-East Asia.

Randy Clark, since that life-changing night in Toronto, on January 20 1994, has travelled to over forty-two nations to preach the gospel, heal the sick, deliver the oppressed, equip the saints, and impart the anointing of the Spirit for a multiplication of ministry. Brazil has been a hot spot where he has seen tens of thousands of healings and miracles. Randy has taken numerous teams of young people on mission trips and seen them equipped, mobilized and released into power ministries for Kingdom advancement.[373]

---

371 Steve and Christina Stewart, Impact Nations, impactnations.com.
372 Spread the Fire, March/April, 1995, Daina Doucet & Gail Reid, pp. 16-17.
373 Global Awakening website, (accessed May 30, 2013)

John and Carol Arnott: Catch The Fire and Partners in Harvest

The family of churches called Partners in Harvest, coordinated originally by Fred and Sharon Wright but, since 2009, by Dan and Gwen Slade, consists of about six hundred churches and ministries worldwide, with one hundred and fifty of those considered as "Friends in Harvest". Three ministries, in Eastern Europe, South America and Africa, have grown into their own movements but are still part of the PIH family.

There are over thirty churches in the Ukraine. Vania and Sadi Rorato oversee about thirty churches in Brazil, four in Uruguay and one in Ecuador. And, although Iris Ministries, led by Rolland and Heidi Baker of Mozambique, Africa, is counted as only one PIH church, it is actually comprised of well over ten thousand churches that have been planted over the last fifteen years throughout Africa and beyond.

The first Catch The Fire church to be planted outside of Toronto was in Raleigh, North Carolina. It was founded by Catch The Fire World Co-Vice Presidents, Duncan and Kate Smith. They have also founded the Catch The Fire School of Revival in Raleigh, which is a radical, supernatural leadership and church planting school.[374]

Duncan, a missionaries' kid, was raised in Africa. He feels most at home preaching the gospel with signs and wonders following, and ministering the Father's love and revival fire in third world countries, particularly Niger, in Africa.

Duncan Smith has also traveled and ministered with Terje Liverod, from Norway. Terje does "Extreme Missions", ministering to Muslims in unreached areas of Africa, where the name of Jesus has never been heard before. Duncan and Terje will go into these villages and many will turn to Jesus after a lame person is healed or a blind person receives their sight. Terje now hosts a Catch The Fire School of Ministry at his church in Tonsberg, Norway. These students have an opportunity to go on extreme missions as part of their training.[375]

---

374 Duncan and Kate Smith, Catch The Fire website, http://www.catchthefire.com/churches/raleigh-usa
375 Connie Sinnott, email to author Jerry Steingard, October, 26, 2013.

Other Catch The Fire churches have been started in:

London, England, with Stuart and Chloe Glassborow
Oslo, Norway, with Jostein and Reidun Hagan
Montreal, Quebec, with Gerry and Marcia Plunkett
Houston, Texas, with Buck and Anna Eaton
Novo Hamburgo, Brazil, with Anderson and Miriam Lima
Sydney, Australia, with Daniel and Robyn Lambert
Halifax, Nova Scotia, with Evan and Shawna Maxwell, along with
Elaine and Charlie Passey
Calgary, Alberta, with Darrin and Daphne Clark

These Catch The Fire churches all come under the Partners in Harvest umbrella.[376]

There are a growing number of Catch The Fire offices and teams worldwide that are being raised up to teach their schools within their own nations and also into the mission fields near them, resulting in multiplied fruit for the Kingdom of God.

Gerry and Marcy Plunkett pastor Catch The Fire Montreal and oversee the establishment of a French-language School of Ministry in 2013.

Chloe and Stuart Glassborow, who are the pastors at Catch The Fire London, have regional coordinators and teams all over the UK and minister particularly into Kenya.

John and Pauline Arnott (no relation) from Melbourne, Australia, together with Nicola Tancock, have a growing number of team members who assist them in numerous schools within Australia, as well as taking the one week Leaders School of Ministry (ILSOMs) into the mission fields around them of India, Philippines, Papua New Guinea, Fiji and Indonesia.

Werner and Babette Jöchle in Switzerland, head up the Catch The Fire Central Europe office, and their ministry particularly into Germany has been growing greatly in the past couple of years.

---

376 Catch The Fire website www.catchthefire.com

Connie and Jeremy Sinnott have been spending half of their time now in training up these team members globally and releasing them to run in the power of the Holy Spirit with the teachings of the heart values that God has been imparting through this move of God.

The Toronto School of Ministry is now called Catch The Fire College, which offers the Heart module, Advance module, Worship module and internships. Catch The Fire Colleges have also been established in Montreal, Canada, South Africa, the UK, Norway, the USA and Brazil.

Since 1995, approximately two thousand youth have gone through the training schools—an army of passionate lovers of God who have been healed up and equipped for Kingdom service. These students all received ministry for the healing of the heart, the revelation of the Father's love, and a fresh impartation of the anointing of the Spirit. Graduates have grown in the disciplines of intimacy with Jesus, passionate worship, Bible study, prayer, soaking in His presence, journaling, and learning to hear God's voice in the "secret place".

With a clearer sense of their identify and destiny in Christ, they have scattered around the globe to serve and minister with compassion and boldness as they follow the Father's initiatives, in the anointing and power of the Holy Spirit. Many have done internships in existing churches and many have gone on to plant churches.

In recent years, the school of ministry has expanded their training and equipping schools to include adults. The Toronto church has also offered adult training schools such as: the three-week Leaders Schools, held every January and July (a total of 1,200 have gone through the school) and the Father Heart Training Schools (about 300 have attended this school). As well, the Toronto leadership has conducted their one-week International Leaders School in nations around the world, equipping pastors and leaders with the tools of revival.[377]

God has not only raised up each one of these apostolic streams with their particular flavour and calling, but they have also been significantly enriched and shaped over the years by the DNA and values of John Wimber and the Vineyard movement. We honour and bless them and

---

[377] www.catchthefire.com website and email from Gordon Harris, August 21, 2013.

thank the Lord for them. I commend the apostolic centres and renewal streams that I am most familiar with in North America:

Catch The Fire in Toronto (John Arnott)
Morningstar Ministries in South Carolina (Rick Joyner)
International House of Prayer in Kansas City (Mike Bickle)
Church of the Rock in Pasadena, California (Che Ahn)
Apostolic Network of Global Awakening in Mechanicsburg, Pennsylvania (Randy Clark)
Bethel Church in Redding, California (Bill Johnson)

Significant Fruit: the Father Heart Revelation Spreads

Fresh revelation of the life-changing messages of the Father heart of God, intimacy with Jesus, learning to hear God's voice, the need for repentance and forgiveness to restore wounded hearts and the mandate of extending the Kingdom into the marketplace through equipping, empowering and mobilizing of the saints, all continue to make inroads within the body of Christ worldwide.

An example of this would be Pastor Gideon Chui. At the Partners in Harvest Conference in Toronto, on September 23 2013, Gideon Chui, the Chinese pastor from Vancouver who roared like a lion in the spring of 1994, came and shared with the Arnotts and other pastors. He wanted to thank the Toronto leadership for not shutting him down when he experienced the prophetic act of roaring. These prophetic-intercessory encounters were in reference to the Lord declaring that He was going to free the Chinese people.

Gideon also wanted to give an update of how God has been using him. Gideon Chui and David Damien, both leaders from Vancouver, met with five leaders of house church movements in China at a conference they organized in Hong Kong in 2012. These leaders represent over fifty million believers in China. They no longer want to be considered generals but fathers in a unified movement and desire to incorporate the Father's love and healing of the heart.[378]

These revelational truths, combined with the sweet and infectious anointing of the Spirit, are being imparted through people who have already received and are willing to go and minister and give it away. "Freely you have received, freely give." (Matthew 10:8) We have often heard the expression, "You only get to keep what you give away". Already the Father heart message has begun to take root in mainstream evangelical Christianity, with authors who are not necessarily aligned with this revival, such as John Eldredge and Wayne Jacobsen, writing books on the Father's love.

Significant Fruit of Friendship and Interdenominational Unity

Through all of this, new friendships have developed across denominational lines, particularly among pastors and leaders. One exciting example would be the friendship that has formed among some of the revival leaders. Six couples: John and Carol Arnott, Randy and DeAnne Clark, Bill and Beni Johnson, Rolland and Heidi Baker, Che and Sue Ahn, and Georgian and Winnie Banov have formed what is called the Revival Alliance. Aside from on-going communication and ministering together from time to time in training events, conferences and mission outreaches, they seek to set aside one week every year to vacation together and just hang out as close friends.[379]

The Next Wave

Rick Joyner had a vision in 1987 of two waves of revival coming. He is convinced that the world has been experiencing the first wave and a harvest of souls for the past two decades. This will provide more workers for the coming revival wave and harvest that is expected to be unprecedented in world history. Rick Joyner believes we are in the

---

378 John and Carol Arnott, citing Gideon Chui speaking at PIH conference at Catch The Fire Toronto, September 23, 2013.
379 Ibid.

quiet lull, in-between time with a tsunami wave of revival and harvest about to hit at any time.[380]

At the Catch The Fire 2013 Conference, celebrating the twentieth year of annual conferences in Toronto, Ken Gott, from Sunderland, England, honoured Catch The Fire with an incredible exhortation that I believe will serve well to close this chapter, and lead into the next.

You know if you ask a business, 'What is your core business?' then they will say we do a lot of things but we [have a core focus]. We just need to understand that the core business of Catch The Fire, is transforming lives. They do a lot of other stuff; training people, schools like you have heard and planting churches but the core business of this ministry is transforming lives. It is because [transforming lives] is the core business of Jesus...The nature of God is not just to give you a little touch and just get you over that little difficulty and deal with that, that problem, but it is to transform. Genesis 1: 1 it says, 'In the beginning God created the heavens and the earth and the earth was without form and void and darkness was on the face of the deep. The spirit of God was hovering over the face of the waters.'...There is always purpose in what God does and the purpose of the Holy Spirit hovering was to bring transformation of a significant kind. When we look at what was created that day, or in the space of 6 days, compared to what was before, there is no comparison. When God touches our lives that is the kind of transformation that He purposes. The same Holy Spirit was hovering again hundreds of years later, not over the face of the deep now, but over an upper room. The first time was to bring in creation, [the next time he was] hovering with purpose to birth the Church. The same Holy Spirit comes with the same transforming power and it had the same effect. These are 120 people without purpose, frightened out of their lives, but when He came and when that transformation happened, 3000 men are saved because of the boldness of [Peter's] preaching. Twenty years ago the same Holy Spirit hovered over a

---

380 Rick Joyner, November 22, 2011, http://www.morningstartv.com/featured-video-week/harvest-revival-tsunami-imminent

Vineyard church [in Toronto]. The same Holy Spirit with the same transforming effect; with the same purpose. This time to release and transform millions and millions and millions of lives all over the world! What God did that day is already historic; has already been chronicled in history. The effect at creation was transformation; the effect in the second chapter of Acts was transformation; and the effect on the 20th of January 1994 was transformation. And that transformation of people's lives has gone on now for nearly 20 years! All over the world! I am one of them! ...I want to tell you that it is going on and on and on. It is not stopping here! The glory of the latter house will be greater than the glory of the former. What we have seen in the last 20 years, I am willing to believe will pale in comparison to the next 20 years![381]

---

381 Ken Gott at Catch The Fire Conference 2013, Session G. http://www.youtube.com/watch?v=skd8b7wbjCo (accessed December 11, 2013)

CHAPTER 17

Where's the River Going?

"... so where the river flows everything will live." —Ezekiel 47:9

"Perhaps what we have experienced at Airport Vineyard is phase one of something that's even bigger."[382] —John Arnott, 1994

"This visitation of the Holy Spirit has brought incredible and wonderful changes to my life, my family, Harvest Rock Church and, indeed, throughout the world... This is only preparation for the greatest revival and the greatest ingathering of harvest in the history of the Church..."[383] —Che Ahn

I'll conclude this section about the twenty years of the Toronto Blessing with a series of prophecies given by Christian leaders and credible prophetic voices that relate to what we could anticipate in the coming days and years. I pray that as you read them, weigh them and pray into them, that they would stir faith in your heart and inspire your mind and imagination to believe and contend for so much more of God's Kingdom to come to earth as it is in heaven.

Che Ahn

I am firmly convinced that the revival toward which we are headed will dwarf anything in recent memory or the history books! This visitation of the Holy Spirit (in Toronto) has brought incredible

---

382 John Arnott, quoted by Doug Koop, Christian Week, December 13, 1994, p. 20.
383 Che Ahn, Into the Fire, Renew, 1998, p. 23.

and wonderful changes to my life, my family, Harvest Rock Church and, indeed, throughout the world… This is only preparation for the greatest revival and the greatest ingathering of harvest in the history of the Church It is only appropriate He would begin by addressing the foundations of our closest relationships! For when the harvest comes, in many ways we will be 're-parenting' scores of new converts. We will be 'reproducing' after our own kind. If our marriages and family lives are suffering, what kind of example and impact will we have on the harvest?

The Church in America is not yet ready to handle the harvest or His holy and glorious presence when the fullness of revival comes. That is why He is calling us as His Church to be holy as He is holy, and to go ever deeper. For us to be truly holy, we must have true repentance. True repentance comes when we comprehend the root sins in our lives. In this renewal, the Holy Spirit is doing just that.[384]

R. T. Kendall, 1998

I believe that we are in the embryonic phase of the greatest work of the Holy Spirit in this century—and it wouldn't surprise me if it turns out to be the greatest movement since the early Church. It is what I've looked forward to all my life, and it is only the beginning. In fact, what we've experienced up to now is what Paul Cain calls the 'appetizer', and the main course is at hand.[385]

Fred and Sharon Wright, 2007

In his excellent book, *The World's Greatest Revivals*,[386] Fred Wright makes clear his belief that the Toronto Blessing will be followed soon after (20-40 years from the 1994 high-water mark) by another "tsunami-wave" revival, characterized by the re-discovered revelatory truths of the Bride & Bridegroom paradigm. He argues that this sequence allows

---

384 Ibid., p. 150.
385 R. T. Kendall, Foreword to the book In Search of Revival, Stuart Bell, Destiny Image, 1998, p. vii.
386 Fred Wright, The World's Greatest Revivals, Destiny Image, 2007.

us to interpret "because He [the Father] first loved us" we can now reciprocate that love to our Bridegroom.

John Crowder, 2009

The greatest harvest the earth has ever seen is just at hand. And it will largely come through a radical movement of love-crazed, end-times martyrs, whose ecstatic lives will usher in the Last Great Awakening... Forerunners have seen what is on the horizon... There are dispensations of God throughout the course of time when the hand of the Almighty moves with untold zeal and fury to showcase His glory to the nations of the earth... These were times of revolution... This last-day revival will be like every preceding great awakening combined, super-sized and coupled together with miracles never before seen by the human eye.[387]

John Arnott, 2013

We kept going, one more day and here we are twenty years on. It has its ebbs and flows. It's not as intense as in the early days when people were bouncing in chairs, thrown to the floor, roaring. I love it when Holy Spirit comes in and highjacks the meeting! One of my fears was 'O God, please don't let this end. We are so desperately in need of this. Please, Lord, one more day, one more day.'

I was reading John 14, where it says, 'I'll send you another Comforter and He will be with you forever.' It jumped off the page. This dynamic presence is going to be with us forever. 'Lord, we get to keep this?' and He spoke back 'Yes, you get to keep this'. So I started to say, 'This is a revival that will never end.' It goes until Jesus comes. There's a faith element and a sovereign element in there certainly.

I've been expecting another wave to come for a long time. It hasn't come yet but I really think it's coming. What has happened is that the whole world has been seeded with hundreds of thousands of people who know what this is now... So, when God blows on it all again, a

---

387 John Crowder, The Ecstasy of Loving God, Destiny Image 2009, pp. 293, 314, 316.

lot of people are going to know what it is and what to do...

I asked the Lord, 'What is this? What are you doing?' Instead of explaining Himself, He just said, 'I am going easy on you now so you won't be totally shocked or undone when the real power shows up.' It's the message of the Father's love. It's about falling in love with Him and being rooted and grounded in love; otherwise you'll use Him to build your ministry.

John talks about David Minor's prophecy from 1987 about two winds. The first wind would be a wind of holiness unto the Lord that would blow out pride and jealousy. The second wind would be a wind of the Kingdom of God, bringing the fear of the Lord, power, signs and wonders, and a great harvest of souls. John does not view the first wind of holiness to mean "straight-jacket good behavior, but transformation of the heart." He also sees in this prophecy a warning that "if you don't get on board with the first wind, you will not get on board with the second. If the first scared you, the second will scare you to death."

When asked for his thoughts regarding the historical tendency of the leaders of the previous revival to be the first to criticize the next wave of revival, John replied, "Help me Jesus! When they exceed my threshold, Lord, give me grace to bless it and love it anyways. I just want them to hold on to orthodoxy, sound doctrine, the cross and the gospel."[388]

Prophetic Voices

Bob Jones, 1984

In April 1984 The Lord told Bob Jones that in ten years there would be the first of three waves of revival. The first wave would be characterized by new wine, which would release refreshment and joy and produce humility in the body of Christ. In the future, a wave of fire (conviction, passion, holiness, evangelism, signs and wonders) would come, followed

---

388 John Arnott, interview in Toronto, June 14, 2013, Bruce Mason & Jerry Steingard.

by a wave of wind (significant increase of miracles and angelic activity), leading ultimately to the end of this age and the return of Christ. Each wave would build on the last wave, not replace it. And these three waves would come in reverse order of the outpouring described in Acts 2, on the day of Pentecost, which was: wind, fire, and wine.

The Lord showed Bob Jones that this first wave of wine would not only bring refreshment and healing of hearts, but that it would be used by the Lord to offend the mind to reveal the heart. God would be testing hearts. He would be seeking hungry and humble hearts. Many people would be offended by the first wave of new wine and miss out and perhaps find it very difficult to enter into the later waves of fire and wind.[389]

Paul Cain, 1996
Paul Cain delivered a prophetic word to John and Carol Arnott on September 14, 1996. A portion of that word is as follows:

> The Lord has initiated the Toronto Blessing, not man… He has refreshed His people in order to prepare them for the next level of visitation… We are now at the place of the Lord's threshing floor… The Toronto Blessing has gathered the wheat and chaff during this visitation… God is preparing the wheat to go on to the next level… Others (the chaff) will be blown away by the next wind, or fall… You are to rise and stand to the occasion… You are to lead the people on to the next level, from appetizer to the main course… The days ahead should be employed for preparation for the next thing God will do.[390]

---

389 Word of Bob Jones given to Mike Bickle in 1984, can be heard or read on Mike's website, Kansas City prophetic history, Joseph's dungeon: the power of the Spirit and humility, May 4, 2013. http://mikebickle.org/resources/resource/1645?return_url=http%3A%2F%2Fmikebickle.org%2Fresources%2Fseries%2F38 (accessed Aug. 20, 2013).
390 Paul Cain's prophetic word, From Appetizer to Main Course, Spread the Fire magazine, December 1996, p. 5.

Marc Dupont, 2001

While Marc Dupont was with Rolland and Heidi Baker in Mozambique in 2001, the heavy presence of the Lord came upon them and Marc received this weighty word, The Coming Release of the Glory of God:

> The Lord is saying in these days that there is coming a release of the glory of God, first to His leaders and then to His church because, like Moses, we need to be consumed by the glory of God, to soar from glory to glory.
>
> His glory is coming to the nations. The Lord says that His holiness is going to fall... The Lord is looking for those men and women who will bend the knee and toss down their crowns of authority and gifting, for those who will be caught up in the holiness of God. We are going to have a message of the joy of the Lord, but beyond that we're going to have a message of the holiness and consuming fire of God. Just as the seraphim could take the fire of God and touch the lips of messengers like Isaiah, so these leaders who embrace the holiness of God are going to be carriers of the fire of God. In this consuming holiness of God, there will be miracles, signs and wonders.

> THE BRIDE WILL PLUCK THE FRUIT OF THE NATIONS.
> It will be easy to pluck the fruit from the tree because on either side of this River there will be trees. The River comes from the throne of God. The trees will be abundant in fruit and there will be different types of fruit for every season. There will be fruit of repentance, signs and wonders and radical evangelism. Do not disbelieve. His glory is coming to the cities of the nations. His glory is coming to the nations. These nations will be given as an inheritance to His Son.
>
> The Lord says, I have been preparing this from before the creation of the world. I have destined the bride to rise up, to dance in the harvest, to run in strength and glory, in wholeness and purity. The bride will rise up and work the harvest. Did I not say that during the times of wars and rumours of wars, earthquakes, famines and droughts, do not be deceived, do not be afraid and do not let your hearts grow cold?

The gospel shall be preached to all nations and all people. At such a time as this I say to you, do not let your hearts go cold. Let your heart explode with my love... Let your hearts be consumed by the person of my Son Jesus.

The fire that fell at Pentecost will grow and consume the whole world. Do not be afraid. My perfect love is going to chase out every part of fear in your hearts. Boldness will be upon you to tread upon the serpent, to tie up the lions, to go against the false lions that roar... The true Lion of the tribe of Judah is on the prowl. He is going against the false gods. Even as the Lion of the tribe of Judah overthrew in the 80's and 90's the false god of atheism called Communism, so now the Lion of the tribe of Judah is going against the false god of Islam. It will fall and it will fall very rapidly.

DAYS OF ACCELERATION

These days are days of acceleration. There used to be gaps of hundreds of years between revivals, then decades between revivals but now there will be a few years between revivals. This second wave is now upon you and the false god of Islam is going to fall very quickly. The harvest is coming and the bride is being raised up, prepared, matured and made holy. The grand, great, glorious and fragrant bride with the perfume of the oil of the Holy Spirit that is purified by the fire of the Holy Spirit, that is strengthened by the power of the Holy Spirit. This bride is being raised up because My Son is coming back very quickly. When you look at the globe and see the complexities of problems, finances and politics, wars and rumours of wars, deceit and corruption, understand that this globe will get very small in my hands, and it will be getting smaller and smaller. The fire that fell at Pentecost will fall on small meetings but then it will grow and will consume the whole world.

THOSE WHOM GOD WILL USE

I'm not looking to conferences or to conference speakers. I'm not looking to large programs or to sleek presentations, to the clever workings of man. I'm not looking to strategies that come out of church

1995 - EARLY MEETINGS IN 272 ATTWELL DRIVE, STILL MEETING
HERE TO THIS DAY

1995 - GUY CHEVRAU CELEBRATES 150,000 COPIES SOLD ON THE
OUTPOURING'S SECOND ANNIVERSARY

board meetings. I'm looking for men and women of fire from the least of them, from the 4 and 5 year-olds to 80 year-olds. There is a fresh fire, a fresh wind of the Spirit coming, and I'm going to use those from the least of them to the greatest of them. If they will humble themselves and draw near as Moses said, 'I must turn aside and gaze upon this marvel,' I will re-commission them, and I will send them out. I will anoint them and re-anoint them.'It's time to step into the holiness of realized destiny.'

It will not be a laborious thing—my presence will go with them, my presence will give them rest. I say to you, for such a time as this, for such a day, an hour and a moment as this I have created you. You have a destiny upon you to whistle for the nations, not to strive for the nations, but my Spirit is whistling for the nations. The nations shall come and you shall not be consumed by the complex problems of this world, by financial problems or strategies or politics. But you shall go with the freedom and the power of abundance. I came that you might have abundance and that you might give that abundance away with the abundance of my Holy Spirit. I have called you, and you are a people of destiny... It is time to step into the holiness of realized destiny. Holy, Holy, Holy am I, and I'm putting a burning message within you that will shake the religious beliefs of people, that will transcend the religious beliefs of Muslims, of Buddhists, of materialists, of agnostics. It will shatter their pre-conceived ideas and their vain philosophies...

WHERE THE RIVER WILL FLOW

The Lord says that just as the fire of Toronto went to the ends of the earth, and it went to Mozambique, so the fire of Mozambique is coming back to Toronto and it's going back again to the ends of the earth.

Did I not say to you a decade ago that I would do things in Toronto that have never been experienced, revival that will bring the nations to Toronto? But now I say to you, this fire that was the River of refreshment will be a River of fire. It will go, just as it has gone, with joy to the ends of the earth. It has gone from one of the great financial centers to one of the poorest places on the face of the earth and come back. Now it will go out again.

The fires of God are upon the world. Do not say that this world is complex, that this world is big. It is just a small globe in My hands and I am breathing again. The second stage, the new form has come but now the winds of the Spirit are coming and this body will have life, life like never before.

THE PREVAILING SPIRIT OF THE BRIDE

Did I not speak to you about the sword of the Spirit that will be a prevailing sword? I am giving you a prevailing spirit if you will walk in humility before me. If you will be desperate for me, if in the secret places you will be humble before Me, I will raise up a bride with humble desperation for her lover. You will not be confounded by pride, nor wrapped up in religious thoughts or religious programs, but if you will be humble before me in the secret places, I will give you the treasures of the secret places. Everywhere you will go, the treasure will be life and abundance. I do not ask for what you cannot give Me; I do not ask for things that you cannot do. I only ask for your hunger and humility. 'Where there is an increase in God's presence there is an increase of provision.'

I can see the sword of the Lord with a wide double-edged blade. To wield it, the sword requires both hands on the handle. I can see the handle. It's pure, solid gold. The Lord says that whoever holds on to this sword must be pure in heart and lay down his life. The tip of the blade and the edge of the blade can sever evil, but for the people who handle this sword, it will take their whole beings, their hearts and souls. It will take both hands. The Lord says the point of contact is for war. The sword can touch, sever and kill evil, but the handle is pure gold. It is the glory of the holiness of God that can only be handled by purity.

GLORY ON THE MEEK AND INSIGNIFICANT

All the problems in the world are going to shrink in the revelation of the glory of God. When there is an increase in God's presence, there is an increase of provision.

The Lord says that He had chosen this little, insignificant church

1994 - THE ORIGINAL BUILDING ON DIXIE ROAD, AT THE EN[...] RUNWAY

1995 - EARLY MEETINGS IN 272 ATTWELL DRIVE, STILL MEETING HERE TO THIS DAY

1994 - THE ORIGINAL BUILDING ON DIXIE ROAD, AT THE END OF THE
RUNWAY

1995 - EARLY MEETINGS IN 272 ATTWELL DRIVE, STILL MEETING
HERE TO THIS DAY

1995 - EARLY MEETINGS IN 272 ATTWELL DRIVE, STILL MEETING HERE TO THIS DAY

1995 - GUY CHEVRAU CELEBRATES 150,000 COPIES SOLD ON THE OUTPOURING'S SECOND ANNIVERSARY

1996 - JOHN ARNOTT BEING INTERVIEWED ON 100 HUNTLEY STREET

1996 - JOHN AND CAROL ARNOTT WITH HEIDI AND ROLLAND BAKER

1996 - A VIBRANT TIME OF WORSHIP AT THE NIGHTLY MEETINGS

1997 - FRED WRIGHT AND CAROL ARNOTT PRAYING 'ON THE LINES'

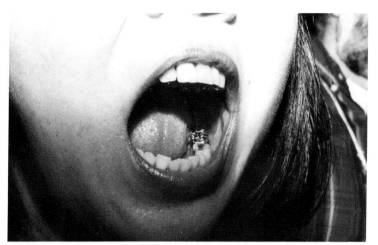

1996 - ONE OF THE EARLY INSTANCES OF THE 'GOLD TEETH'
PHENOMENON

1996 - ONE OF THE EARLY INSTANCES OF THE 'GOLD TEETH'
PHENOMENON

1997 - JEREMY SINNOTT

1997 - MINISTRY TEAM VOLUNTEERS

1998 - THE ENTIRE MINISTRY'S STAFF TEAM

1998 - MINISTRY TIME

1999 - PEOPLE GATHERED IN WORSHIP

2000 - THE FIRST KIDS CAMP AT HARVEST RETREAT CENTRE

2001 - JOHN AND CAROL ARNOTT AT A CONFERENCE

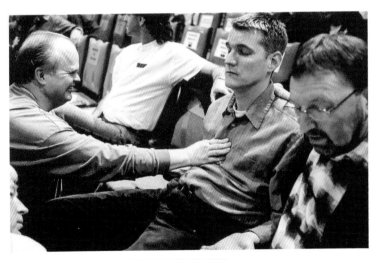

2002 - DUNCAN SMITH RECEIVING PRAYER

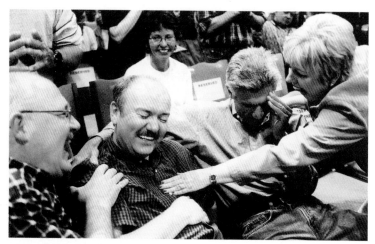

2002 - KEN GOTT RECIEVING PRAYER

2004 - WORSHIP

2004 - JOHN AND CAROL ARNOTT

2004 - RANDY CLARK AND DUNCAN SMITH

2007 - CHESTER AND BETSY KYLSTRA ON STAGE WITH JOHN ARNOTT

2013 - MARC DUPONT PRAYING FOR JOHN AND CAROL ARNOTT

2009 - WORSHIP AT THE FRESHWIND YOUTH CONFERENCE

2013 - WORSHIP AT THE PASTORS & LEADERS CONFERENCE

2013 - JOHN ARNOTT PREACHING AT THE PASTORS AND LEADERS CONFERENCE

2013 - DUNCAN SMITH RECEIVING PRAYER FROM CAROL ARNOTT

2013 - RT KENDALL PREACHING AT THE PASTORS AND LEADERS
CONFERENCE

2013 - STEVE LONG RECEIVING PRAYER FROM CAROL ARNOTT AND
KATE SMITH

2013 - PRESENT DAY EXTERIOR OF 272 ATTWELL DRIVE

2013 - PRESENT DAY EXTERIOR OF 272 ATTWELL DRIVE

on the end of the runway to start this revival, to pour out His Spirit, and that He has chosen the least, poorest and most desperate nation to pour out His Spirit. There is a link and a bridge between the two. God will choose the foolish things to confound the wise. God began a revival in the poorest nation, a nation torn by war, flooding and corruption, intense poverty and land mines to start a revival in the whole of Africa. The move began in a small church at the end of the runway, in a city that had never experienced revival, and used that to begin a move that would go to the nations. God chooses the obscure, humble, out-of-the-way places and out-of-the-way people. People have said, "Why did He go to Toronto?" Because He chooses the humble. God chose an obscure place at the end of a runway in 1994. From there it went to an out of the way place in the world. Now it's coming back again.

The Kingdom of God is breaking forth... and the Lord will bring another wave of hungry, thirsty people, and they will go with the bread of His presence. The Lord says the days of hard work are over. We're not going to run anymore. We're going to ride, to mount up with the wings of eagles, to ride on the chariots of fire."[391]

Marc Dupont, July 2006

You have done well in carrying this child of revival. Just as Mary carried her child, with the reproach of those who viewed the child as illegitimate, so you, too, have carried the child with reproach and derision. Along the way, there has been great joy. Just as the future prophet, John the Baptist leaped in his mother's womb, so there have been many who have leaped, laughed, and cried for joy as this child of promise has grown and grown.

But know this; the time of the birth of the child is at hand. Indeed

---

391 Marc Dupont's prophetic word, posted July 1, 2002 on the revival magazine website http://revivalmag.com/article/coming-release-glory-god; also posted December 15, 2001 in Spread the Fire magazine. Prophetic word came to Marc Dupont while with Rolland and Heidi Baker and three of their leaders one afternoon under a tree, behind the outdoor platform, late in 2001. The glory of the Lord fell heavily upon them for about an hour. Source: telephone interview with Marc Dupont, September 4, 2013.

you have had a mighty visitation, but I say, ask of me for another visitation even as Manoah, the future father of Samson, asked for a second visitation, and I will give it to you. Fear not, I delight in giving you the Kingdom (Judges 13). This is not a time for saying the best has come and gone. This is a time to say God saves the best for now. Ask of me for wisdom and My Presence, even as Manoah asked for a second visitation and I will, indeed, give it to you. And this will be the time the child, which you have carried with reproach, shall be fully birthed. And the wise will come with worship (frankincense) and gold (provision). But they shall also come with myrrh, a great desire, born of My Holy spirit, to die to self and give themselves wholly over to Me.

During the first visitation, I poured out joy and the new wine to awaken My people to My Kingdom of righteousness, peace and joy. In this second visitation, I will do that and more. I will pour out a burning passion for My glory and My holiness. Indeed, your meetings with Me will be a place where the future Isaiahs and the future Moses will be sent out. The first visitation was unto My joy, this second one will be unto My Kingdom coming on earth as it is in Heaven.

And know this, I am pleased with how you have borne the reproach of this child without bitterness or shame. You have not retaliated against those who have reproached you for carrying this child of My Spirit. Neither have you been dismayed by those who have thought they knew better. I am pleased with the heart and the faithfulness by which you have carried this child that too many have not understood. But, now, like never before the wise in My Spirit are going to come and are going to go out in a new revelation of My glory, compassion, power and ways. The cry that is going to resonate throughout this move will be 'holy, holy, holy is THE LORD GOD, THE ALMIGHTY, WHO WAS AND WHO IS AND WHO IS TO COME' (Revelation 4:8). Indeed I shall pour out a revelation, even as I did to Isaiah, that the whole earth is filled with My Glory.

You have seen the little sheep come and find refreshment and encouragement, but now you will see the Lion and the Lamb sit down together. You will become a Lion's den, where the future apostles and prophets who will embrace holiness, humility and a hunger for Me will be sent out from. Pour yourselves into these future leaders and the reward of lightning bolts of My Presence will set many, many cities and regions on fire with My Glory.

Indeed, you believed, but found it hard to believe years ago when I told you I was about to do things in your lives and cities that had never happened before. Know this deep within your soul, I am still the one who promises that your eyes have not seen, your ears have not heard, and it has not entered into your minds all that I have prepared for you. My promise of Matthew 25:29 is coming upon you; *'For to everyone who has, more shall be given, and he will have an abundance.' Amos 3:7-8: 'Surely the Lord GOD does nothing unless He reveals His secret counsel to His servants the prophets. A lion has roared. Who will not fear? The Lord GOD has spoken. Who can but prophesy?'*[392]

Kat Kerr, 2009

Canada is the gateway to the world. A tidal wave is coming to Canada of His fire.[393]

Bob Hartley, 2012

Bob had an angelic visitation while in Redding, California, in the middle of the night, on September 7, 2012. Here is an excerpt of this word:

He (the angel) said that he was sent to confirm the reality of the intention God has in His heart to take His people from 'revival' into 'reformation' and that now is the time for the inauguration of this transitional development. Beyond this, he reported that this reformation, issuing from the refreshing presence of the Lord, would ultimately lead to the fulfilment on earth of biblical prophecy—the time of the restoration

---

392 Marc Dupont's word, compiled by Fred Wright, Dan Slade, Prophetic History of Partners in Harvest, 2007, (unpublished), pp. 21-22.
393 Kat Kerr, December 6, 2009, Gateway Harvest Fellowship, Barrie, Ontario, author was present, also CD recording.

of all things…

The children of God will see, comprehend, and enter more fully into our promised inheritance. We have lived too far below our privileges. A much greater portion of God's precious promises are available to us in this age than we have imagined. The messenger made it very clear that many people have pushed their expectations of fulfilled promises off into a future age to avoid the challenges associated with contending for them here and now…

The Lord is inviting us to become 'inside-out' rather than 'outside-in' people. The difference between these two things is monumental. We will find our 'rest' in God, and God will find His 'rest' in us. This is what will make us much more useful to Him. We will learn to walk in the 'easy yoke' of Christ…

The messenger of the Lord declared that whole cities and nations have divine identities and callings upon them that they do not yet know. The Lord will scale the hope reformation up to global proportions. A great number of hope reformers will rise up and offer individuals, families, organizations, businesses, schools, towns, cities, and nations an encounter with the genuine presence of Christ…[394]

Andrea Aasen, 2012

Andrea, a leader with Patricia King's ministry in Cambodia, gave a prophetic word, on November 2, 2012. Here is a portion of that word:

… And I then saw Isaiah 40:3 and Malachi 3:1—and I saw the Body being aligned in body, soul, and spirit. There was a huge angel with a great tuning fork striking it, and as he struck the sound was released, and with each strike I saw the breath of God coming forth, but His breath was fire and the Life was in the Fire. The Body was being prepared, and the Purifier / the Helper came (I was taken to see Jesus' body in the tomb being prepared and then His rising and the release

---

394 Bob Hartley and Michael Sullivant: The Hope Reformation Room: An Angelic Encounter, posted July 23, 2013 bobhartley.org Deeper Waters Ministry, Voice of Hope. http://bobhartley.org/bob-hartley-and-michael-sullivant-the-hope-reformation-room-an-angelic-encounter/

of the Spirit/our helper coming to dwell in our midst... and I saw the prophetic that was released in that moment to be 'activated' now). And another angel came and sounded a great trumpet, and I saw it shaking and crumbling mountains. And I heard the Julie Meyer song, 'Prepare the Way of the Lord' sounding, echoing, in great weight. And then I saw into Matthew 3:11-12, where I saw Angels of Fire coming with the wind, and burning up all the chaff. And God said a 'fresh fire' is coming like never before... a corporate baptism of fire. He said it's a 'restoration of fire'... and I saw the same angel of restoration that had visited previously, and again His eyes danced with fire... and this time he looked on the face of the nations and the nations looked back, and I saw Him pointing to Jesus... and I saw the eye of the Lord and [the] eyes of His people, and He was looking at us, but we were looking back... it was a restoration of 'first love'.[395]

Gary Morgan

Australian prophetic voice, Gary Morgan prophesied several years ago that when a flood came to Toronto, it would signal a coming outpouring of the Spirit with signs and wonders. A significant flood hit Toronto Monday night, July 8, 2013.[396]

According to the news media,

Monday's rains, measured at 126 mm for the day, set an all-time record for Toronto Pearson Airport, breaking a record that had stood for nearly 59 years. What's more amazing is that this new record was set in just 7 hours, whereas the previous record was set over 22 hours of rain, when Hurricane Hazel hit the city on October 15, 1954.[397]

---

395 Andrea Aasen's prophetic word called "Revival is Coming", Visitation and Vision, November 2, 2012, posted February 22, 2013, http://www.australianpropheticcouncil.com/?p=1993

396 Steve Long's email a few days after flood; also John Arnott's email July 29, 2013, stating he believed the word was from six or seven years earlier.

397 Yahoo News Canada, Toronto storm sets rainfall record amid flash flooding, traffic chaos, July 9, 2013, Scott Sutherland, http://ca.news.yahoo.com/blogs/geekquinox/record-rains-toronto-cause-nightmare-flash-flooding-power-135320259.html, accessed July 22, 2013.

Patricia King, 2013

At the Dare to Dream Conference in Owen Sound, Ontario, July 25-27, 2013, both Stacey Campbell and Patricia King gave powerful messages on the subject of the next move of God. Both of them are carrying in their spirit an anticipation of an imminent outpouring of God that they described as a "baptism of fire."

Patricia King, on July 26, declared that,

A move is coming—the greatest move ever is going to come suddenly, like a monster wave. It will be different than the ones in the past. It's always different than you expect, but better. It will be a holiness revival.

Patricia also shared that she had been given a vision from the Lord in 1980 in which she saw a tsunami wave coming. Then she saw a map of Canada with fires breaking out and consuming the map; it ended up being a gold bar.

She believes that God also spoke to her about Isaiah 60:1-3, which commands God's people to arise and shine with the glory of God upon them in the midst of deep world darkness. Patricia believes the Lord told her that, in the next move of God, He will shine on many and it will be recorded that a group were called "the shiners."[398]

Tommy Hicks, 1961

The American revivalist who was used mightily by God in Argentina in the 1950s, Tommy Hicks, believed the Lord had given him a prophetic word on July 25, 1961.

I wish to quote a portion of that word:

God is going to take the do-nothings, the nobodies, the unheard of,

---

398 Patricia King, Stacey Campbell, Dare to Dream Conference, hosted by pastors Zak and Karen-Marie Gariba of Jubilee Celebration Center, Owen Sound, Ontario, July 25-27, 2013, author Jerry Steingard has the CDs.

the no-accounts…and [is] going to give to them this outpouring of the Spirit of God… the last days will have a double portion of the power of God… my people, in the end times, will go forth as a mighty army and shall sweep over the face of the earth… I watched these people as they were going to and fro over the face of the earth. Suddenly there was a man in Africa and in a moment he was transported by the Spirit of God, and perhaps he was in Russia, or China or America or some other place, and vice versa. All over the world these people went, and they came through fire, pestilence, famine, persecution, nothing seemed to stop them… God is going to give the world a demonstration in this last hour as the world has never known… as these people were going about the face of the earth, a great persecution seemed to come from every angle… suddenly from the heavens above, the Lord Jesus came, and said, 'This is my beloved bride for whom I have waited. She will come forth even tried by fire. This is she that I have loved from the beginning of time.'[399]

Let me conclude this chapter and this section with a significant quote from the British revivalist, Arthur Wallis. In his book, Rain from Heaven, Wallis declared:

Distress for the nations and tribulation for the church is predicted by the Spirit for the time of the end. But growing darkness will only make the light shining from God's people seem all the brighter. God will conclude this age as He commenced it. Great power and glory in the church, great victories over Satan, but in the context of great persecution and opposition. But the difference will be that what was then confined to one small corner of the globe will, in the end, be worldwide. I believe that the greatest chapters of the church's long history have yet to be written, and that it will be said of the generation that brings back the King, 'This was their finest hour.'[400]

---

399 Tommy Hicks, Revival End-Times Vision, www.revivalcentral.com/Prophecies.html
400 Arthur Wallis, Rain from Heaven, Bethany, 1979, p. 124.

PART 2 – A HISTORY OF THE TORONTO CHURCH

CHAPTER 1

A Detailed History of the Toronto Airport Church

While the first part of this book is focused primarily on chronicling the Toronto Blessing, some people – especially church leaders, church planters and revivalists - may find a detailed history of the Toronto church itself interesting and helpful. Here is the story of our little church at the end of the runway.

Small Beginnings

In the spring of 1987, while living and pastoring in Stratford, Ontario, John and Carol Arnott began a kinship group in west Toronto, in John's mother's living room. In the Spread the Fire magazine, John wrote, "What was to become the Toronto Airport Christian Fellowship started from that humble beginning. Several from our Stratford church came along every week, and we began to have a weekly cell meeting in my mother's home."[401]

In May of 1987, Blaine Cook and a ministry team from the Anaheim Vineyard came to Toronto to conduct a healing seminar. The Canadian Vineyard leader, Gary Best, as well as Andy Park and Brian Doerksen, came from the Langley Vineyard on the west coast to Stratford and

---

401 John Arnott, Spread the Fire magazine, Issue 1 – 2004, p. 5.

Toronto in September of 1987 to build relationships with the Arnotts and their congregations, as well as to model, teach and train in the area of intimate worship, which has always been a vital part of the DNA of the Vineyard movement.

After John's mother passed away, towards the end of 1987, the first kinship moved over to Ian and Rosalind McLean's home. A second kinship began at Connie and Jeremy Sinnott's home, in Willowdale, in February 1988. The weekly kinships were complemented by monthly celebrations, held at Bloorlea Middle School in Etobicoke.

By May of 1988, they officially launched the church, having started a third kinship and now meeting all together every Sunday afternoon. Initially it was called Vineyard Christian Fellowship Toronto. It was only after another Vineyard church started downtown Toronto, with Tony Romano, that people started calling the Arnott's church the Airport Vineyard in order to distinguish between the two. So soon John and Carol changed the name of their Vineyard to the Toronto Airport Vineyard Christian Fellowship (TAV).[402]

After about six months, they moved from Bloorlea to Silverthorne Collegiate. John and Carol conducted the morning service in Stratford, then whisked off to Toronto for the 3 PM service. This was a one and a half hour drive. In the fall of 1990, John, with help from Jeremy Sinnott and others, launched a weekly half-hour radio program that included Vineyard worship music and John sharing and teaching. This ministry lasted almost a year.[403]

Around this time, TAV leased a unit in the industrial plaza, just west of Pearson International Airport, on Dixie Road, just south of Derry Road, in Toronto. Marc Dupont prophesied to John and Carol, in late January 1991, that they were to make plans to leave Stratford and move to Toronto in order to prepare for what God had in store for them there.[404]

Starting in July 1991, the new Toronto church plant changed their afternoon services to Sunday mornings. John and Carol came twice

---

402 Email from Connie Sinnott, October 20, 2013.
403 Several telephone conversations with Connie Sinnott, August 21-29, 2013.
404 Conversations with John Arnott; telephone conversation with Marc Dupont, September 4, 2013.

a month to the Toronto meetings and twice a month remained in Stratford.[405] John and Carol Arnott's last Sunday as pastors of Jubilee Vineyard in Stratford was June 14, 1992.[406]

Pastoral Staff

Assistant pastors Paul and Sandy White and Dale and Linda Bolton launched out from the Airport Vineyard in 1993 to plant Vineyards in Scarborough and Thornhill respectively.

Just prior to the 1994 outpouring, the pastoral staff at TAV consisted of senior pastors, John and Carol Arnott; worship pastors, Connie and Jeremy Sinnott; women's ministry and equipping pastor, Mary Audrey Raycroft; Brian West; youth pastor, Ian Ross; and prophetic pastor, Marc Dupont. They also had a number of volunteer leaders such as Jim and Diane Paul, who would later plant a church in Hamilton.

Connie recalls John saying, "You can tell how big a puppy is going to grow by the size of its feet." The size of the pastoral staff of this fairly small (three hundred and fifty, including children) and infant church pointed to something big coming. They just had no idea how big.[407]

Connie and Jeremy Sinnott, became the church worship leaders at the outset of the Toronto Vineyard church plant. My brother, Rick Steingard (who would come on staff as a soundman by late 1994), came across this new Vineyard work in Toronto and told our sister, Connie, and her husband, Jeremy, about it, suggesting that they check out the kinship, the monthly celebrations and an upcoming seminar.

The Sinnotts had been in the Christian music group, Hakamu, for years and, at that time, were leading the group, Rejoice. They were naturally drawn to the intimate Vineyard worship music as well as the love and grace flowing out of John and Carol Arnott. It wasn't long before John found out that Jeremy was a gifted guitar player and that both had worship leading gifts. John was then able to release the Stratford musicians, which included Jeff Duncan and Carrie Seddon, from having

---

405 Jubilee Vineyard, Stratford, elder's notes, May 16, 1991.
406 The Beacon Herald newspaper article, dated Thursday, June 11, 1991; also author's daytimer.
407 Connie Sinnott's talk in Australia, November 5, 2012.

to travel from Stratford. John also put away his autoharp.

Connie was the first person to be hired, part-time. She became the church secretary and children's ministry worker in the fall of 1988. Jeremy came on payroll part-time as worship leader and associate pastor in the summer of 1991. The Arnotts and Sinnotts all came on full-time staff in August of 1992. Jeremy had been a teacher for one year and principal of People's Christian Schools (elementary and high school) for seventeen years prior to coming on full-time with the church.[408]

Jeremy and Connie have continued as associate pastors/worship leaders and more recently also as international trainers, taking the messages of intimacy with God, healing of the heart and renewal out to the nations.

Marc and Kim Dupont moved with their family from San Diego, California, to Toronto in May of 1992. Marc, who has an international itinerant prophetic ministry called Mantle of Praise Ministries, came on as part-time pastoral staff at the Toronto Airport Vineyard. In 1998, he and his family returned to the States to be on the part-time staff with Ron Allen at the Fort Wayne Vineyard in Indiana. Some time later, they made the Dayton, Ohio Vineyard, with Doug Roe, their church home base. After leaving Toronto, Marc continued to be an invaluable prophetic resource to the Toronto church and was part of the apostolic leadership team of Partners in Harvest.

Ian Ross, a businessman, was invited by John Arnott to join a team on a mission trip to Nicaragua in March of 1992. Ian and I first met on this trip. As roommates, we hit it off nicely because we both loved to joke around with puns. This mission trip was a life-changing experience for all of us as we saw God do an abundance of signs and wonders before our eyes. In March of 1993, Ian again went to Nicaragua with the Arnotts and saw virtually a whole village receive salvation, healing and deliverance. Ian was ruined for anything else. These experiences, plus sitting under the teaching and ministry of Jack Winter on the Father's love, particularly at the Singing Waters Retreat, near Orangeville, Ontario, transformed Ian's life.

---

408 Connie and Jeremy Sinnott retelling the story at an Australian meeting, November 5, 2012, recorded; also email from Connie to author, August 23, 2013.

Ian and his wife, Janice, came on staff part-time in September of 1993. Ian was laid off that month from his work so he actually gave himself full time to the church. Ian's responsibilities included building up small groups and facilitating prayer meetings. When the historic day arrived, January 20, 1994, Ian was there to see God burst onto the scene. Early in the renewal, John said to him, "Ian, do you realize that Azusa street is now just a parking lot, and if this (the Renewal) ends, I still want a church." With so many the visitors coming each week, the small groups helped keep some sense of church family.

In the renewal, Ian oversaw the daily prophetic intercession meetings, with hundreds of folks from around the world attending, while his wife, Janice, oversaw the reception desk. Ian also assisted John on stage during renewal meetings and conferences and also began to travel around the world ministering the revelation of the Father's love. In 1998, Ian and Janice left the staff in Toronto in order to give themselves to itinerant ministry to the nations, sharing the message of the Father heart of God. Of the almost two-dozen nations visited, Mozambique, with Iris Ministries, would be the most life-changing for Ian. He has gone back repeatedly.[409]

Prior to coming on the Toronto staff, Mary Audrey Raycroft had ministered internationally and inter-denominationally for a number of years with Christian Services Association, a Canadian-based teaching and outreach organization. Mary Audrey became pastor of equipping ministries and women in ministry. She is an excellent Bible teacher, exhorter and equipper in things of the Spirit. During the renewal, Mary Audrey gave oversight to the training and care of the prayer ministry teams and also became the founder of the annual Releasers of Life Women's Conference which continued in Toronto for many years. As of this writing, in the midst of talk of retirement, she continues to be quite active in ministry. Her husband, Bill, went to be with the Lord a few years ago. Mary Audrey has also authored a book on the history of the Toronto blessing, entitled *Once Upon a Revival*.

---

409 Ian Ross' email to author, August 29, 2013; Connie Sinnott's email August 21, 2013; John Peters, The Story of Toronto, p. 25.

In the spring of 1993, Steve Long, a local Fellowship Baptist pastor, attended a prophetic school at Toronto Airport Vineyard, led by Mark Virkler, Marc Dupont and Dennis Wiedrick. Steve heard the Lord's voice clearly for the very first time. He started to journal and sought to hear God's voice more regularly. At one point in his journey, he felt the Lord speak to him about serving a person of vision and helping them accomplish their vision. He also believed the Lord said that this person was John Arnott. So, Steve went out for breakfast with John prior to 1994 and told him, "I think I'm supposed to work for you and serve your vision." John and Carol had actually been praying and asking the Lord to bring them someone to help them fulfill their vision.

The fact that Steve quoted John and Carol's prayer caught John's attention.

On Monday, January 25, 1994, Steve Long came to his first renewal meeting. February 1, his pastors, John and Anne Freel, of Credit Valley Community Baptist Church, loaned Steve out to the Toronto Airport Vineyard. Steve officially came on full-time staff in early June of 1994 as administrator and conference planner. Steve has been instrumental in the behind-the-scenes planning and logistical organization of the roughly half a dozen major conferences every year, as well as the ongoing renewal meetings, since the beginning of the outpouring in 1994. [410] Steve and Sandra would eventually become senior pastors of TACF when John Arnott turned sixty-five, as well as Vice-Presidents of Catch The Fire World, along with Duncan and Kate Smith.

Fairly soon into the renewal, the Toronto church added others to the leadership team as well as the support staff. Within the first two years, they had well over fifty people on the part-time or full-time payroll—for everything from janitorial, grounds, café, book resource centre, administration, and the training school of ministry.

---

410 Steve Long, recorded interview by author, June 3, 2013.

Church Facilities

The newly sprouting Vineyard church met in the Silverthorne Secondary School in Etobicoke for Sunday services for more than a year. This arrangement was combined with renting office space at 3889 Chestwood Drive, in Downsview, for staff meetings, training seminars and counseling.

They moved in 1990 to their first leased home in an industrial mall at 6915 Dixie Road, which is just south of Derry Road and west of the Toronto Pearson airport.

When the outpouring of the Spirit hit on January 20, 1994, this ordinary congregation was in this nondescript warehouse, at the end of one of the airport runways, next to a cornfield.

News got out quickly that God was showing up at this little church and soon crowds were lining up for hours, in the frigid Canadian winter weather, to get a seat in the nightly meetings.

The modest-sized auditorium seated roughly three hundred and fifty to four hundred people. A little more seating space became available by mounting the sound booth high up on a platform on the back wall. Sound technicians had to climb a vertical ladder to get up to it. Thankfully, this was done just prior to the January outpouring. With more than four hundred coming to the meetings, the room adjacent to the auditorium, which was normally used for children's ministry and training events, became an overflow room. John Adams was the soundman and responsible, initially, for video recording. About a month or two into the renewal, my father, Bill Steingard, set up a video feed for the several hundred people in the overflow room. He also became responsible for video recording the meetings and conferences for close to a decade.[411]

John Arnott temporarily found a larger venue at a nearby rental hall, the Capital Banquet and Convention Hall, on Dixie Road. They also utilized the old Canada Christian College facility on occasion.

---

411 Conversations with Connie Sinnott, August, 2013; recorded interview with Steve Long, June 3, 2013; first-hand knowledge by author.

But, with the assistance of Dave Hobden, they continued to search for a larger and more permanent venue to accommodate the crowds of close to one thousand each night. I remember talking with Connie and Jeremy Sinnott, as well as others, about this challenge of overcrowding and the need for more space. We were thinking in terms of a facility that could handle about one thousand people, while John Arnott, with great apostolic faith and vision, believed for so much more.

Finding a Bigger Building: The Move to Attwell

The first annual Catch The Fire conference, October 12-15, 1994 was held at the Regal Constellation Hotel, which was on the opposite side of the airport from the Dixie church building. The main convention room could accommodate three thousand and the second room about twenty-five hundred. Five thousand were in attendance during the day and at night the place was packed out. [412] There were 500 people from Korea in attendance.

In November 1994, The Regal Constellation Hotel was booked for a Prophetic School. Steve Long had a dream from the Lord two weeks before the conference that prepared him and the leadership for a curve ball. In the dream Steve was asked, "What happens if the Regal Constellation calls you and has the right to kick you out?" The next day, he got a call from the hotel informing them of the change of plans. Thanks to the dream, Steve was ready to ask for all the things that were needed—the hotel was obliged to find them another venue that was as good or better than theirs, shuttle buses and chairs. The hotel also provided fifty dollars a night accommodation. [413]

So the Toronto church used the huge building at 272 Attwell Drive, which was open and empty due to the fact that the building was in bankruptcy. This very facility had been rented by TAV in June 1994, for the two nights of renewal meetings with John Wimber.

---

412 Steve Long interview, June 3, 2013
413 Ibid

Shirley Smith, Verda Foeller and their intercessory team prayed through the building before these meetings and then came to John saying, "We believe this is our building." So John Arnott and Dave Hobden, who had been assisting John in searching for a larger facility, put in an offer to purchase the building. To their disappointment, they found out that someone else had just taken possession of it. However that arrangement did not last very long.

While using the empty Attwell facility for this November Prophetic conference, the gentleman from the bankruptcy court, who had an office upstairs, asked the TAV leaders, "You guys want to lease it? After January, it is available on a permanent basis." With limited seating and parking at the old Dixie building, compounded by much frustration in the on-going negotiations with the landlord regarding a renewal of their soon-to-expire lease, this offer of a lease at the larger Attwell facility was a massively delightful opportunity that seemed to have God's fingerprints all over it.

Toronto Airport Vineyard signed the new lease for Attwell Drive, which was actually cheaper than the Dixie building. After the conference was over, TAV never went back to the old Dixie building but carried on with church services and renewal meetings at the new facility. TAV simply continued making the old lease payments until it expired a number of months later.

Within a month of leasing the Attwell building, issues related to the bankruptcy were sorted out and the building was now available for purchase. On the first anniversary of the outpouring, January 20, 1995, this three thousand-seat exhibition and conference centre, the former Asian Trade Centre, officially belonged to the Toronto Airport Vineyard. A property that was valued at roughly seven million dollars when first built, around 1985, the church was able to purchase for two point two million dollars.[414] The old Dixie facility was later leased by another church, The Potter's House Christian Centre, which continues to the present day.

---

[414] Steve Long, recorded interview, June 3, 2013; also: interview with John Arnott, June 14, 2013; Christian Week newspaper, article by Doug Koop, "Airport Vineyard Still Flying High", December 13, 1994.

Dave Hobden was awed by God's leading: "He did all this for us without even working up a sweat! Imagine what He'll do with some of the really important things if we trust Him."[415]

God miraculously provided a more spacious place that was right next to the international airport and a cluster of hotels. This new church home would become a more permanent meeting place for divine encounters between heaven and earth. It is no coincidence that the name, Toronto, is a First Nation's name for "the meeting place." Nor is it accidental that the street is "at the well." It reminds me of the details pertaining to the Azusa Street revival ninety years earlier. The glory came to Los Angeles, "the city of angels", to a dilapidated barn on Azusa Street, a Native American term for "blessed miracle". And both cities, at the time of their respective heavenly visitations, were considered to be the most cosmopolitan cities in the world. Like on the Day of Pentecost in Jerusalem, the Holy Spirit loves to show up where the nations are represented.

Marmac

Many leaders close to John Arnott, including myself, did not have the faith for a leap to such a large venue. However, John did have the faith and vision. As it turned out, this building soon proved to be inadequate.

In 1995 we purchased the building next door, 268 Attwell Drive, for office space, youth ministry and to establish a training school of ministry. Parking was still a challenge. Administrator Steve Long worked out some temporary arrangements for parking at the Seventh Day Adventist church across the street and with some neighbouring businesses. Eventually, we would acquire more property for parking and in 1998, we acquired a third building at 10 Marmac, one block away, for the School of Ministry.[416]

By October 1995, TAV had seventy-eight people on staff, of which about fifty were full-time.[417]

---

415 Dave Hobden, quoted in Spread the Fire magazine, January 1995, pp. 14-15.
416 Steve Long, interview, June 3, 2013; also Steve Long's talk at Catch The Fire Conference, September 28, 2013. Marmac, as it became affectionately called by the SOM students, was sold in 2005.
417 Doug Koop, article, Christian Week, p. 4.

A Typical Weekly Church Schedule in 1995

By 1995, the Toronto Airport Vineyard Christian Fellowship was holding eighteen meetings per week:

Sunday:	Morning Service
Monday:	Evening Alpha course
Tuesday–Sunday:	Renewal meetings each evening
Monday–Friday:	Pastors and leaders' information meeting each morning
Monday, Tuesday, Thursday and Friday:	Prayer and intercession each afternoon
Wednesday:	Ontario Renewal Network (prayer and sharing with two hundred local pastors)[418]

The Toronto Airport Vineyard Christian Fellowship had tripled in size from three hundred and sixty members in 1994 to one thousand in regular attendance in 1995.[419] The church has also offered a weekly outreach to feed and clothe the homeless.

Administering Renewal

In the January/February 1995 *Spread the Fire* magazine, the first issue of this new magazine, edited by John Arnott and Daina Doucet, John sought to help people understand the general framework of how they administered the renewal meetings and sought to facilitate the grace of God that was being poured out:

> At present, we are structuring our meetings to run about two and a half hours, as follows:

---

418 John Arnott, The Father's Blessing, Creation House, 1995, p. 238.
419 Ibid.

Worship	7:30–8:15 PM
Testimonies	8:15–8:45 PM
Offering, announcements, song	8:45–9:00 PM
Preaching/teaching the Word	9:00–9:40 PM
Invitation for salvation, re-commitment	9:40–9:50 PM
Specific words, ministry for healing	9:50–10:00 PM
Service dismissed	
General ministry time	10:00 PM"

This basic outline, however, does not reflect the holy chaos that was often the norm. The leaders welcomed and longed for the Lord to come and do whatever He saw fit in any way and at any time. They knew the Holy Spirit could be trusted. If you ask for bread He is not going to give you a snake or a scorpion. And the Holy Spirit often came and vetoed or hijacked the meeting, particularly during the testimony times. Occasionally the scheduled speaker was unable to give his message and ministry time often went on until one or two in the morning, with some people needing to be carried out to their cars in order to close the church doors for the night!

John Arnott's article in *Spread the Fire* goes on to explain,

At ministry time, we invite the Holy Spirit to come and touch, bless and fill God's people. We found it very helpful to tape lines on the floor eight feet apart in the ministry section to help 'organize' the general ministry time. Our new facility has helped immensely with more room. We no longer need to stack the chairs. People are encouraged to stand on the lines, face the platform and enter into worship. Visiting pastors and leaders are invited to assist and help the ministry team by 'catching' and making sure people are in a safe place to receive ministry.

Our ministry team is made up of people from our own church and other nearby churches. They are extensively trained and coached; beginning with the healing of their own hurts... We cannot 'give away' what we haven't first received. Our own hearts must be healed and freed, finding our significance in God's love for us. And so we say, 'Walk in God's love, and then give it away'... I have watched our teams night after night, lovingly serving and giving it away, needing only the knowledge that the Father uses them with a word, a prayer and a powerful touch, to bless someone hungry and thirsty for more of Him. They do it for hours, with happy faces, month after month, going home late and tired but very fulfilled in the Father's love, and content He will again use them as a blessing. Because of the ministry team, the effect of ministry is multiplied. We are able to give quality time to people again and again, 'soaking' them in the Spirit of God Who gives them wonderful change and transformation...

We want pastors and leaders to see the value of 'soaking' and continual prayer, so we model 'soaking prayer' from the platform with several testimonies. The results are dramatic...

We operate with six different ministry teams. Each is under a team captain and teams rotate one night per week. Each team member will work with an assistant (usually a visiting pastor or leader) who helps him or her with 'catching' people who fall during prayer. This gives visiting pastors an opportunity to observe and learn from our team members.

To summarize, we see our function as releasing among God's people a new love affair with Jesus. How long will it last? Who knows? Two years? Ten years? Where's it heading? We believe toward a harvest.[420]

The Toronto Airport Vineyard made it clear that they were positioned to serve the body of Christ as a "spiritual watering hole" or "international filling station", for as long as people continue to come.[421]

Prayer and Care Ministry, 1995

In early 1995, John Arnott brought Al and Helen MacDonald, of Stratford, on staff at the Toronto Airport Vineyard to establish the

---

420 John Arnott, article: How We Minister and Administer, Spread the Fire magazine, January/
  February 1995, pp. 7-8.
421 Ibid.

Prayer and Care ministry, which is, prayer counselling and healing of the heart.

One day, Pastor Akihiro Mizuno of Japan prayed for Al MacDonald in the main auditorium at the request of John Arnott. Al collapsed to the floor and began to speak in tongues. The pastor recognized the prayer language as Japanese and got very excited to hear him shouting such declarations as "God is number one over Japan" and "Jesus is number one over Japan". Sometime later, when Al and Helen were on one of two ministry trips to Japan, they saw t-shirts in storefront windows stating, "Mazda is #1" and "Toshiba is #1." But they knew that ultimately God is #1.[422]

Itinerant Team

Not only were tens of thousands of spiritually hungry people swarming to Toronto, but the Toronto church also began sending out members of their itinerant ministry team to the ends of the earth. In the early days, aside from their staff members, such itinerants included those mentioned in the following paragraphs.

Curtis Hinds, an itinerant evangelist, prior to coming to TAV in 1992, came into this renewal burned out and very works-oriented. Once his heart was healed and refreshed, Curtis began to receive invitations to preach again and was asked to come on the pastoral staff. Over time, Curtis felt led of the Lord to plant churches as well as to establish orphanages for street children in Brazil.

Jim Paul and his wife, Diane, were members of TAV from its beginnings. They went on to plant a church in Hamilton, Ontario. Jim began to travel to the nations and impart the anointing as well as minister prophetically.

Ray Young, a former itinerant Pentecostal evangelist, had his heart healed by the unconditional love of God and went out preaching in various countries in 1995.

Peter and Heather Jackson were both hit by the Spirit's outpouring

---

422 Personal interview with Al MacDonald, July 29, 2013; also John Arnott.

in January 1994. They have laughed, prophesied and carried the message of the Father's love to leaders and churches around the world. They have also been on staff as founding directors of the school of ministry as well as frequent speakers at the Toronto renewal meetings and the annual "The Party is Here" summer conference.

Gordon Grieve, a local fundamental Baptist pastor, who was "ambushed" by renewal in December of 1994, repented for his forty-two year mindset that did not believe in the supernatural gifts operating today. Gordon, as a preacher and prophetic intercessor, also began to travel the world.[423]

Local Hotels and Businesses

With so many believers making the pilgrimage to Toronto to meet with God, hotels in the vicinity saw their revenues up by twenty-five percent in 1994 and 1995. Some hotel owners and staff even came to the meetings out of curiosity as to why a church has brought such increase to their businesses.

Wes Campbell quotes John Arnott as saying,

> "You know something is happening when hot dog vendors set up shop at the entrance of the church parking lot and end up finding Jesus!"[424] This Sri Lankan couple, Joseph and Maria, have become members of the church and continue to run their hot dog stand out front, marked with a banner that says, "Jesus is Lord!"[425]

On Easter Sunday morning of 1998, Faustin and Marina Fernando and family came to visit TACF for the very first time. Faustin was the food and beverage manager at the nearby Travelodge Hotel. I'll let him tell his story:

---

423 Melinda Fish, From Toronto to the Ends of the Earth, Spread the Fire, Issue 1, 2001, pp. 12-13.
424 Wes Campbell, Welcoming a Visitation of the Holy Spirit, Creation House, 1996, p. 179.
425 John Arnott, recorded interview, June 14, 2013.

In the breakfast room of the hotel one day, I was called by a waitress to witness a lady on the floor. I rushed to check the situation and I found a whole bunch of people around her laughing. The scene seemed very strange to me to see a lady on the floor and everyone laughing. When I enquired what was happening, one of them said they were praying for her. I had never seen this type of prayer. Curiosity led me to find out that this group of people go to Toronto Airport Christian Fellowship Church. On Easter Sunday of 1998, I took my family to visit the church. We sat at the back of the auditorium and we were amazed with the type of church it was, with people dancing and people lifting their hands to worship. Towards the end, John Arnott gave an altar call. I grew up in a Catholic church and I have prayed to Jesus but never heard about having a personal relationship with Jesus. As a family, we knew this is what we want to live for the rest of our lives, so we walked the aisle to give our life to the Lord.

A year and a half later, Faustin came to work as food service manager at TACF. After various staff roles, in 2008, Faustin came on the pastoral staff at the church and now he and his wife, Marina, pastor the Mississauga campus.[426]

The Freshwind Youth Conference has taken place for many years now every spring during the Easter weekend. From April 9 to 11, 1998, youth pastors Kim Unrau and Ahren Summach had the chairs removed from the sanctuary to allow room for dancing. The highlight of the conference was the Saturday afternoon meeting that was held at Nathan Phillips Square, the largest open-air public square in Toronto. Four thousand youth attended, Rick Leaf's band played, TACF distributed five thousand hotdogs to street people and onlookers. Ottawa evangelist, Bill Prankard, and British Columbian youth evangelist, Nolan Clark, and others, preached. God's power swept through the crowd with a number of salvations and healings. Kim Unrau reported that some of the conference youth invited punkers with green, spiked hair and dog collars to the evening meeting. They came, and during the altar call

---

426 Faustin Fernando, email correspondence, September 18, 2013.

for salvation, they responded by coming forward to receive Christ.[427] Freshwind continues to this day and is well-attended by youth of all denominations around Toronto. If you call a church in Toronto and inform them you are calling from Catch The Fire, chances are you may be directed to their youth pastor.

SARS Outbreak 2003

Between February and September of 2003, Health Canada reported four hundred and thirty eight probable or suspected cases of "severe acute respiratory syndrome, or SARS, resulting in forty-four deaths in Canada, mostly in the Greater Toronto area.[428]

Twenty-five thousand residents of Toronto were placed in quarantine. With Toronto being the only city outside of Asia to be significantly impacted, it received enormous media coverage. "The concerns of international media eventually led the World Health Organization (WHO) to issue a travel advisory. On April 23, 2003, after the first peak of the SARS outbreak, WHO recommended that travellers only visit Toronto if a trip was absolutely essential." This advisory was lifted in less than a week when they believed the SARS outbreak to be over. However, a second wave struck by late May and through the summer. The travel advisory had a devastating economic and social impact on Toronto.[429]

Worship Team

Just before the SARS epidemic, TACF had a worship team on full-time staff, including Nuno Marques (drummer), Kelley Warren (vocals and flute), Rob Critchley (keyboards and lead vocals), Owen Hurter (electric and acoustic guitars and lead vocals), Mike Hughes (bass guitar). Luke Sinnott was on staff as bass guitarist and assistant chef for a time. The whole worship staff team (except for Jeremy and Connie Sinnott and

---

427 Steve Long's article, Fresh Winds Blow, Spread the Fire magazine, June 1998, p. 26.
428 Canadian Medical Association website, http://www.cmaj.ca/content/171/11/1342.full
429 Canadian Environmental Health Atlas website, SARS Outbreak in Canada, http://www.ehatlas.ca/sars-severe-acute-respiratory-syndrome/case-study/sars-outbreak-canada

Rob Critchley) were laid off due to a decline in finances at the time of the SARS epidemic. In total, forty full and part-time staff members had to be laid off during this time.[430]

After twelve years of nightly meetings (except Mondays), the Toronto church cut back to three to four nights later in the week, then eventually to just Friday nights as a "Come Holy Spirit" night. The leadership has learned that you don't keep a thing going for the sake of it. You follow what God is doing fresh. You follow the river wherever it goes and seek to "live in a culture of revival". At this time, they found that God was very much on the intercession.

Training Schools

God has been establishing many apostolic resource centres throughout the world in recent years. Equipping and training schools tend to spring up in virtually all of these centres.

The Toronto Airport School of Ministry began in September 1995, drawing young and intensely eager students from around the world. The founding directors were Peter and Heather Jackson. The Jacksons had planted the Barrie Vineyard in 1989 and, prior to that assignment, they had been ministry counselors at Daystar Ministries with Jack Winter in the United States.

David and Charmaine Hicks, former worship leaders and elders at Stratford's Jubilee Vineyard, came on staff with Peter and Heather Jackson. They became the directors after the third school term, at the end of 1996. Afterwards, New Zealanders, Stuart and Lynley Allan became the directors, followed by Gordon and Cathy Harris who have served from 2003 to the present.

Gordon and Cathy Harris and Mark Virkler established a two-year Bible school, first called Spirit Ablaze Bible Institute, in the fall of 2000. It was housed in the Marmac building, one block away from TACF. By the fall of 2001, Spirit Ablaze was transformed into the School of Ministry and was renamed the School of Biblical Studies. A School of

---

430 Connie Sinnott, email correspondence with Jerry Steingard, August 27, 2013.

Worship was also established and led by Mark and Darlene Dunn for a time, with input from Jeremy and Connie Sinnott.

The schools moved out of the Marmac building in 2005 and temporary arrangements were made with a hotel until renovations were completed in the firehall portion of the 268 Attwell Drive building in April 2006.[431]

I had the privilege of teaching on revival and church history in the School of Ministry for the first few years, then taught an expanded course on revival and church history in the Bible school for about a decade, along with courses on Christian Doctrine, World Religions and Cults.

Approximately two thousand youth have gone through the training schools—an army of passionate lovers of God who have been healed up and equipped for Kingdom service. These students all received ministry for the healing of the heart, the revelation of the Father's love, and a fresh impartation of the anointing of the Spirit. Graduates have grown in the disciplines of intimacy with Jesus, passionate worship, Bible study, prayer, soaking in His presence, journaling, and learning to hear God's voice in the "secret place". With a clearer sense of their identify and destiny in Christ, they have scattered around the globe to serve and minister with compassion and boldness as they follow the Father's initiatives, in the anointing and power of the Holy Spirit. Many have done internships in existing churches and many have gone on to plant churches.

Family Camp

In 1990, the Toronto Airport Vineyard began a wonderful tradition of hosting a week of family camp, every summer, for their church as well as the Vineyard churches in the province. After the first two years of family camp at Round Lake, near Ottawa, the Stayner Missionary Camp was used for the next seven summers.

John Arnott invited many amazingly anointed speakers to minister

---

431 Gordon Harris, email to author, August 21, 2013.

at these increasingly popular family camps. This was a fabulous time of building relationships within the Vineyards in Ontario (and some from Michigan and New York state) as well as great recreation, training and ministry. The renewal that broke out in 1994, of course, took ministry to a whole new level. Ministry was often quite loud and intense and, since this campground was next to the small town of Stayner, it created logistical problems with meetings and ministry that went late into the evening. The camp management eventually disallowed our group to rent their campground.

The church purchased a campground on Penuel Lake, north of Huntsville, Ontario in 1999. The camp was named "Harvest Retreat Centre" and provided family, youth, children's and Partners in Harvest leaders' camps. It also hosted healing retreats for the Toronto church and Partners in Harvest churches. The camp was sold in 2004.

Names for the Toronto Church

As mentioned earlier, when officially launched in 1988, the church was called Vineyard Christian Fellowship Toronto but to avoid confusion with a second Vineyard in the city, it was changed to Toronto Airport Vineyard (TAV).

On the second anniversary of the outpouring, January 20, 1996, TAV was no longer a member of the Association of Vineyard Churches. The name, therefore, was changed to the Toronto Airport Christian Fellowship (TACF).

The church changed its name once again, in 2010, to Catch The Fire Toronto. In recent years, the Toronto church has been planting satellite campuses, with local pastoral teams located around the Greater Toronto Area.

In addition to the nearby campuses, Catch The Fire churches are being planted around the world. The first church plant was by Toronto staff members, Duncan and Kate Smith, in Raleigh, North Carolina. Churches have been planted wherever a hotbed of support for revival values have been found, including London, England; Oslo, Norway;

Montreal, Canada; Houston, US; Novo Hamburgo, Brazil; Sydney, Australia and more. Darrin and Daphne Clark, Catch The Fire Toronto's Children's Pastors for more than a decade, left in early 2013 to plant Catch The Fire Calgary.

CHAPTER 2

Where is Catch The Fire Toronto at Now?

Steve Long estimates that somewhere between four and five million people have come to at least one revival meeting or conference at the Toronto church.[432]

On their website, Catch The Fire Toronto is described as a "multicultural, cell church based in Toronto with campuses all over the Greater Toronto area. We're known internationally as a global revival centre." Catch The Fire is more than four times larger than it was at the beginning of the renewal, even after giving away many people to other churches and church plants. Their goal is to establish two hundred campuses in the Greater Toronto area by 2025.[433]

John and Carol Arnott are the founding pastors of the Toronto church. Steve and Sandra Long are the senior pastors overseeing all the Catch The Fire campuses in the greater Toronto area as well as the new church plants in Canada. John and Patricia Bootsma, spiritual children to John & Carol Arnott, spent some years pastoring the church in Stratford that John & Carol planted, and then returned in 2011 to pastor Catch The Fire Toronto Airport campus and establish a House of Prayer.

The Catch The Fire Toronto website states, "At Catch The Fire Toronto, we value the Presence of God. 'Come Holy Spirit' meetings

---

432 Steve Long's article, Spiritual Milestones and Large Stone Stories, in Revival Magazine, www. revivalmag.com.
433 Catch The Fire website, http://www.ctftoronto.com/campuses (accessed Oct. 28, 2013).

are times that we allow the Holy Spirit to give direction and we press in for more. We usually start with worship followed by worship and ministry. 'Come Holy Spirit' meetings are held every Friday evening at our Airport Campus, unless otherwise stated."[434]

The campuses around the GTA are pastored by men and women who have been raised up through cell groups and schools in Toronto. Many of them would call Steve and Sandra Long their spiritual parents. Many of these pastors have developed fruitful ministries in Toronto and other nations of the world.

Catch The Fire Toronto continues to send out teams to minister at churches and conferences as well as conduct leadership training schools and mission outreaches around the world.

Catch The Fire Toronto senior leaders such as John and Carol Arnott and Connie and Jeremy Sinnott still maintain a full schedule of global travel. Steve and Sandra Long, Mary Audrey Raycroft and Patricia Bootsma, along with their pastoral responsibilities at home are also often out ministering around the world.

Steve Long, the humble Baptist administrator, has grown into a national leader. He especially loves to minister and teach on physical healing, equipping and empowering all believers to walk in a lifestyle of evangelism through divine healing. He constantly brings home faith-building stories that testify of God's miraculous work, which then provokes the congregations to also step out and take risks for God's glory. His wife, Sandra, is a wonderful example of how God takes quiet, shy people and empowers them to become the mighty men and women that God intends them to be under His anointing.[435]

House of Prayer

In 2012, under the direction of Patricia Bootsma, Catch The Fire Toronto opened up the a House of Prayer, which follows IHOP Kansas City's "Harp and Bowl" model of prayers mingled with live worship

---

434 Catch The Fire website, http://www.catchthefire.com/ (accessed May 31, 2013).
435 Connie Sinnott email to author Jerry Steingard, October 26, 2013.

offered to the Lord. Currently the House of Prayer runs in two hour slots about a dozen times each week.

Catch The Fire College

The Toronto school of ministry is now called Catch The Fire College, which offers the Heart module, Revelation module, Worship module and internships. Catch The Fire Colleges have also been established in Montreal, Canada, South Africa, the UK, Norway, the USA and Brazil.

In recent years, they have expanded their training and equipping schools to include adults. The Toronto church has also offered adult training schools such as: the three-week Leader's Schools, held every January and July (a total of 1,200 have gone through the school) and the Father Heart Training Schools (about 300 have attended this school). As well, the Toronto leadership has conducted their one-week International Leaders' School in nations around the world, equipping pastors and leaders with the tools of revival.[436]

Media and Publishing

Thousands of videos from over 10 years of revival meetings are now available on YouTube, thanks to CatchTheFireTV. Seeing a lack of printed revival resources available on the market, especially in foreign languages, Catch The Fire launched a publishing and distribution arm in late 2013. An outgrowth of the original Spread The Fire magazine, Revival Magazine launched in 2011 and publishes inspiring articles online at revivalmag.com

---

436 www.catchthefire.com website and email from Gordon Harris, August 21, 2013.

CHAPTER 3

Where is Partners In Harvest at now?

The current website describes the organization this way:

> PIH is not a top-down, controlling, pyramid structure, rather, PIH
> churches and ministries are autonomous, self-governed entities.
> Leadership of PIH readily provides counsel when asked but will not
> meddle or offer unsolicited advice.

Partners in Harvest has also provided a mechanism called Friends
in Harvest, for pastors and churches that want to continue their
relationship with their existing denomination or association but also
desire to be relationally connected with PIH because of our mutual
love for the river of revival.

By the year 2000, greater clarity came regarding the movement's
core values and heavenly commissions. Jim Curtis of Tulsa Harvest
Church, in Oklahoma, came up with an acrostic to describe those core
values, using the word "Fire":

F Father's Love revealed through the Lord Jesus Christ

I Intimacy, Presence, and Hearing God's Voice

R Restoration of the Heart/Soul

E Extending the Kingdom through the equipping, anointing and
   empowering of the Holy Spirit

The Partners in Harvest mission statement was also clarified by the year 2000: "Partnering to spread the fire of God's love, presence and healing throughout the nations."[437]

To create a place of friendship and encouragement, PIH instituted the concept of "foursomes". These small groups of three to five ministry leaders or two pastoral couples in an area meet regularly for the sole purpose of providing a safe place where personal ministry can occur and real friendships may develop. It is hoped that "foursomes" will function as foundation stones of everything else we do.[438]

The first Partners in Harvest leaders' summer camp was held in August of 1999 at the Deersbrook Christian Ministries farm (where the author and his family lived and hosted a Christian retreat centre), near Creemore, Ontario, north of Toronto. TACF had recently purchased a 640-acre campground that surrounds a lake, north of Huntsville, a three-hour drive north of Toronto, but it was not ready for immediate use.

Partners and Friends in Harvest have also hosted a major conference in Toronto every September or October, often just before the Catch The Fire Conference. This has been a highlight for PIH/FIH pastors and leaders.

PIH eventually formed an apostolic, five-fold, leadership team, called "The A Team", which included prophetic leaders Marc Dupont and Steve Witt, missionary Heidi Baker, as well as John Arnott and Fred Wright. This team was together for approximately half a dozen years.

After working closely and travelling with Fred Wright for a couple of years, Dan and Gwen Slade, who had been overseers of the PIH churches in the Ukraine and Eastern Europe, became the new International Coordinators of PIH when Fred and Sharon Wright retired in July of 2009. The Slades were younger, could speak more than one language, had pastoral and international experience and had come back to Canada for their children's education. It was a smooth transition of

---

437 Partners in Harvest Manual, 2007, p. 5.
438 Ibid., p. 21.

leadership and the Slades are a perfect fit for this assignment.

In time, Fred and Sharon Wright moved to British Columbia and have focused on writing and enjoying being grandparents. We are deeply grateful for their sacrificial service and wise apostolic and pastoral leadership over the years.

Partners in Harvest and Friends in Harvest churches were organized into areas or regions. In each region, a regional coordinator was appointed to help facilitate conferences, area meetings and gatherings for fellowship and encouragement. Local PIH/FIH Family Days, training events and Catch The Fire-type regional conferences are coordinated through them.

The PIH senior team consists of:

John and Carol Arnott: apostolic leaders/spiritual father and mother
Fred and Sharon Wright: founding international coordinators
Dan and Gwen Slade: international coordinators along with others on
their Board of Directors, and those around in the world in leadership
positions of other churches.

Partners in Harvest consists of close to six hundred churches and ministries worldwide. [439] However, one of those churches/ministries is Iris Ministries with Rolland and Heidi Baker of Mozambique, Africa. As mentioned elsewhere, they have well over ten thousand churches in their network alone. Two other apostolic ministries linked to PIH are growing and expanding throughout Eastern Europe and South America.

Let me close with words from PIH international coordinator, Dan Slade:

Partners in Harvest functions as a family and yet as a partnership: As
a family in terms of relationship and as a partnership in terms of the
resources, giftings and blessings that are linked together with each

---

439 Dan Slade, email to author Jerry Steingard, October 31, 2013.

member having a key part. PIH is not a top-down control-orientated organization but functions as a network of autonomous congregations and ministries that link together with each other and with the Lord for mutual benefit and shared mission. We have been birthed in a profound move of the Holy Spirit and outpouring of God's presence which started in January of 1994.[440]

---

440 Dan Slade, letter to PIH ministers in the PIH Manual, 2009, p. 2; also on PIH website, http:// partnersinharvest.org/media/resources/WHO_IS_PIH.pdf

About the Authors

Jerry Steingard

Jerry Steingard holds a Master of Divinity from Regent College, Vancouver, and a Doctor of Practical Ministry from Wagner Leadership Institute. Jerry is author of The Overcomer's Handbook: Preparing for the Best of Times, the Worst of Times and the End of Times. Jerry has pastored for 25 years. In addition, he has taught courses in revival church history, Christian doctrine, and world religions and cults, at the Catch the Fire Toronto School of Ministry for many years. He has also taken ministry teams to more than half a dozen nations. Jerry and his wife, Pam, have three grown children, Jonathan, Michael and Joanna, an amazing son-in-law, Collin Gibson, and daughter-in-law, Jesse, as well as one very cute grandson. Jerry and Pam currently live in Stratford, Ontario, Canada.

John and Carol Arnott

John and Carol Arnott are the Founding Pastors of Catch The Fire Toronto (formerly known as the Toronto Airport Christian Fellowship) and are Presidents of Catch The Fire World. They are also overseers of the Partners in Harvest network of churches around the world. As international speakers, John and Carol have become known for their ministry of revival in the context of the Father's saving and restoring love. As the Holy Spirit moves with signs and wonders, they have seen millions of lives touched and changed through God's power and Christ's love.

John attended Ontario Bible College (now Tyndale College) in the late 1960's and then pursued a successful career in business. In 1980, while on a ministry trip to Indonesia, John and Carol responded to God's call on their lives for full-time ministry. John is known for his teachings on the Father's love, grace and forgiveness and the Holy Spirit's power. He continues to impart wise counsel and provides a strong framework for those who want to see the power of God manifest in their church.

John and Carol live in the Greater Toronto Area. They have four adult children and five grandchildren. They travel extensively while continuing to oversee Catch The Fire and Partners in Harvest networks of churches.

Bibliography (Recommended Books)

Ahn, Ché. *Into the Fire*. Renew, 1998.

Ahn, Ché, editor. *Hosting the Holy Spirit*. Renew, 2000.

Arnott, John. *The Father's Blessing*. Creation House, 1995.

Arnott, John, general editor. *Experience the Blessing*. Renew, 2000.

Arnott, John. *Manifestations and Prophetic Symbolism*. New Wine Press, 2008.

Arnott, John and Carol. *Grace & Forgiveness*. New Wine Press, 2009.

Arnott, John and Carol. *The Invitation*. Catch The Fire, late 2013.

Baker, Rolland and Heidi. *There is Always Enough*. Sovereign World, 2003.

Bell, Stuart. *In Search of Revival*. Destiny Image, 1998.

Beverley, James A. *Holy Laughter & the Toronto Blessing*. Zondervan, 1995.

Beverley, James A. *Revival Wars: A Critique of Counterfeit Revival*. Evangelical Research Ministries, 1997.

Boulton, Wallace, editor. *The Impact of Toronto*. Monarch Publishing, 1995.

By Their Fruits: The Lasting Impact of Toronto in the UK. Word Pub., 2001.

Campbell, Wesley. *Welcoming a Visitation of the Holy Spirit*. Creation House, 1996.

Campbell, Wesley. Stephen Court. *Be a Hero*. Destiny Image, 2004.

Chevreau, Guy. *Catch The Fire*. Marshall Pickering, an imprint of HarperCollins, 1994.

Chevreau, Guy. *Pray the Fire*. HarperCollins, 1995.

Chevreau, Guy. *Share the Fire*. Self-published, 1996.

Clark, Randy. *Lighting Fires*. Creation House, 1998.

Clark, Randy. *Supernatural Missions*. Self-published, 2012.

DeArteaga, William. *Quenching the Spirit*. Creation House, 1992.

Dixon, Patrick. *Signs of Revival*. Kingsway, 1994.

Dupley, William. *The Secret Place*. Self-published, 2011, 2013.

Dupont, Marc A. *The Elijah Years*. Mantle of Praise, 1995.

Fish, Melinda. *Keep Coming Holy Spirit*. Chosen Books, 2001.

Fitz-Gibbon, Andy and Jane. *Something Extraordinary is Happening.* Monarch, 1995.

Helland, Roger. *Let the River Flow.* Bridge-Logos, 1996.

Helland, Roger. *The Revived Church.* Sovereign World, 1998.

Jackson, Bill. *The Quest for the Radical Middle.* Vineyard International Pub, 1999.

Johnson, Bill. *When Heaven Invades Earth.* Destiny Image, 2003.

Johnson, Bill. *Face to Face with God.* Charisma House, 2007.

Johnson, Bill. *Hosting the Presence.* Destiny Image, 2012.

Kendall, R. T. *When God Shows Up: Expecting the Unexpected.* Renew, 1998.

Kendall, R. T. *The Anointing.* Thomas Nelson, 1999.

Kendall, R. T. *The Sensitivity of the Spirit,* Charisma House, 2002.

Kendall, R. T. *Holy Fire.* Charisma House, January, 2014.

Kilpatrick, John. *Feast of Fire,* The Father's Day Outpouring. Self-published, 1995.

Loren, Julia, Bill Johnson, Mahesh Chavda. *Shifting Shadows of Supernatural Power.* Destiny Image, 2006.

Peters, John. *The Story of Toronto.* Authentic Media, 2005.

Poloma, Margaret M. *Main Street Mystics.* Altamira Press, 2003.

Riss, Richard and Kathryn. *Images of Revival.* Destiny Image, 1997.

Roberts, Dave. *The Toronto Blessing.* Kingsway, 1994.

Steingard, Jerry. *The Overcomer's Handbook.* Xulon Press, 2012, 2013.

Stibbe, Mark. *Times of Refreshing.* Marshall Pickering, 1995.

Tenney, Tommy. *The God Chasers.* Destiny Image, 1998.

Tenney, Tommy. *The God Catchers.* Thomas Nelson, 2001.

Virgo, Terry, David Holden, and John Hosier. *From Refreshing to Revival.* Kingsway, 1995.

White, John. *When the Spirit Comes with Power.* IVP, 1988.

Williams, Don. *Revival The Real Thing: A Response to Henk Hanegraaff's 'Counterfeit Revival'.* Self-published, 1995.

Wright, Fred and Sharon. *The World's Greatest Revival.* Destiny Image, 2007

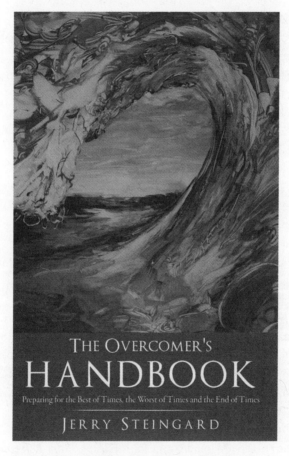

THE OVERCOMER'S
HANDBOOK
Preparing for the Best of Times, the Worst of Times and the End of Times

JERRY STEINGARD

The Overcomer's Handbook

The Power of Thanksgiving

FRED & SHARON WRIGHT

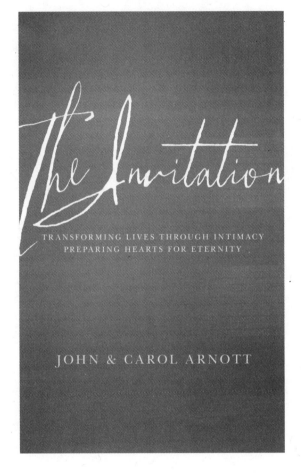

The Invitation
JOHN AND CAROL ARNOTT